Public Safety and Risk Assessment

Improving Decision Making

David J. Ball
Laurence Ball-King

publishing for a sustainable future

London • New York

First published 2011
by Earthscan
2 Park Square, Milton Park, Abingdon, Oxon OX14 4RN

Simultaneously published in the USA and Canada
by Earthscan
711 Third Avenue, New York, NY 10017

Earthscan is an imprint of the Taylor & Francis Group, an informa business

Earthscan publishes in association with the International Institute for Environment and
Development

Trademark notice: Product or corporate names may be trademarks or registered trademarks,
and are used only for identification and explanation without intent to infringe.

British Library Cataloguing in Publication Data
A catalogue record for this book is available from the British Library

Library of Congress Cataloging in Publication Data
Ball, D. J. (David John)
  Public safety and risk assessment : improving decision making / David J Ball and Laurence
Ball-King.
       p. cm.
  Includes bibliographical references and index.
  ISBN 978-1-84971-380-1 (hardback) — ISBN 978-1-84971-381-8 (pbk.) 1. Public safety—
Great Britain. 2. Risk assessment—Government policy—Great Britain. 3. Decision
making—Great Britain. I. Ball-King, Laurence. II. Title.
  HV675.B255 2011
  363.1'070941—dc22   2011008846

ISBN: 978-1-84971-380-1 (hbk)
ISBN: 978-1-84971-381-8 (pbk)

Typeset in Sabon and Frutiger
by 4word Ltd, Bristol
Cover design by Benjamin Youd

Printed and bound in Great Britain by the MPG Books Group

To Zhu Xian

Contents

List of Figures, Tables and Boxes   ix
Preface   xi
List of Acronyms and Abbreviations   xv
Acknowledgements   xvii

1   Clear and Foreseeable Danger   1

2   Risk Assessment – *A Simple Tool?*   16

3   Is Safety Paramount?   33

4   Risk and Safety – *A National Philosophy*   46

5   What Works in Public Life?   53

6   Legal Matters   65

7   Advice – *Whose Advice?*   78

8   A Closer Look at Decision Making   99

9   Adventure Activities – *A Hard Case*   117

10 Risk-Benefit Assessment   135

11 In Search of a New Agenda   151

12 Final Thoughts and Résumé   165

Notes   178
References   187
Index   197

List of Figures, Tables and Boxes

Figures

2.1	Risk judgement in policy making	21
2.2	The first four stages of HSE's risk assessment process	22
2.3	A fairly typical 3×3 risk matrix	23
2.4	An example of a 4×4 risk matrix	25
2.5	The risk matrix as set out by the Cabinet Office	26
4.1	The Tolerability of Risk framework	48
5.1	Trend in leisure accidents by accident location	58
9.1	Fatal accident rates for selected sports	124
9.2	Non-fatal accident rates for selected sports	125
9.3	Respondents' views of AALA's regulatory regime	128
11.1	Recognition, or not, of risks and benefits	155
11.2	The ROAMEF management cycle	159
11.3	The 'Design for play' play space design cycle	160

Tables

2.1	Risks we face	18
7.1	An analysis of six different concepts of 'safety'	79
7.2	Analysis and commentary on HSE's *Principles of sensible risk management*	90

Boxes

1	A sample of media reported stories about health and safety	4
2	Dangerous trees?	12
3	Regina (HSE) v. Porter	13
4	Answer these questions to value your own life	41
5	The 'safe' playground – an ideological battleground	55
6	Council staff worry about regulators not public	60
7	What works? Views from far and near	62
8	Right to swim in Hampstead Heath ponds	68
9	Optimal levels of protection	72
10	Safety measures do not guarantee safety	75
11	Government's principles of managing risks to the public	96

12   The MHSWR – obligations, advice and guidance   106
13   Risk and adventure – thoughts of climbers on managing risk   119
14   Benefit assessment of Plas Dol-y-Moch Outdoor
     Education Centre   142

Preface

This book is motivated by the emergence, over the past few decades, of an apparent clash between the provision of services to the public, and of publicly enjoyed space and activities in general, and a new and vigorous culture of 'health and safety'. The clash is perhaps most felt in the United Kingdom, though it is by no means confined to UK shores and anecdotal evidence suggests it may be taking a hold in susceptible countries distributed around the world. This suggests that apart from its intended UK audience, the messages present within this book might have relevance much further afield, either as a means of addressing an existing situation or as a means to heading it off.

This culture of health and safety with which the book is concerned, and which originated largely in the factory environment, has gradually seeped into service provision, whether the classroom, the health centre, sport and leisure activities of any kind, as well as (for example) the management of the countryside, urban space, parks, theatres and heritage locations. Along with it comes a requirement to do, in some way, risk assessments which must themselves be written down. Of itself, this has created a vast new industry with all its associated costs and burdens. It has also had other subtle consequences. One is that it has the effect of shifting the balance of power for decision making away from front-line public service personnel to a new elite of health and safety practitioners; that is, people who specialize in what is known as 'health and safety' rather than service provision.

Apart from the considerable burden of all this activity and its associated machinery, it has attracted a growing amount of adverse publicity and has thus been the subject of several government inquiries. Although indubitably well-intentioned, it is apparent that health and safety can be taken too far, either in the way of gobbling up resources or through interfering with some other aspects of public life which are valued. It may even, through its unintended consequences, increase risk and put lives at danger. In this way it has been implicated in all manner of bizarre and sometimes shocking episodes, ranging from the trivial, though still for some upsetting, banning of garden gnomes and personal wall hangings in residential care homes, to the harrowing cases of abused children and vulnerable adults who have received too little help too late as a consequence of ponderous or overprescriptive bureaucratic procedures which are themselves by-products of this new approach to safety.

What seems to be lacking in much of the ensuing argument is a clear understanding of the fundamental principles upon which health and safety should properly rest. This applies not only to the wider public and public service professionals who are subjected to it, but also to a fair number of practising health and safety professionals. For example, there is a tendency for risk assessments of public activities to be conducted in a mechanistic fashion and for them to lead inexorably to certain choices, as if the process and its outputs were somehow sacrosanct and above challenge. The fact is, however, that there are many levels of understanding when it comes to assessing risk, let alone how that should feed into decision making, and copious histories which make it clear that important considerations are often omitted or sidelined. One aspect of public service provision is the enhancement of public health, whether physical or emotional, so, as is increasingly recognized, restricting public activities in the name of 'health and safety' can in fact damage health. A simple explanation of this paradox is that 'health and safety', as currently practised in public life, is primarily about safety from physical injury. It is not about health or, if it is, it is about things that harm health, like exposure to some chemicals. It thereby affords scant attention to the health *benefits* of public life, or any other of its legions of benefits.

The purpose, then, of this book is to set out a clear and comprehensible exposé of the inner workings of risk assessment processes, and of their input and role in decision making. Surprisingly, given the present-day level of importance assigned to this topic in Britain and increasingly around the globe, there are few publicly accessible accounts of what makes these things tick, and of the many unresolved issues which lurk there. This may be because the topic transcends so many disciplines – from natural science and engineering to psychology, ethics, economics, philosophy, sociology, law and even neuroscience. But one advantage at least of this transcendence is that 'health and safety', which might outwardly be anticipated a topic of unfathomable dullness, emerges as deeply fascinating! The following questions, for example, which are tackled in this book, illustrate how risk assessment itself is inextricably tied to some basic issues of life:

- Is it true that, as some people allege, safety is paramount?
- How safe should public space and activities be?
- To what extent should concern over safety from injury trump the benefits of public life (benefits include things like healthy exercise, relaxation, education, personal and community well-being, beauty, natural environments, freedom to roam ...)?
- Is there some underlying philosophy of safety?
- What, in fact, does the law require?

The nature of these questions clearly demands answers anchored in considerations which go way beyond the technical domain of risk assessment. But there are even questions about the risk assessment process itself which raise a further panoply of intriguing issues. For instance:

- What is risk, how is it measured in the public realm and with what certainty?

- Is risk assessment objective or subjective?
- What is the relationship between risk assessment and risk management (risk management is about deciding what to do)?
- Were risk assessment to be subjective, whose subjective opinion is relevant in deciding what actions should be taken?
- Do the public life solutions commonly identified by risk assessment deliver improved safety?

Ultimately, by tackling these and other questions, this book seeks to inform and hopefully to re-enfranchise those numerous persons, private or professional, in diverse walks of life, who wish to understand this phenomenon at a deeper level so as to be able to deal with it in a positive and constructive way. Public safety is, of course, an important matter, and for that reason alone it should be viewed and conducted with as complete an underpinning knowledge as possible. However, many professional individuals in fields from healthcare to education, to sport and leisure, recreation, urban design, countryside access and so on, will have their own experiences and concerns which, it is hoped, may be partially understood by reference to this text. Even private individuals, whether or not their lives have been affected by this culture, should benefit from an understanding of the way in which our society handles risk to the public and, of course, of their duties to others and of others to them, which knowledge could even be described as a human right.

A note on the book's structure

To assist readers in getting to grips with the ideas in this book, each chapter concludes with a short summary before embarking upon the next piece of the 'jigsaw'. We are aware that there is some degree of repetition in the text. We venture the explanation that this is because all the diverse topics covered interlock, and we wish to identify and emphasise those linkages as the story unfolds. There are lots of endnotes and references for those who wish to trace the origins of ideas expressed.

The authors

As we see it, this book is founded on the decades-long experience of David Ball coupled with the modern perspective of Laurence Ball-King. David has been Professor of Risk Management at Middlesex University since 1997, and directs, with colleague John Watt, its Centre for Decision Analysis and Risk Management (DARM). Prior to that he was Director of the Centre for Environmental and Risk Management at the University of East Anglia, and spent 14 years with the scientific branch of the former Greater London Council. Over the decades he has worked on a great variety of risk issues on behalf of local, national and international agencies. Of late, he also has extensive experience of the legal system through acting as an expert witness in court cases. His education and background is hard science (physics), in which he first worked for a number of years in the USA and the UK, though he is often thought, nowadays, to be a social scientist.

Laurence, in contrast, has an academic qualification in Risk Management (an MSc), and a degree in economics and politics. His portfolio of risk experience ranges over adventure sports regulation, arboricultural risks, accident investigation, the analysis of financial credit risk and the utility of common tools like risk matrices.

List of Acronyms and Abbreviations

AALA   Adventure Activities Licensing Authority
AALS   Adventure Activities Licensing Service
ACoP   Approved Code of Practice
AHOEC   Association of Heads of Outdoor Education Centres
ALARA   As low as reasonably achievable
ALARP   As low as reasonably practicable
ATP   Automatic train protection
BCA   British Caving Association
BMA   British Medical Association
BPEO   Best practicable environmental option
BPM   Best practicable means
BRC   Better Regulation Commission
BRTF   Better Regulation Task Force
BSI   British Standards Institution
CARR   Centre for Analysis of Risk and Regulation
CPAG   Child Poverty Action Group
DARM   Centre for Decision Analysis and Risk Management of Middlesex University
DCSF   Department for Children, Schools and Families
DCMS   Department for Culture, Media and Sport
ECJ   European Court of Justice
EOC   English Outdoor Council
FAR   Fatal accident rate
FC   Forestry Commission
HMT   Her Majesty's Treasury
HSC   Health and Safety Commission
HSE   Health and Safety Executive
HSW Act   Health and Safety at Work etc. Act (1974)
IOSH   Institution of Occupational Safety and Health
LASS   Leisure Accident Surveillance System
MHSWR   Management of Health and Safety at Work Regulations
MRPP   *Managing Risk in Play Provision*
NCB   National Children's Bureau
NFAR   Non-fatal accident rate

NHS	National Health Service
NICE	National Institute for Health and Clinical Excellence
NT	National Trust
NTSG	National Tree Safety Group
NYCC	North Yorkshire County Council
OMM	Original Mountain Marathon
ONS	Office of National Statistics
PSF	Play Safety Forum
QALY	Quality Adjusted Life Year
RBA	Risk-benefit assessment
RoSPA	Royal Society for Prevention of Accidents
RRAC	Risk and Regulation Advisory Council
RRC	Regulatory Reform Committee of the House of Commons
RSA	Royal Society for the encouragement of Arts, Manufactures and Commerce
SCES	Select Committee on Education and Skills
SFAIRP	So far as is reasonably practicable
SME	Small and medium enterprise
ToR	Tolerability of risk framework
TUC	Trades Union Congress
UN	United Nations
VCS	Voluntary and Community Sector
VSCG	Visitor Safety in the Countryside Group
WTP	Willingness to pay

Acknowledgements

We would like to thank those many individuals who have helped us by providing inspiration, encouragement, suggestions and critical commentary, in some cases extending over many years. We are particularly grateful to colleagues John Adams, Marcus Bailie, Mike Barrett, Keith Baverstock, Harry Collins, David Crossland, Tim Gill, Huw Jones, Bill Leiss, Shaun Lundy, Joe Morabito, David Seedhouse, Bernard Spiegal, Robin Sutcliffe, Michael Thompson and John Watt.

We wish to thank Helen Ball-King for the illustrations, and HM Cabinet Office and the Office of Public Sector Information for permission to reproduce Crown Copyright material.

Crown Copyright items are reproduced with thanks under Open Government Licence v1.0.

Last but not least, we express our gratitude to Earthscan's editorial staff, especially Anna Rice, Alison Kuznets and Nick Ascroft, and 4word Ltd for seeing this work through to publication.

1
Clear and Foreseeable Danger

At some time during the last 30 years actions carried out under the banner of 'health and safety' started to intrude upon public and private life – that is, life away from the office or factory – in a way previously unknown. This intrusion has not been universally benign, and has increasingly given rise to varying degrees of irritation and even ridicule. The phenomenon can be observed above all in countries like the UK and some other western-style, English-speaking countries around the world, from Australia and New Zealand to North America, but also to some extent in other cultures, India and Singapore for example, where western-style thinking has footholds. It appears, also, to be spreading.

Where this influence came from, and with what rationality and what legitimacy, is a question deserving of an answer. In the UK, in the present decade of the 2010s, barely a day passes without a media story denouncing some incident in which health and safety has impacted unfavourably upon public life. Some stories are distortions and some are daft, but others have grains of truth, substance even, giving rise to a widening sense of anger, frustration and despair. There is also a suspicion that some interventions in the name of health and safety may be causing more harm than good. By 2010 the situation was such that the British government felt compelled to asked Lord Young, a respected business leader, to report on the operation of health and safety laws, and the growth of what it called the 'compensation culture'. As Prime Minister David Cameron put it:

> *Good health and safety is vitally important. But all too often good, straightforward legislation designed to protect people from major hazards has been extended inappropriately to cover every walk of life, no matter how low risk.*
>
> *As a result, instead of being valued, the standing of health and safety in the eyes of the public has never been lower. Newspapers report ever more absurd examples of senseless bureaucracy that gets in the way of people trying to do the right thing and organisations that contribute to building a bigger and stronger society. And businesses are drowned in red tape, confusion and the fear of being sued for minor accidents.*
> *(HM Government, 2010)*

As noted, this phenomenon is not unique to the UK, although it may, for reasons to be described, be more strongly felt in this land. Indeed, there are no particular reasons why it should be, unless one thinks that British people have some unusual trait predisposing them to situations of this kind. This is because health and safety, risk assessment, and the kind of thinking which accompanies these activities, is an international phenomenon propagated by governments and multinational institutions and international standards.[1] We are aware, from our own contacts and observations, that what is happening in the UK is observable to varying degrees in countries around the globe.

This pilgrimage, as some may see it, which is ostensibly about making things safer, is in some situations impossible to ignore. Set foot outside of your home and you may be regaled with warnings and unsolicited advice of variable quality on all manner of things connected with your personal safety and well-being. This continues whether your journey is by pavement, bus, underground or train. Even before venturing out there is a constant stream of the same transmitted over the airwaves. At night, when most people are trying to relax or put their children to bed, one may be reminded that you may never see them again because 'toxic smoke can kill'. There is, of course, a time and place for everything, but other questions simmer alongside the momentary stress engendered by this activity. For instance: 'Do these actions actually make people safer?'; 'Is there an ulterior motive for them?'; 'Might some of these measures undermine health-giving, community-enhancing activities?'; 'Who is paying for it all?'

As Lord Hoffmann, one of Britain's most-esteemed Law Lords, remarked of his own experience a few years earlier: '... people suddenly began to notice (other) ways in which activities which they used to enjoy were disappearing because authorities responsible for those activities were afraid that it might be said they had not taken sufficient steps to avoid an accident' (Hoffmann, 2005).

One should, nonetheless, tread carefully. We ought not to forget that it hasn't always been like this. In its pioneering days, health and safety made huge inroads into the annual toll of workplace accidental deaths and disease. In just one British industry alone, coal mining, the number of workers who died in accidents fell from what is now a barely imaginable 400 plus per year in the 1950s to about 20 in the 1980s. Although output of coal roughly halved over that period because of pit closures, this is by no means enough to discount the dramatic gain in safety. Those who brought it about should be immensely proud, and as we hear of the continuing toll of mining deaths in China, the USA and New Zealand, and near-misses in Chile, it is something for which others of us should be deeply thankful.

Today, though, everyone in the United Kingdom is aware of the steady stream of anecdotes about 'health and safety', some of which appear to lack any sense of proportion. In 2006, Bill Callaghan, then Chair of the Health and Safety Commission (HSC), which was at that time overseer of the primary regulatory body, the Health and Safety Executive (HSE), became so irate that he felt obliged to issue a press release entitled: 'HSC tells health and safety pedants to "get a life"' (HSC, 2006a). Unfortunately, and now some years later, these stories continue. They range in significance from the ludicrous and entertaining to the tragic. They are so widespread that most people can recount their own personally experienced examples. This is a serious matter for two principal reasons. On the one hand it serves to discredit and undermine safety procedures which, when properly conducted, are obviously very much in the public interest. Hence the 'clear and foreseeable danger' of this chapter's title – a reference to the threat which could ensue should the wider health and safety movement be discredited, and lose public and political support. On the other hand, in public life, and as Lord Hoffmann and others have noted, it has deterred and sometimes prevented people of whatever age from enjoying their free time, public space and social activities which, amongst other things, promote health and community. It also goes without saying that the pursuit of safety does not come free: it consumes stunning amounts of public and private money.

The causes of this situation have been ascribed to many things. Marcus Bailie, Head of Inspection for the Adventure Activities Licensing Service, has traced its British origins back to a Welsh mining disaster in 1966 in which a colliery waste tip slumped onto the village of Aberfan, killing 144 people, mainly school children (Bailie, 2007). As Bailie recounts it:

> *months later Lord Alfred Robens, then Chairman of the National Coal Board, was still trying to justify to the people of Aberfan the actions of the Coal Board, the mine owners, and the government in the face of the physical and psychological damage which had all but obliterated a generation of their village. By and large he failed, was later heavily criticized, but famously never apologized.*

In the period to come, in his quiet and private moments, it would be easy to imagine Robens' horror of a world where injustice on this scale could happen in the name of work. Horror, and perhaps an initial determination to ensure it never could happen again. If ever there was a 'something must be done moment' this was surely it. If this was indeed his motive then just three years later Robens got his opportunity, when he was asked to Chair a government commission to look at the management of health and safety in the workplace, and to prepare a report. As will be seen later in this book, the subsequent Robens Report of 1972 set out the vision, and the resulting Health and Safety at Work etc. Act of 1974 set out the detail. But how then, in the space of a little over 30 years, have we moved from the public clamour for safer workplaces to a broad recognition that it has all gone a bit too far? The Nanny State – children suffocated in cotton wool – and the abandonment of anything which could cause harm, irrespective of whatever benefits may be thrown out with the bathwater, is becoming the enemy (*The Times*, 2006).

Fingers have been pointed at far more immediate causes of this condition. These include: false attribution ('Nowt to do with us guv!'); cowboy health and safety professionals lacking qualifications or experience;[2] the 'ignorant' public; exaggerated, even 'fabricated', media stories; a risk-averse society; a wave of managerialism which hinders people using their mental faculties; the 'litigation society',[3] generally attributed, though with little evidence, to America; no-win-no-fee solicitors; the 'evil' tendency of insurers to settle claims out of court; the cost of public liability insurance; 'red tape' and paperwork mountains; self-protectionism by some agencies; a lack of communication skills; inappropriate use of 20/20 hindsight after an accident; performance targets; 'soft-hearted' courts and the deep-pocket syndrome; and unaccountable advisory and regulatory agencies.

It is probably true that all of these things have at times contributed to the situation which now exists. Box 1 provides a sample of mainly recent headlines, stories and internet postings which illustrate the breadth of the issues

---

Box 1 *A sample of media reported stories about health and safety*

The daft and the dubious

'Banned gnomes can return home' – A Metropolitan Borough Council apologised to a tenant who had been told to remove two gnomes, a pottery tortoise and a welcome plaque from outside her home. It said there had been a 'misunderstanding' of its fire safety rules (*The Times,* 1 December 2009).

'Pair told door plaque unsafe' – A housing association required an elderly couple to remove their wall hangings and flowers, citing health and safety: 'We recognise that health and safety requirements sometimes seem over the top. However, the safety of our residents must always come first' (http://news.bbc.co.uk/1/hi/puffbox/hyperpuff/audiovideo/england/7606636.stm)

'Outplayed – but some people still think we're conkerors' – Tom Whipple reports that conkers have been banned by one school because of fear of nut allergies, and another because they could be considered as an 'offensive weapon'. A third school requires children to wear goggles (*The Times*, 5 October 2009).

'Chemical reaction. Students prevented from experimenting in laboratories are soon lost to science' – Scientists and government advisers are warning that a heavy focus on exams, combined with fear of wayward Bunsen burners and volatile reactions in test tubes, are elbowing experiments out of the school day ... because of safety concerns. It's the difference between flicking through an Italian recipe book and trying to make your own cheese ravioli from scratch. *The Times*, 5 October 2009).

'Swimmers at an outdoor London pool have been warned they will have to leave the water if it rains too much because of health and safety rules' (*London Evening Standard*, 9 May 2009).

Worrying

'It's not just the discs that have lost their way' says Anatole Kaletsky of a junior official who lost 25 million tax records in HMRC's internal mail. 'The worrying thing is that Britain's data protection regime will prevent you finding out when you last paid your own utility bill unless you remember an obscure password, yet it fails to prevent 25 million bank accounts being disclosed' (*The Times*, 22 November 2007).

'The zombie health and safety inspectors should be replaced with a risk commission' says Simon Jenkins in the *Guardian*. 'I puzzle over what can be done to replace this puritan revolution. Its health and safety apparat enjoys a power similar to that of the military. Its work is enhanced if it can scare us witless. This apparat exploits the politics of fear much as does the military' (*The Guardian*, 22 June 2007).

'Verity, I say unto you: trust the mums' – Libby Purves reports on modern trends in parenting. 'Natural responsiveness to babies is actively discouraged; formulaic managerialism, which wrecks everything from education to broadcasting, is seeping into motherhood. We are encouraged to see babies as a management challenge ...' (*The Times*, 30 October 2007).

'Extra billions fail to raise school standards' – Greg Hurst reports a Conservative spokesman as saying. 'Huge sums of money have been spent on fortnightly initiatives and bureaucracy, which are burying teachers under a mountain of paperwork and rarely lead to improvements in education' (*The Times*, 2 December 2009).

'Who knows best?' – According to *The Times*, Wikipedia volunteer editors are complaining of a rise in 'Kafkaesque bureaucracy and rules' to stifle rogue incidents of misinformation (25 November 2009).

'Government advertisements are bad for our health' – 'Why scare us, when reality is bad enough?' says Mary Dejevsky. 'Using public transport these days increasingly resembles a descent into Dante's nine circles of Hell,... I find a huge black and brown advert warning me – or rather the male of the species – that "drinking causes damage you can't see". Except that here you see it all too well: a blood-red jagged flash amid some indeterminate innards, possibly a brain ... There's one for women, too, on another bus stop, showing a similarly brutal red gash obtruding from a bra. Entering the Tube train, I face a diagram derived from the schematic map of the London Underground that assumes I must be in urgent search of treatment for Sexually Transmitted Diseases. There are clinics everywhere, it implies; if you want to, you could be seen right away ... On alighting, the message becomes darker still. The frantic appeal "Stop, No, Stop Please, No ..." appears against the background of a desperate woman apparently about to be raped. "Please stop taking unbooked minicabs", orders Transport for London's footnote – as though nothing untoward ever happened at its own unmanned stations or black-cab drivers were all saints ...' (*The Independent*, 26 February 2010).

Intriguing

'Surgeons flout care guidelines' – On finding that surgeons do not obey health service guidelines during operations, Nick Freemantle, Professor of Clinical Epidemiology and Biostatistics at Birmingham University, writes: 'Nothing is impossible for the man who doesn't have to do it himself' (*The Times*, 2 November 2004).

'Floods caused by managing rivers for habitat biodiversity' – A correspondent describes the conflict between managing rivers as habitats and safeguarding people's homes from flooding (*The Times*, 25 November 2009).

'A row over plans to erect a fence along the riverside in Otley has taken a new twist with Leeds City Council deciding to seek fresh legal advice over the issue. The plan to erect the £165,000 fence at Wharfe Meadows Park followed a council-commissioned safety review carried out by the Royal Society for the Prevention of Accidents (RoSPA), which advised putting up a fence. But the idea of fencing off a section of the open riverside has angered many residents in the town, and more than 1,000 people have signed a petition urging the council to scrap the plan ...' (*Yorkshire Evening Post*, 15 March 2007).

Disturbing

'Health and safety in "crisis" says Lord Young's Headline from an IoSH's conference in Glasgow. '... in the eyes of the general public, health and safety is regarded, "at best, as an object of ridicule, at worst, a bureaucratic nightmare"' (24 March 2010).

'Children arrested for building a tree house' – Police today stood by their decision to arrest and take DNA swabs from three 12-year-olds for trying to build a tree house (*Birmingham Mail*, 25 July 2006).

'If this is modernity, let me stay in the public sector cave' says Joe Moran. 'The paradox of the New Labourite managerialist revolution in the public sector is that it seems on the surface to be neurotically control-freakish, but in reality it is the antithesis of management: it is un-management. In its search for an objective, formal system that will somehow drive the process independently of all those untrustworthy, self-interested human beings, it creates a strange, parallel world made of paper and PDF files, populated by clean fonts, bullet points and abstract nouns like "excellence" and "transparency"' (The *Guardian*, 23 March 2010).

'Ofsted "feeding fears"' – Ofsted has been attacked by council leaders for 'feeding people's fears' over child safety. Town hall chiefs said Ofsted was too concerned with its own reputation and focused on procedures and process rather than the welfare of children (*The Times*, 24 November 2009).

'Chainsaw madness' – Victoria Moore reports that '... urban trees are being chopped down at terrifying speed because of ludicrous health and safety concerns and cautious insurance companies' (*Daily Mail*, 13 August 2007).

Deeply disturbing

'Mine shaft probe "to reopen" after new evidence emerges' – A woman died from injuries sustained after falling into a disused mineshaft in Ayrshire. Senior fire officers maintained that safety rules had prevented the rescue (BBC News, 1 May 2010).

Simon Jenkins writes: 'In the case of Baby P, the real scandal appears to be not so much the failure of the family – families "fail" every day – nor the failure of supervision. The scandal seems to lie in why that supervision failed. A local agency of government was so hard-pressed by regulation and monitoring that its social workers spent 60% of every day in front of a computer safeguarding their information trails, rather than doing the job of looking after children' (*The Guardian*, 10 March 2010).

'There is no need for this (risk assessment) to turn into a paperwork nightmare. Pages and pages of risk assessment for simple school trips are not only unnecessary but unhelpful' says Judith Hackitt, Chair of HSC (31 October 2007).

'London's prosecutors stand in the dock' says the *London Evening Standard* over news that there are serious failings in prosecutors' performance in most London boroughs. Keith Starmer QC 'concedes that his service's performance in London is lacking and says that moves are being made to switch more resources into front-line work' (16 March 2010).

'... rules and regulations now governing police procedures are putting victims' lives at risk' says Rachel Royce (*Spectator*, 6 December 2003).

Signs of hope

'Safety first but keep it sane' says Sir Bill Callaghan, chairman of the HSC (Public Agenda, 31 July 2007).

'We strongly recommend that the Risk and Regulation Advisory Council should now be dissolved and replaced by a Public Risk commission, an important part of the new regulatory architecture in the wake of recent crises of confidence in existing risk management approaches and oversight.' In 'Response with responsibility' by the RRAC (May 2009).

In search of balance

'But something is seriously awry when teachers feel unable to take children on school trips, for fear of being sued; when the Financial Services Authority, that was established to provide clear guidelines and rules for the financial services sector and to protect the consumer against the fraudulent, is seen as hugely inhibiting of efficient business by perfectly respectable companies that have never defrauded anyone; when pensions protection inflates dramatically the cost of selling pensions to middle-income people; where health and safety rules across a range of areas is taken to extremes' says Tony Blair at UCL (26 May 2005).

'"Elf and safety" stories should carry a warning' says Rob Strange, Chief Executive of IOSH. '... we've started to see health and safety become a political punch bag, left to swing with repeated right hooks from predictably aggressive elements of the media' (*The Independent*, 15 March 2010).

'Odd cut and bruise better than sterile childhood' says Sarah Womack. 'The Royal Society for the Prevention of Accidents said parents were too risk averse, particularly after the abduction of Madeleine McCann in Portugal, and youngsters should be allowed to bruise and cut themselves' (The *Daily Telegraph*, 12 June 2007).

'Climb every mountain, taste the salt of risk' – Libby Purves reports, following Prince Edward's controversial suggestion that the risk of death is part of the attraction of the Duke of Edinburgh award scheme for young people' (*The Times*, 2 November 2009).

'Advice to avoid sun should be lifted, say cancer experts' – The head of Britain's drive to cut soaring skin cancer rates said the advice to restrict sunbathing is 'draconian and unnecessary' and should be lifted (*The Independent*, 31 January 2004).

and the worries that people have. There is no shortage of supply. The impacts affect both individuals and society at large. The perceived causes reflect many of those just listed.

The primary regulator, the HSE, tried to ward off the obvious threat which this posed to its own worthy mission, which is to reduce harm, and that of the health and safety profession in general, by publishing on its website a satirical item called 'Myth of the month'. This sought to debunk some of the stories as they come up. It also published some *Principles of sensible risk management*, including a list of things to avoid (HSC, 2006b). These will be discussed in more detail later. But right now the observation is made that these media stories were only in varying degrees myths. As Judith Hackitt, Chair of the HSE has said, there is at least an element of truth behind these stories (Hackitt, 2008).

Why and whither this book?

The preamble sets out, if it were needed, that there are some serious questions around health and safety as practised beyond what is commonly understood as the workplace, which warrant examination. And intimately connected with health and safety is the business of risk assessment, something we nowadays hear about daily, but which a few decades ago was seldom spoken of, except by a few professionals mainly in the heavy industries.

'Sorting out all of the causal factors', as Adrian Voce, director of Play England, has rightly said in the context of children's play provision, but with more general applicability, 'will not be simple. The barriers are many and complex' (Play England, 2008a). And in the wider realm of public activities in general, the UK Risk and Regulation Advisory Council (RRAC) has shown how numerous agencies, including the courts, insurers, standards-setters, single-issue campaign groups, regulators, assorted experts and others all have a finger in the pie (RRAC, 2009), and somehow consort, inadvertently or otherwise, to promulgate aversion to risk.

So what can be done? One of the things surprisingly lacking in the public arena is a straightforward explanation of what makes, or should make, health and safety tick. Unexpectedly, obvious questions are not readily answered, even by some health and safety professionals.[4] For people who feel that maybe they have suffered at the hands of excessive health and safety demands, or for those who just want to improve their understanding, answers to the following questions might be useful:

- What exactly is risk assessment?
- Is it objective, in a factual or scientific way?
- If it's not objective, then whose subjective opinion counts?

Having got to grips with that, another suite of questions could come to mind:

- Is safety of supreme importance, overriding all else?
- Is the aim (as often alleged) to minimize or eliminate risk?

- What does the law actually require?
- Should one treat legal requirements as minimum requirements for, say, ethical reasons?
- Is there a UK or international philosophy on safety and risk, and, if so, what is it?
- What do you do if proposed safety measures impinge unreasonably on other facets of public life or public space?
- Who are the real experts?

By examining these questions, this book seeks to inform and re-enfranchise people who feel they have lost out in some way through strictures of health and safety, and secondly to support a more considerate application of risk assessment, specifically in the domain of public space and activities, from whence most of the friction seems to originate. In doing this, the aim is not to discredit health and safety, but to aid understanding. Unbridled application in public life of things going by the name of 'health and safety', which may or may not work, and without checks and counterbalances, is potentially damaging. It could actually do more harm than good, whether to people's health, safety and well-being, or through disrupting healthy activities, or just by wasting people's time and making them poorer.

The dawning of risk assessment

By way of brief background, it is worth recalling that although the use of the language of risk has burgeoned in recent decades, this way of thinking has always been present. Human activities which bear a resemblance to modern day, record-keeping style risk assessment have been sourced back over a period of 5000 years (Covello and Mumpower, 1985).[5] The story can be traced from there through Greek and Roman civilizations and to western Europe, where it had a significant boost during and following the period known as The Enlightenment. There it was picked up in particular by the

fledgling insurance industry, and later by the mid-20th century it was assimilated by other industries: nuclear, offshore oil and gas, rail transport and so on, where it continues to be usefully applied.

So far as safety of individuals from accidents is concerned, the ancestry of this particular interest is far more recent. Over little more than a century, a gradual change in thinking about the nature of accidents has occurred (Green, 1997). At one time these were attributed to fate, 'acts of God' or just bad luck. Today, though, the pendulum has swung sharply towards a view which, in extremis, regards all accidents as having identifiable causes, thereby being preventable.[6] This position, in other contexts referred to as 'zero tolerance', has considerable superficial appeal until you ask: 'Is it achievable?'; 'Who pays?'; and 'Will it have any unintended consequences?' And of course, if this zero-tolerance road is taken, it all too easily opens the door to unlimited culpability, so providing a powerful fillip for the 'compensation culture'.

More recently, a very significant landmark was established when, in 1974, a major piece of legislation, the UK's Health and Safety at Work etc. Act (HSW Act), was passed, the ripples from which were felt worldwide. The Act, which was immensely farsighted, even revolutionary, essentially brought in a set of general, goal-setting principles for guiding the conduct of health and safety. This was in place of earlier piecemeal and increasingly voluminous safety requirements, which were becoming unmanageable through their sheer quantity and complexity.

A second novel and very significant feature of the HSW Act was that it applied not just to factories, but also captured for the first time those people *affected* by work activities, including employees in local government, hospitals, education and other services. It also impinged upon members of the public because, as Section 3 (Part 1) of the Act says:

> *It shall be the duty of every employer to conduct his undertaking in such a way as to ensure, so far as is reasonably practicable, that persons not in his employment who may be affected thereby are not thereby exposed to risks to their health or safety.*

As it is interpreted, these undertakings could be a school, forest, country park, city square, theatre, stadium, playground or the seaside, or some other place of leisure pursuits. The Health and Safety Executive (HSE), which along with local authorities is the agency which implements this regulatory framework,[7] has said of that change as follows: 'in the mid-1970s, this latter provision provoked widespread astonishment' (HSE, 2004a). In retrospect, and in view of all the strange outcomes noted across the breadth of public life, it might be considered that astonishment was warranted.

Interestingly, the HSW Act does not itself use the term 'Risk Assessment'. That term came in with the 1992 Management of Health and Safety at Work Regulations. Thus, most working adults will remember risk management as a generally successful, everyday, common sense, flexible ingredient of modern living, which existed before the phrase risk assessment entered the scene.

A few recent histories

In January 2009, Oliver Letwin MP, the then Conservative policy chief, attacked what he described as 'rule-based regulation'. This, he said, was inappropriate when applied to complex activities (Letwin, 2009). The examples he gave were the dreadful death of Baby P and the global banking crisis, which affected millions and also, in its own way, killed people. In both cases the rule-based systems, one for protecting children from abuse, and the other for ensuring the stability of the banking system, had been largely obeyed, but had failed terribly and catastrophically. Oliver Letwin's proposition was that rule-based systems of control, which had been steadily introduced over the previous decade or so, were inferior to the old-fashioned professional judgement which they had largely replaced.

What links Baby P, the banking system, and public health and safety? The answer is that all are subject to the requirements of some form of risk assessment and risk management, and the way in which these activities are conducted has a direct effect upon the decisions which are made. As noted, during the last century, systems for assessing risks developed rapidly, primarily in the heavy industry sector including offshore oil and gas, nuclear power, mining and so on, where they have been very effective in reducing the toll of injuries. With the passage of the HSW Act, the simpler versions of the methodologies and protocols developed in these sectors spilled over into public life, and now impact upon almost every aspect of life.

To demonstrate the pervasiveness of the impact on everyday life, it is worth considering a few examples. One which hit the headlines in 2008 was the proposition by the British Standards Institution (BSI) to introduce a British Standard on tree inspections (Box 2). According to one source (*The Times*), and under the ironic banner headline 'Barking mad', this would have required many of those with a tree in their garden to pay for regular inspections, some by professional arboriculturists (*The Times*, 2008a, b). While superficially logical, this ignored the fact that the risk to the public of harm from falling trees is miniscule, and the reality that the prospects of reducing the risk below the current level are remote and comparable to finding a microscopic needle in a gargantuan haystack.

Within the education sector, the legal case of R v. Porter is no less perturbing, though in a different way. In 2006 the Health and Safety Executive brought a criminal prosecution against the headmaster of a small private school. This followed a fall by a young boy in the school playground which resulted in a minor head injury. Tragically the child, who was taken to hospital for a precautionary check, picked up an infection while in hospital of which he subsequently died. The headmaster was initially convicted by jury, but in 2008 the Court of Appeal quashed the sentence (see Box 3 for some details).

In retrospect, it is hard to believe that the attempted prosecution did anyone any good: it extended the suffering associated with the already tragic event and embarrassed a normally much-respected regulator. Inexplicably, research showed that the school in fact had an outstanding safety record which would have been the envy of the vast majority of other schools. This was seemingly attributable to its caring culture.

Box 2 *Dangerous trees?*

During late 2007 one of us was invited to join a British Standards Institution (BSI) working group on the risk posed to public safety by falling trees. The interest of the BSI had been prompted by some arboriculturists following a few legal cases, in which landowners had been prosecuted over injuries to members of the public caused by falling trees. In these cases the usual allegation was that insufficient care had been taken by the tree owner to manage their tree, and that they should have inspected more regularly. Although reluctant, sensing trouble ahead, I agreed to join the group while making clear my position, which was that any method of inspection to be recommended should be commensurate with the seriousness of the threat. This was because it was already known that there were on average about six fatalities a year in Britain attributable to falling trees, and that given that there were upwards of tens or even hundreds of millions of candidate trees, the inspection regime required would have been monumental. Further, since tree failure prediction is an art rather than a science, and because failure often occurs in storms, it was improbable that the number of fatalities could have been reduced without a massively precautionary programme of tree pruning and felling, which would have destroyed many places of beauty.

In the summer of 2008 the Risk and Regulation Advisory Council (RRAC) entered the arena, where the temperature was rising, and issued a press release condemning the plan by the BSI to implement a new, demanding and costly inspection regime, which would affect every person with a tree in their garden. In its 2009 report the RRAC commented as follows:

> *Industry insiders brought their concerns (about the BSI initiative) to the Council, worried that important parts of our natural and cultural heritage could be needlessly swept away by new demands in the name of public safety, without taking account of the actual risk, or the myriad benefits we derive – and take for granted – from the continued presence of millions of trees across Britain's rural and urban environments.*

Rick Haythornthwaite, Chair of the RRAC, is quoted as follows: 'This is a perfect example of how the pressure to regulate to minimise public risk can lead to wholly undesirable outcomes if left unchallenged.'

A spokeswoman for the BSI later defended its position: 'We issue standards in all sorts of areas, including businesses such as estate agents'; and went on to say that everyone was free to comment on the draft standard (*The Times*, 2008a).

The Times (2008b) itself had this to say in its leader:

> *Only God can make a tree. But it takes the British Standards Institute to protect us from its trunk and disorderly dangers. It is drawing up the first national standard for tree safety inspection. Under this, a tree specialist will inspect the trees in your garden every three years; every five years a professional arboriculturist will give them a more rigorous inspection in order to anticipate growing problems.*

An average of only six people a year in the United Kingdom are killed by falling trees. You are more likely to be struck by a runaway bike, bull or bullet. Of course, any mortal accident is sad. Of course, arboriculturists would like to be empowered to inspect all trees. And, of course, somebody will have to pay for such hyper-safety. Guess who? But Occam's axe should be applied to all such wild wood schemes: rules about trees should not multiply except from absolute necessity. In this forest of unnecessary regulation the BSI is way out on a dodgy limb.

Box 3 *Regina (HSE) v. Porter*

Regina v. Porter refers to a legal case in which the Health and Safety Executive brought a prosecution under the HSW Act against the headmaster of a small private school in North Wales. The main facts of the case were that a boy of just under four years was playing in the playground at break time in July 2004 and went to a known out-of-bounds area, where he jumped down the last few of a flight of steps (about 60cm) while pretending to be Batman, fell over, and banged his head. He was taken to hospital for a check and found to have a relatively minor head injury with no skull fracture nor even a laceration of the skin, but while there he picked up a hospital-acquired infection from which he died a month later. After some delay, the HSE prosecuted the headmaster for failing to assure health and safety. Key elements of their case were the allegation that the school's risk assessment was insufficient and that the supervision ratio at playtime should have been much higher (a figure of two staff to 26 children was mentioned). In the first instance the headmaster was convicted by the jury, but in 2008 the Court of Appeal quashed the sentence.

Most people who know of this case are bemused as to why it was brought. This, even before they knew that the school had a proven safety record which would have been the envy of other schools; that the 2:26 ratio had been set for classroom educational purposes and was not designed for use at break time, when it was arguably impractical and probably undesirable; and that nobody could find anything wrong with the steps.

Lord Justice Moses, on giving his judgment, said that for risk to be of concern it had to be real and not fanciful, adding that there was no objective standard, but one way or the other there would be important indicator factors, none of which might be determinative but many might be of importance; for example, evidence of any previous accident in similar daily circumstances (Court of Appeal, 2008; Harrington and Forlin, 2008).

One widely reported impact of the drive for freedom from risk of injury is its effect upon an entire generation of young people and children (Gill, 2007; Guldberg, 2009). There are by now many surveys which maintain that the state of childhood and youth in Britain is little short of dreadful. For instance, in 2009 the Child Poverty Action Group reported the outcome of a European survey of youth well-being. Of the 27 member states surveyed, the United Kingdom came near worst at 24th (CPAG, 2009). In 2007 a UNICEF survey found similarly: Britain, despite its affluence, was the worst country in the West to be a child. The report's author, Professor Bradshaw of the University of York, is quoted as saying: 'We are not the poorest country in this league table, we are, in fact, the fifth richest. And yet we consistently come a long way behind the average ... It's a pretty bleak picture' (*The Times*, 2007).

The pressure for safety is of course by no means solely responsible for the state of childhood and youth, but neither is it innocent. As Helene Guldberg says in her book: 'The key thing that could be holding children back is today's safety-obsessed culture, and low expectations of what they are capable' (Guldberg, 2009: 3).

There is copious evidence of childhood prohibitions in the name of safety. A 2002 study by the Children's Society and Children's Play Council found that children have been prohibited from playing with water, climbing trees, using playground equipment, riding bikes and skateboards, and even making daisy chains. Adrian Voce has said that in relation to formal playgrounds: 'A lot of play equipment is designed with the primary focus on safety, offering little opportunity for play that offers risk and challenge' (Play England, 2008a). And as long ago as 1995, Peter Heseltine, an expert on children's play, warned:

> We (the Standards committee) have recommended removal of anything dangerous ...
>
> We have emasculated equipment. We inspect far more than necessary .... We have covered everything in protective surfa-cing ... We have made playgrounds so monumentally boring that any self-respecting child will go somewhere else to play – somewhere more interesting and usually more dangerous. And quite right too ... (Heseltine, 1995)

Summary and way forward

Although much of the evidence described here could be dismissed as anecdotal, it seems improbable, given the sheer volume, that there are not serious under-lying issues. Safety promotion, like health promotion, is important, but there is a clear and foreseeable danger that it could lose its credibility if things continue on the current road, and the implications of this could be of a global dimen-sion. In developing countries health and safety is often lacking, so its reputation needs to be maintained if its valuable messages are to be propagated.

Secondly, individuals, communities and society are paying a real toll. Even though the (true) story of an elderly couple having to remove their pictures and wall hangings from their home (Box 1) is foolish, it caused genuine personal upset. At the societal level, the impact upon generations of children and young people is nothing short of alarming, and the tree inspec-tion gambit alone, if it had been implemented, could have generated substantial additional expense for taxpayers without measureable benefit, while actually putting the nation's tree stock in jeopardy. And these are but a few of the many examples. Likewise, the threat that many people in public life feel in the light of attempted prosecutions like R v. Porter, even when overturned, is a source of stress and anxiety which hangs over their lives and conditions their activities.

One way of getting to grips with this situation, if partially, is through understanding. To this end, the rest of this book is about explaining the nature of risk assessment as normally used in public life and, from there, about how people make decisions. The latter is the most important part, in fact, because risk assessment is not an end in itself, but the first stage of a process which leads to decision making. Decision making, which some people call risk management, rests on many foundations, and so the discussion will range over science, economics, ethics, the law, psychology, philosophy, sociology and even neurobiology. It is hoped in passing that this will reveal that even a subject like 'health and safety', often presumed to be as unremarkable as ditch-water, can in fact be deeply fascinating.

2
Risk Assessment – *A Simple Tool?*

In the UK the requirement to do risk assessments came in with the Health and Safety at Work etc. Act of 1974, although as noted in chapter 1 it wasn't at that stage specifically mentioned. The requirement arose because the Act said that risks should be reduced until they were 'as low as reasonably practicable', a term whose meaning will be discussed in detail later because of its extreme importance in the world of safety, both nationally and internationally. For the moment it need only be said that without doing some kind of risk assessment you cannot decide if the 'reasonable practicability' requirement has been met. The general requirement to do a risk assessment became explicit with the Management of Health and Safety at Work Regulations of 1992 and 1999, which say in Regulation 3 that 'Every employer shall make a suitable and suffi-cient assessment of the risks to health and safety ...' (HSE, 2000: 4).

Prior to the present era of risk assessment, say about 40 years ago, the approach to workplace safety had mainly been one of complying with relevant legislation, where it existed,[1] or if there were none, with regulations, Codes of Practice (CoPs), standards and published advice specific to each job in hand. The difficulty with this, as was pointed out following the investigation by Lord Robens' Commission in 1972,[2] was that there was simply too much written advice available. This had accumulated over the years in an ad-hoc fashion such that the sheer volume and complexity of it was beginning to overwhelm even its most dedicated followers. Something simpler was required, something which set out the *general principles and duties*, and this was where the HSW Act came to the rescue.

The language of risk

Before going on to discuss the nature of risk assessment it is necessary to understand a bit of terminology, particularly with respect to words like hazard and risk, and also to think about the meaning of the word 'safe' or 'safety'. Though these words are used in everyday language, they have to some extent been captured by this new professional interest, so taking on more specific meanings. However, it is not quite that straightforward because even within the professional sphere words like 'risk' have no universally agreed definition and mean different things to different people at different times.[3] Therefore, you have to be careful when you use them, otherwise misunderstandings can quickly arise. Even experts can be guilty of sloppiness in their usage of the language, or maybe it is just unavoidable because words like 'risk' and 'hazard' are not just the property of experts who wish to appropriate them. Whatever the reason, you need to be wary if you are having a conversation with someone, or reading a text, that the meaning of these words is suitably agreed and clear.

Hazard

This at least is fairly straightforward and refers to something which is a potential source of harm. In the workplace it could refer to a piece of machinery, a flammable or corrosive substance or even a badly adjusted office chair. Within public life countless hazards are continuously encountered and examples could be a riverside path, architectural features in a city square, a cobbled street, a wooded area or sports and leisure activities. Note that not only objects but activities too can give rise to hazards. In 2008 health and safety officials considered a victory parade for Manchester United Football Club, who had just become champions of Europe, a hazard too far and it was prohibited (The *Guardian*, 2008). This gave Manchester the dubious status of being the only city in memory not to give a civic welcome to its victorious team. Many other public activities, from fêtes to pantomimes, have been classified as hazards and some have in this way been prohibited (e.g. Mayhew, 2007).

Risk

Once a hazard has been identified, the term *risk* usually refers to the probability that it could cause some specified type of harm.[4] If you do not like the word 'probability' try 'likelihood' or 'chance'. In common parlance they mean pretty much the same thing. As for the type of harm, in the context of public safety this ranges from a slight injury, such as a scratch or bruise, to a single death or multiple deaths. Sometimes it is about psychological harm or perhaps property damage.

In stating what the risk associated with some hazard is, you need to be careful to specify a number of things. One of these is the consequence you have in mind. For example, a firework display could start a fire or it might cause personal injury, and the associated probabilities (risks) are likely to be very different for these two consequences. Secondly, the period of time over which a risk is measured is also important and should be made clear when it is stated. Is it the chance that a person will get hurt each time she encounters a hazard, using an electric hedge trimmer perhaps, or is it the chance that the person will be hurt during a specified period of use, say a year? Or is it the chance that any member of an entire community will be harmed during a specified period? Depending what you have in mind, the answers will be quite different. It is surprising how often these important dimensions of risk are glossed over or ignored when risk assessments are reported, yet they can be a source of considerable misunderstanding and even lead to spectacularly different conclusions.

Table 2.1 *Risks we face. All are risks of dying (see text for a discussion)*

Hazard	Risk	Source
'Smoking'	One in 3	Bast, 2002
Smoking (10 cigarettes a day)	One in 200 per year	BMA, 1987
Falls (all ages)	One in 18,000 per year	based on ONS, 2005
Falls (1–14 years of age)	One in 900,000 per year	based on ONS, 2005
Being a pedestrian	One in 93,000 per year	DfT, 2008
	3.6 per 100 million kilometres	
	3.7 per 100 million journeys	
	15 per 100 million hours	
Riding a pedal cycle	One in 440,000 per year	DfT, 2008
	3.1 per 100 million kilometres	
	12 per 100 million journeys	
	38 per 100 million hours	
Being on a motorcycle	One in 100,000 per year	DfT, 2008
	11 per 100 million kilometres	
	190 per 100 million journeys	
	430 per 100 million hours	
Fairground ride	One in 2.3 million rides	HSE, 2001
Playing soccer	2 per 100 million hours	Ball, 1998
Mountaineering	30–60 per 100 million hours	Ball, 1998
Release of radioactivity from nearby nuclear power station	One in 10 million	BMA, 1987

Some examples of hazards and the associated risks as reported by various agencies are listed in Table 2.1. The first two entries are about smoking. One originates from a British Medical Association publication (BMA, 1987) and the other is taken from an anti-smoking campaign billboard in the USA (Bast, 2002). Can they both be right? The answer lies in the detail. The main reason for the apparently huge discrepancy is that the billboard figure of 1 in 3 is actually an estimate of the risk of dying from smoking during a lifetime, not one year. It possibly omits to acknowledge the timescale because it seeks dramatic effect in order to shock people. But there are other subtleties lurking behind both figures. For example, the effect of smoking on the body is complicated and some effects are more scientifically verified than others. The extent to which more speculative consequences of smoking have been included is not clear in either case. To find out, it would be necessary to investigate the derivation of the numbers. Likewise, there is a tendency for smokers to take less exercise and drink more alcohol than non-smokers, and these too will affect risk, so there is also a question of the extent to which these 'confounding factors', as they are called, have been left in or removed from the risk estimates.

The next two entries, describing the risk of dying through falling over, are relatively straightforward. They are both averages over the entire population of Britain, which is around 60 million. What is interesting is that the risk for young people is far less than the average over the entire population. This is because the risk of serious consequences following a fall is much higher for the elderly.

The next three entries compare the risks of different ways of travelling: walking, cycling and riding a motorcycle. The first line in each category gives the risk of dying per year, but uses the population of Britain (circa 60 million) as the denominator. On this basis, being a pedestrian appears more risky than riding a pedal cycle and even a motorcycle! This is because these numbers ignore the fact that the number of people using these modes of transport is very different. It is obviously useful, therefore, to consider how many people actually use each mode of travel and to work out the risk for that population alone. This is what the other numbers do, but there is still the question of whether you should work out the risk per distance travelled, per journey or per hour of travel. In terms of distance travelled, the three modes have figures of 3.6, 3.1 and 11, which are not hugely different. On the other hand, a comparison on the basis of risk per hour of travel shows motorcycling to be by far the most dangerous mode. There is not in fact a right answer to the question of which of these statistics is preferable, but you do need to be aware of the effect this choice can make, especially if you are comparing one hazard with another.

The estimated risks for the leisure-related activities in Table 2.1 – riding at the fairground, playing soccer and mountaineering – are specific to those people taking part in the activity and are not averaged over the UK population, so they say something about the degree of danger associated with each pastime. The final estimate, of the risk of living near a nuclear power plant, is of a very different nature and origin. Unlike the other estimated risks in this table which are based upon statistics of past events, this estimate is based on the prediction, using sophisticated computer models, engineering experience and scientific knowledge, of the likelihood of a radiation release and its subsequent effect on the health of the population, which in turn requires knowledge of how the radiation would disperse and the relationship between human dose and ill health. Estimates of this kind are very demanding to arrive at, involve lots of assumptions and are often very uncertain.

Difficult as these numbers are to interpret, you might also begin to wonder why numerous risk assessments simply specify a risk as either 'high', 'medium' or 'low', leaving the meaning deeply obscure.

Safe or safety

If there is a word to avoid, this could be it. On the one hand, the words 'safe' and 'safety' mean such different things to people, including professionals, that they are best circumvented; although if this proves impossible, and it may do because they are so frequently used, be careful to state what you mean. On the other hand, if you should be so rash as to say that some activity or thing is 'safe', then you may be interpreted as having guaranteed zero risk, which, being a virtual impossibility, would render you a hostage to fortune.

The difficulty can be understood by considering the often-asked question: 'Is it safe?' For many people, this probably means: 'Is there any chance at all that something could go wrong?' But for the person who comes around to check your gas boiler, or fire safety on your premises, it probably means: 'Does it comply with (say) the industry standard?' This is not the same thing because standards are not normally written with risk elimination in mind, because it's difficult if not impossible to achieve, as well as expensive, and people wouldn't pay for it or put up with the inconvenience of the draconian measures required, and so there have been compromises.

For other people, say those concerned with things like drinking-water quality or air pollution, the question is more to do with whether certain threshold levels of contamination have been exceeded, because for many contaminants, providing you can keep the dose low enough, there are few or no harmful effects. This is not true of carcinogens, however, which are generally considered to have no threshold. However small the dose you get of a carcinogen, there is still some risk of cancer, even though it may be very tiny. So if you are being screened in a hospital or dental surgery by use of X-rays for some health condition, the X-ray dose, because it is a carcinogen, will expose you to some risk. The issue of 'is it safe?' then becomes a complex judgement about the relative risk of using X-rays and the benefits of their use in assessing your health.

This final example, of the medical use of X-rays, is actually closest to the kind of decision making which ought to go on when managing health and safety risks to the public. This is because it is a question of balancing the benefits of some thing or some activity against the dangers which it poses. As will be seen, this is not necessarily the way it is done.

Other terms

A few other terms are worth mentioning. 'Individual risk' is one sometimes encountered. This refers to the chance of a particular individual (real or imagined) sustaining a specified level of harm. The term is often used to differentiate it from situations where a hazard could harm a lot of people in one go, as with a major flood. Individual risk is relatively easy to measure if historical information is available on, say, the number of accidents associated with some activity and the number of people who have taken part. The examples in Table 2.1 are of individual risk.

Another term introduced recently is 'societal concerns'. This was defined very clearly in HSE's landmark publication, *Reducing risk: protecting people* (HSE, 2001: 12). The term refers to hazards which might lead to sociopolitical repercussions even though the risk and the consequences themselves might not appear to warrant such a degree of concern. It could be said, though it is unlikely the HSE were thinking of such trivia at the time, that MPs who claimed expenses in order to furnish their duck ponds would be dicing with societal concerns. Likewise the risk from dangerous dogs, perhaps the blanket closure of airspace because of volcanic ash, those of mobile-phone masts and the MMR vaccine could fall into this category, because of the public concern generated and hence the political upheaval associated with them.

A subcategory of societal concerns is that of 'societal risks.' These are hazards which differ from other hazards in that they could be catastrophic; that is, kill or harm a lot of people in one go, as in an aircraft crash, dam collapse, Chernobyl-type incident or bank failure. Most day-to-day health and safety hazards to which the public are exposed are largely devoid of these characteristics so we need consider them no more, but if they do apply, advice on their assessment has been published by HM Treasury (HMT, 2005).

The essential differences between risk assessment and risk management

As with the word 'risk', there are no universally agreed definitions of 'risk assessment' and 'risk management', but a major distinction of which one should be very aware is the difference between them. 'Risk assessment' refers to the systematic use of information to identify hazards and estimate the associated risks. 'Risk management' is about the next stage of the process: *what to do, if anything, about the risks identified.* Thus, whereas risk assessment may be a wholly or at least partly a technical or even scientific process, risk management is emphatically not.

This is because risk management, which is basically about decision making, should, as made abundantly clear in the new international standard (ISO, 2009), consider the policy background including objectives of the agency responsible for the hazards, as well as legal, social, ethical and economic aspects, and clearly these cover a lot more ground than purely technical considerations, even though these are important. It is sometimes not appreciated by technical persons who do risk assessments, or their recruiters, that they may not be qualified, authorized or in an intellectual position to make risk management decisions.

Figure 2.1, which is taken from the Cabinet Office's 2002 report on the management of risk, illustrates the point about the differing requirements of risk assessment and risk management. The left-hand box, headed 'Risk Identification', is about the identification of what in this text are called hazards. This can be done based on research into, say, the health effects of some new chemical or through studying the historical record of incidents, or

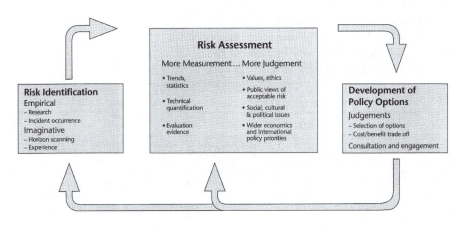

Source: Crown Copyright, Cabinet Office (2002: 34)

Figure 2.1 *Risk judgement in policy making*

by observation and experience. The central box, although labelled risk assessment, is what we would prefer to call risk assessment *and* management, because it goes beyond the purely technical matter of assessing the risk associated with some hazard into matters of ethics and policy. The left-hand column in this central box shows the various 'technical' inputs which constitute pure risk assessment. The right-hand column refers to the judgemental elements which necessarily influence any decision about what to do. In dealing with public safety, these judgemental elements will inevitably entail human values and ethical considerations, public attitudes and policy matters.

Conducting risk assessments

There are numerous methods available for assessing risks.[5] In heavy industry, numerical methods which rely upon detailed engineering knowledge are widely used. In the insurance sector there is considerable use of historical claims data and this has the great benefit, providing circumstances have not changed, of being anchored in some sort of objective reality. When it comes to forecasting future risks, as in global climate change, or flu pandemics, this requires deep scientific understanding of how these things might come about coupled perhaps with the use of sophisticated computer models. Whatever method is used, it is important to somehow test it against actual observations of past events to ensure so far as one can that the theory is sound and the models are realistic.

In the case of risks to the public of the kind addressed in this book, the more sophisticated engineering-style approaches are of little relevance because, for one thing, there are so many decisions to make, mainly of a small-scale nature, and it would be impractical. It is far more common for simplified procedures of the kind described in documents like HSE's *Five steps to risk assessment* (HSE, 2006a) to be used. The five stages which this particular approach advocates are as follows:

- Look for hazards.
- Decide who might be harmed.
- Evaluate the risks and decide on precautions.
- Record the findings and implement them.
- Review and update the assessment as necessary.

Step 1: What are the hazards?	Step 2: Identify who is exposed, particularly vulnerable groups	Step 3		Step 4: By whom, and when will it be done?
		What are you doing already to manage the risk?	What further action is necessary?	

Figure 2.2 *The first four stages of HSE's risk assessment process*

The publication *Five steps to risk assessment* also includes a pro forma to help people meet their responsibilities, a version of which is shown in Figure 2.2. This is clearly a much more simplistic approach than the Cabinet Office's example above which, in so far as models go, is a good one as it actively identifies the need to consider the context within which risk is being assessed, and the fact that decisions about what to do are not purely technical.

Prioritization

Another device which is commonly used by risk assessors is known as the 'risk matrix'.[6] Figure 2.3 shows a typical 3×3 version of this, with three levels of severity of consequence and three levels of probability. The matrix doesn't have to be 3×3. Versions ranging from 2×2 to 10×10 have their followers. Whatever the size, the normal procedure is to place each hazard which has been identified in one of the boxes. In the 3×3 example in Figure 2.3 this would be done according to whether the probability was judged to be low, medium or high, and the envisaged harm to be low, medium or high.

Some people use these devices to prioritize their tasks, according to the rule that hazards falling in the top right-hand corner would generally attract more attention than those in the bottom left. To assist this it is sometimes the practice to give a numerical score to each level of consequence and probability and multiply them together, as has been done in Figure 2.3, so that hazards in the top right-hand box in this case would have a 'risk score' of nine.

However, beware of applying mathematics to things which are not inherently mathematical. In this case, for example, 1×3 is *not* the same as 3×1. More on this later.

Risk assessment – *is it simple?*

The HSE, in its *Five steps to risk assessment*, has endeavoured to keep things simple so that people responsible for everyday hazards are not unduly burdened. Their document is aimed at smaller firms and presumably public service bodies who are responsible for what are considered to be routine and everyday hazards, rather than the kinds of complex and serious risks associated

Consequence	Probability		
	Low (1)	Medium (2)	High (3)
High (3)			Risk score (3×3) = 9
Medium (2)			
Low (1)			

Figure 2.3 *A fairly typical 3×3 risk matrix (note that if no explanation is provided of what is meant by low, medium and high on the axes, its meaning for the reader will be a matter of speculation)*

with major chemical industries or intercity express trains, which obviously warrant more sophistication. Even so, the truth is that it isn't so simple and furthermore the task is highly subjective, meaning that different people could well assess a hazard very differently. There are a number of reasons for this.

Failure to be explicit about benefits

Arguably the most serious deficiency in risk assessment, when applied to public places and activities, is the failure to be explicit about the benefits of the place or the activity. *Five steps ...*, for instance, makes no mention of benefits, and the probable outcome therefore is that they will be ignored or at the least undervalued.[7] This means that the risk assessor's recommendations will be driven by the desire to relocate hazards from the top right of Figure 2.3 towards the bottom left and little more. Indeed, in the 1998 version of *Five steps ...*, the requirement is stated as follows: 'The important things you need to decide are whether a *hazard is significant*, and whether you have covered it adequately so that the *risk is small*.'

Emphasis on making risks small, or minimizing them, can be found in many documents about health and safety (Elmonstri et al, 2009; Diamond et al, 2009). Strictly speaking this is wrong wherever it is applied, including in the workplace, because the actual legal requirement is to reduce risks so far as is reasonably practicable.[8] In public life a change of emphasis, from reducing risk so far as reasonably practicable to minimizing risk, can have other implications. If your only consideration were to reduce risk, then public life as we know it would end. All water bodies, ponds, rivers and lakes would have to be fenced off if not filled in, all plants with even mildly toxic parts would be banned, and sporting events would not be permitted because of the obvious risk of injury. Of course, risk assessors are not so unworldly as to be unaware of the benefits of public space and activities, but with no formal requirement to consider benefits the extent to which these figure in final recommendations about what to do is likely to be vague, uncertain, and vary from person to person, situation to situation and time to time. This variability may well be a major contributor to the profusion of anecdotes in public life about 'elf and safety', as described in chapter 1.

Likewise, the dictum that risk should be minimized without further ado can be achieved by moving the risk somewhere else, outside of your immediate sphere of interest perhaps, and hence appear to be successful from the narrow perspective, but potentially at the expense of society.

How far to reduce risk?

There is another important question to be answered. With reference to Figure 2.3, hazards with high consequence and high risk appear towards the top right of the matrix, and the challenge for the risk assessor is usually seen as shifting these hazards towards the lower left corner by reducing the severity of possible consequences, or reducing the risk, or both, by the means available. But is it necessarily the case that this should be done and, if it is, how far ought it to go?

To this effect it is not unusual to see risk matrices with the boxes coloured in shades of grey or, with greater panache, from red to green, as a means of

	Risk – unlikely	Risk – occasional	Risk – probable	Risk – frequent
Severity – critical				
Severity – high				
Severity – moderate				
Severity – low				

Figure 2.4 *An example of a 4×4 risk matrix*

differentiating between the high-risk–high-consequence hazards and other hazards. Figure 2.4 shows a simple 4×4 matrix with these features, here as shading. Typically these matrices come with the presumption that hazards in the darker areas should be relocated to the lighter-coloured regions.

It should be recognized that the act of dividing up the matrix into zones in this way, either by shading or colouring the boxes, or sometimes by inserting a 'boundary line' between what are thought to be the more serious hazards and the less serious hazards, could be tantamount to making risk management decisions. It is going well beyond the domain of assessing risk, which is what is required to simply locate each hazard in its cell in the matrix. As has been discussed earlier in this chapter, decisions about what to do about identified hazards should be considered against the policy background of the agency responsible for the hazards (e.g. does it wish to support certain physical activities or social events, even though it is known that some people may be injured merely through being there?), as well as legal, social, ethical and economic factors. It is clear that the decision process is one requiring careful consideration by those who are experienced in those issues, and care should be taken that this thoughtful process will not be replaced by a box-ticking-cum-colouring exercise.

In this way, as with many approaches which appear at the outset sound, an initially sensible and intuitive process can be taken to illogical and inappropriate lengths. The point is illustrated by a risk matrix published a few years ago by the Cabinet Office (2002), which has some rarely seen though very informative features (Figure 2.5). While this matrix has a boundary (the thick black line) drawn on it, the legend holds valuable information as to how the information on the matrix should be interpreted. For the hazards marked as crosses, on the lower left side, only monitoring and planning is required. More interestingly, even for some hazards (those shown as lighter ellipses), which fall on the wrong side of the boundary, no further action is required. This admission, that some higher-consequence and higher-risk hazards can remain untreated, is very unusual – most risk matrices imply that anything falling in that zone must be shifted towards the bottom left of the diagram. Similarly,

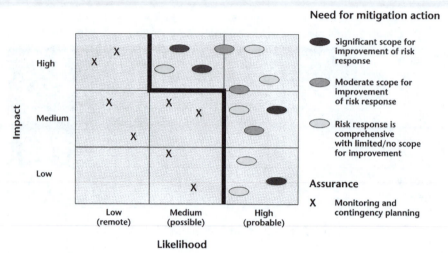

Source: Crown Copyright, Cabinet Office (2002: 48)

Figure 2.5 *The risk matrix as set out by the Cabinet Office*

most statements by people responsible for hazards, and sometimes by politi-cians, imply that higher-consequence accidents will not be tolerated. Understandable though this desire is, it cannot always be achieved unless you believe in risk control at any price. Even then, it may still not be possible.

The justification given by the Cabinet Office for not taking that approach, as clearly set out in the notation accompanying their figure, and which is refreshingly sensible, is that there will in some cases be limited scope for further risk reduction, everything reasonable having already been done. Maybe another justification which could be used in relation to risks of public life is that the benefits of the activity, space or object would be harmed by safety measures and need to be protected.

How to locate hazards on the risk matrix?

The problems of interpreting the risk matrix have been described, but there are also problems in locating hazards on the matrix, and in producing 'risk scores' if you go down that route. They are quite obvious when thought about, so it is surprising how often they are ignored or seemingly pass unnoticed.

Firstly, for any given hazard, say the simple hazard of tripping, there is a range of consequences which could ensue from a stumble, to a head injury, an upper limb fracture and in very unfortunate circumstances even a fatality. Each of these consequences has its own probability. So, in placing a mark within a single box on a risk matrix, an assessor is performing some highly complex mental computation and expressing the output as a single point (Ball-King, 2009a).

This mental gymnastics is not assisted by the fact that the axes of the matrix seldom go up in uniform steps, such as one unit of harm, two units, three units etc., but go up in steps of ever increasing size.[9] A consequence of death, for example, would clearly fall at the high end of the consequence scale, and a minor injury at the bottom end, but there is no simple arithmetic which says how many minor injuries are equivalent to a death. So the level of mental arithmetic involved in contemplating where to locate a hazard on the risk matrix, though seldom discussed, is severe.

One ruse for avoiding this difficulty has been to take the route of the 'worst-case scenario'. That is, for any hazard, think of the worst thing that could happen and use that as the consequence when completing the matrix. There are several problems associated with this subterfuge. One is that even apparently trivial hazards have been known to seriously injure or even kill people if circumstances conspire. The counterargument might then be to use the most likely consequence, but that just returns you to more mental gymnastics, little different from the previous. And, in any case, there is a political (policy) judgement implicit in this choice of 'most likely' or 'worst case', which is another example of how the technical process of risk assessment can inadvertently trespass upon the risk management or policy process.

A second problem of the 'worst-case scenario' approach is that it encourages a highly risk-averse society. If people want to live in a risk-averse society, that of course is a political choice they are entitled to make. But the proposition here is that this important decision should not be permitted to creep in via some unobserved or undisclosed artefact associated with the peculiarities of tools like risk matrices.

Use of risk assessment 'scores'

It has been mentioned that a common tendency is to put numbers along each axis on the risk matrix, as was done in a simple way in Figure 2.3. This 'allows' risk scores to be calculated by multiplying together the values on the two axes for any particular hazard. We are extremely sceptical of this way of working. Some would even describe this practice, maybe correctly, as a 'gross abuse' which could only be perpetrated by 'disengaging (the) brain' (Garlick, 2007: 27). If you do this kind of thing, a hazard appearing in the high-consequence and medium-risk box of Figure 2.3 would generate a score of $3 \times 2 = 6$. Quite often a matrix will be accompanied by a legend which says something along the lines of: hazards giving rise to risk scores greater than or equal to 6 require immediate action; those scoring 2 or less need only to be monitored; and those between require something in-between. While this approach might have a little bit of utility, it is important to recognize that what is being done is again in no way scientific. For a start, where the axes are defined in qualitative terms (high, medium and low), points along them are purely ordinal and not cardinal.[10] This means it is simply wrong, and deceptive, to multiply them together. If you finished third in a flower show and won fifth prize in a raffle, your overall achievement could not meaningfully be described as 15.

A second reason why this kind of maths is misleading is, as Garlick points out too, because the scales on each axis, as mentioned above, are grossly nonlinear (i.e. do not go up in even steps). If the consequence level 3, for instance, were death and consequence level 1 were minor injury, then hazards appearing in the lower-right and top-left boxes would both score 3, seemingly of equal priority in terms of risk score. But one is a 'low' risk of death and the other is a 'high' risk of minor injury. Seldom, in reality, would these be considered to amount to the same thing. Some risk assessors attempt to escape this conundrum by drawing bigger and bigger matrices with more and more gradations, or by using different scales on the two axes. In most cases this is no more than a ploy and fails to fully address the underlying issue.

Thirdly, this procedure of creating a risk score is often said to be as an aid to prioritizing control actions. Clearly this once again trespasses on the policy domain by its use of numbers, in this case not very good numbers, to make decisions. As in the example from the Cabinet Office (Figure 2.5), high scores do not necessarily warrant more action than low scores.

Subjectivity and objectivity

For risk assessment to anchor itself in reality, it is necessary wherever possible to ground it in facts and observations. This is why actuaries are such important people in the insurance industry and business – they have knowledge of past events which can provide guidance for the future. In terms of public safety, however, risk assessments tend neither to refer to nor use statistics, even where statistics on past or similar situations exist (e.g. as in the case R v. Porter, where the safety record of the school was initially ignored), making them subjective.

However, it is well known that many places, including public places that look dangerous, have few accidents, and that locations that look innocuous can have a high rate of accidents. There is copious research into why subjective risk assessments can deviate from reality. A key element which emerges is that intuitive decision making of this kind is subject to various forms of mental bias. The American risk expert Louis Cox has produced a summary of no less than 17 psychological factors which affect judgement and which apply equally to lay people and experts (Cox, 2007: 38). These include things like the 'availability of images'. If you have experienced directly, or even indirectly through a recent news story or even a Hollywood film, some memorable accident, you will be inclined to rate the probability of a recurrence as higher than it actually is.

This deficiency can have serious consequences for people's judgement and self-protective behaviour. After the 9/11 attack many Americans shunned air travel in favour of cars, even though cars are a more dangerous means of getting about, resulting in unintended deaths of drivers and pedestrians rivalling in numbers those of the attack itself (Blalock et al, 2005).[11] Likewise, the extent to which people rely upon personal intuition versus thoughtful analysis will depend on the person's numeracy, age and gender. None of this is conducive to either objectivity or reproducibility unless one is very careful, even extending that care to one's own mental processes.

Cox has also made a very thorough study of risk matrices and reaches the following disturbing conclusions:

> *Inputs to risk matrices (that is the severity and risk categorizations) and resulting outputs (risk ratings) require subjective interpretation, and different users may obtain opposite ratings of the same quantitative risks. These limitations suggest that risk matrices should be used with caution and only with careful explanations of embedded judgments.*

and ...

> *Risk matrices do not necessarily support good (e.g. better-than-random) risk management decisions ... (Cox, 2008)*

Interestingly, Worcestershire County Council (amongst others) also advises against the use of technical or numerical scoring systems in the context of its 'Learning outside the classroom' guidance (Gill, 2010: 19), as does Play England's *Managing Risk in Play Provision* (Play England, 2008b). Indeed, as will emerge later,[12] there are probably even deeper issues surrounding the use of risk assessment in public life, to do with the surprising complexity of these hazards.

In passing, in 1996, Gordon Hayward of the Consumer Safety Unit of the Department of Trade and Industry, published an insightful paper on the actual risk versus the perceived risk of a large range of consumer products, ranging from hedge trimmers to garden forks and electric blankets. He obtained the data on actual risk from accident statistics and the perceived risk data from a consumer survey (Hayward, 1996). Consumer products are, of course, similar in nature in some respects to items in public space. Hayward concluded as follows:

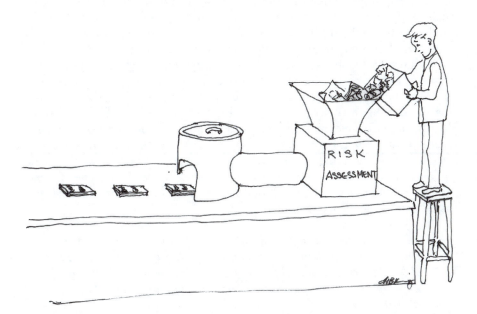

> *People's perception of comparative danger of products is clearly an unreliable guide to the actual risk of injury of a product in use.*

and ...

> *The need for objective criteria for priority setting is therefore clear.*

This, of course, concurs with the Cox thesis that subjective assessments do not necessarily support better-than-random risk-management decisions.

Alternative approaches to decision making

Of course, some risk assessors are well aware of the problems described above. One route often used is not to apply conventional risk assessment at all,[13] but to resort to other strategies such as following what is otherwise described as 'best practice'. In fact, some years ago Baruch Fischhoff and colleagues described three main approaches to risk assessment and decision making (Fischhoff et al, 1981), which were given the following names: formal analysis, bootstrapping and professional judgement. The one referred to as 'formal analysis' is most akin to conventional risk assessment,[14] but, as they described it, is conducted at a much higher level of sophistication in situations where major policy decisions have to be made. These high-level approaches are seldom suitable for decisions about public safety unless some major event is being contemplated, or if a policy decision is being made which will be rolled out across a lot of circumstances, thereby having regional or national implications. This is because, for one thing, it takes far too long and requires much data. This makes it inappropriate for situations where a myriad of circumstance-specific, local-scale decisions have to be made, as in much of public life. Nonetheless, it should not be totally discarded even in this context, because it does make use of numerical information which conveys some realism to risk estimation.

Turning to 'bootstrapping', this is an alternative approach designed to circumvent the above difficulties of formal analysis. It can take two forms. One is to refer to standards and written codes of practice, and follow their advice. The other involves searching for historical precedents. How, for example, have other people managed this hazard and how is it working out? There is certainly merit in this approach so far as risks to public safety are concerned because it is never going to be easy to predict with certainty how the public will react to some new public space or some new activity. Practical experience is therefore immensely valuable. Not only this, but as Fischhoff and colleagues have said of proponents of bootstrapping:

> ... *risks cannot be analyzed adequately in any short period of time. Rather, society achieves an acceptable trade-off between risks and benefits only through a protracted period of hands-on experience that allows for trial-and-error learning. (Fischhoff et al, 1981: 79)*

Of course, an obvious weakness of bootstrapping is its strong bias towards the status quo and the assumption that past decisions are right for the future. Additionally, in the case of new hazards, there may be no relevant experience against which to compare. However, most public safety issues are not of this nature.

Besides this, there are other potential problems. In the case of standards and codes of practice, these are not necessarily based upon risk assessment, and their relevance to your circumstances may only be marginal. They may even have been written with entirely different issues in mind (Herrington and Nicholls, 2007). And the business of 'bootstrapping' to what is going on elsewhere is not *necessarily* a good guide to risk either, though it could be the best you have. Since the law currently requires a risk assessment, this needs to be thought about carefully.

The third approach, referred to as 'professional judgement', brings up yet more interesting issues which will be revisited at various points in this book. Normally, professional judgement would be expected to rely on the technical knowledge and judgements of appropriate experts in a field. These persons might have expertise, say, in the design of engineered structures such as footbridges or traffic management schemes used in public space. But in situations where the issue is to consider not just the safety of some public place or activity, a further kind of knowledge is required – knowledge about the benefits which might, say, include those of a health-giving activity or the beauty of an object or place, and from that how to arrive at a reasonable balance or 'trade-off' between risk and benefit. Making decisions of this kind is quite different from deciding about the structural integrity of some facility. Both may be important in given circumstances, but require different kinds of expertise.

There is a powerful and contemporary argument that these kinds of decisions should not be delegated to technical people because they are about values; that is, the relative importance of different things that people care about. Although people undoubtedly do care about safety, in public life they value many other things besides, and these should be factored into decisions about what to do. If appropriate recognition is given to the fact that the ultimate client is the general public, then professional judgement may be the best way to determine what is desirable and practical. However, one must bear in mind that there is no necessary link between expertise in a substantive area like, say, engineering, or the ability to check for compliance with standards and expertise in decision making about public life. A key requirement would be to emphasize the needs of the specific client, which for public activities would normally be, ultimately, those of the general public. This raises the crucial question of the kind of professionals who are best placed to make these judgements.

Summary

During the latter part of the 20th century risk assessment developed substantially in heavy industry. In 1974, with the passing of the Health and Safety at Work etc. Act, many other sectors including local government, hospitals and education were brought under this umbrella, and the approaches pioneered in industry began to spill over into public life. As noted in chapter 1, this period of transfer did not pass without difficulties.

Consideration of the industry approach suggests that these difficulties are attributable to a number of causes; in particular, their failure to give sufficient if any overt recognition to the benefits of public places and activities. Coupled with a widely held belief, actually erroneous, that the purpose of risk assessment is to minimise risk, this has put considerable pressure on all kinds of public activities which people previously enjoyed.

Risk assessment, as practised in public life, is also found to be highly subjective, and not at all the scientific or technical process which it sometimes is made out to be.

At times risk assessment is used in such a way that it trespasses well beyond the technical domain into that of policy where its legitimacy may be further open to question.

3
Is Safety Paramount?

Were one to judge the answer to the above question of the paramountcy of safety by the number of hits generated on typing the words 'safety' and 'paramount' into an internet search engine, then the answer would surely be affirmative. In 2011 these words conjure up millions of hits.

However, a problem soon emerges. According to the first few pages of these hits, all of the following are paramount: swimming pool safety, public safety, foreign travel safety, pesticide safety, two-wheel safety, medical safety, patient safety, construction safety, gas safety, environmental safety, air travel safety, safety against fraud, and so the list goes on. Given that the word 'paramount' means 'requiring first consideration' (Concise OED, 8th Edition), the obvious question which follows is: 'How can *all* of these concerns be first?' Perhaps the question can be partially avoided by the ruse that 'safety in general is paramount'. But is it, and who says so?

Certainly there are many people out there who champion causes, sometimes very worthy ones, and who fervently believe in the importance of the issue which is the focus of their attention. Thus, it should come as little surprise that the Health and Safety Executive, whose job it is to regulate workplace safety, has proposed the following as an example of the position which a factory or business might adopt with respect to health and safety:

> *We believe nothing is more important than safety ... Not production, not sales, not profits. (HSE, 1997)*

This tendency has not passed unobserved. As Lord Hoffmann has said of the HSE:

> *Their mission is to reduce the number of accidents. A fall in numbers of people suffering accidental injuries is the measure of their success. And so, while no doubt they take into account the wider consequences, they do not have to strike a balance between safety and liberty. That is a matter for the court ... (Hoffmann, 2005)*

So this is one important issue: the potential conflict in some circumstances between the quest for safety from injury and liberty. There is another one though. With any unconstrained proposition which seeks to prioritize some particular thing over other things, there is the question of its satiability. However safe an activity is, there is always a residual risk, but the dictum 'Safety is paramount' would still seemingly require further action. So where does it stop?

Such statements are also essentially political because they express a preference for some good, in this case safety, over other goods. Other goods that might contend with safety in terms of their importance include environmental protection, healthcare, provision of jobs, a sound economy, a reliable supply of electricity and gas, journey times on public transport, the authenticity of a historical building, the educational benefits of a school outing, cookery classes, the health benefits of leisure activities, enjoyment of wilderness, psychological well-being, sense of community, the right to roam, and the beauty of a riverside walk or city square.

According to Her Majesty's Treasury (HMT, 2003), when considering whether some change should be implemented or not, all the relevant costs and benefits to society should be considered, including the wider social and environmental costs and benefits, even if they have no market price.[1] In the case of a safety intervention, for example, in deciding whether a measure which will improve safety is to be implemented, one should consider the benefits of the measure; that is, how much safer things will become, the cost of the measure, and any other consequences, intended or not, which might arise. In order then to decide what to do it is common practice to rely upon the work of the 19th-century Italian economist, Vilfredo Pareto, who introduced the concept now referred to as Pareto efficiency.

According to this principle, there is an overall improvement in the welfare of society if, when a change is made, at least one person benefits and nobody loses. All changes which satisfy this condition should, logically, be sanctioned. However, this pure version of the Pareto criterion is seldom achievable. This is because with most interventions there are some losers.

Consider a plan to create a skate park for teenagers in the middle of a popular public area or to create a sculpture park, or to open up a new riverside walk. All of these things provide benefits for some people, but for others they might create annoyance, disturbance or nuisance, or they may have to pay, through taxes, for something of no interest to them. And some of the options, especially perhaps the skate park, may locally increase the risk of injury.

Nonetheless, even though the Pareto criterion is breached because there are losers, it still might overall be in the interests of society to go ahead with these plans if there is an overall societal gain and nobody is too badly affected. This is where the 'modified Pareto criterion' comes in. Thus, economists Nicholas Kaldor and John Hicks made the Pareto criterion into a much more useful decision rule by a simple adjustment. Essentially what this modified form of the Pareto rule says is that an intervention is rational, and socially desirable, provided those who gain from it could, in theory, compensate those who lose. Based on this rule, if there is a net positive advantage to society as a whole of taking an action, then subject to any other issues, it would be logical to proceed.

To refer back to the above examples, it would be logical to proceed from a societal perspective if the gains in, say health and amenity to those who lived nearby and enjoyed the facility, outweighed the disbenefits, including the increased taxes, to whoever experienced them. Note the use of the words 'in theory'. Under the Kaldor-Hicks criterion, it is *not* a condition that this compensation is given!

Is health and safety exempt from economics?

Many people, particularly those who think that safety is paramount, are either unaware of, or disregard, the idea that safety should be subject to economics. Money simply does not enter into the equation for them, and the mere mention of such a fact can evoke shock, bewilderment and instant dismissal. But if they think that safety is above monetary consideration they are wrong.[2] The United Kingdom's approach to all kinds of decision making is anchored substantially in the prudent use of resources, whether those resources are to be used for healthcare, safety, environmental protection, flood defence or whatever. Essentially, the bedrock of decision making is cost-benefit analysis. As will be revealed later, there is more to decision making than a crude tally of costs and benefits of measures, but this is the starting point and one from which logic dictates that significant deviation should require good justification.

To demonstrate the truth of the above, and the pervasiveness of this approach in our society, four contrasting examples are now given from the following sectors: railway safety; healthcare; environmental management; and occupational safety. These sectors span a wide range of services and issues, but as HM Treasury says, things like health, safety, time saving, environmental quality and the like, although being 'non-market goods', are all things which matter to people when decisions are made, and should therefore be valued wherever possible (HMT, 1991: 19).

The case of Automatic Train Protection

In 1988 two commuter trains collided outside of London's Clapham Junction station and a third train ran into the wreckage, killing survivors of the original crash. Thirty-five people died and over 500 were injured. This sparked a major inquiry, with many recommendations for preventing further rail deaths (DoT, 1989). One recommendation was to fit a system known as Automatic Train Protection (ATP) to the rail network as a whole.[3] All trains are of course fitted with an array of safety systems, one being a warning system which alerts drivers who are about to prompt a hazardous event known as a Signal Passed at Danger (SPAD). SPADs have been perhaps surprisingly frequent occurrences, there being about 300 per year in the UK not so long ago, but most were very minor events causing no harm. Retrofitting of ATP to the UK rail network would virtually eliminate the risk of SPADs. Essentially, ATP is a computerized system which automatically applies the brakes if a driver fails to heed a signal, and at first glance it appears logical that it should be installed. However, a risk assessment, combined with a cost-benefit assessment, showed that ATP fell outside of the normal safety investment criteria in use at the time. What this means is that, in effect, the cost of the system, which was estimated as in the region of £1 billion in 1989, was deemed by government to exceed the benefit in terms of life saving.

To make such a comparison, however, it was necessary to have an estimate of the number of crashes avoided and hence lives saved which ATP would bring about: and, secondly, some idea of the appropriate amount of money which should be allocated to save a human life. The first of these quantities is relatively uncontentious and can be obtained by the use of one form of risk assessment based on the analysis of historical accidents. Andrew Evans and Neville Verlander of University College London reported such an analysis in 1996. By looking at accidents which had occurred on the rail network, and deciding whether or not they were of a type which ATP would have prevented, they were able to estimate the number of fatalities per year which the non-fitting of ATP would bring about. The answer was around three to four per year (Evans and Verlander, 1996).

Now supposing that any ATP system adopted would have a lifetime of 20 years indicates that it would save around 70 lives, and this at the then cost of £1 billion. The implied cost per life saved is thus £1 billion divided by 70, or £14 million per fatality avoided for network-wide installation. This figure of £14 million per life saved was also arrived at by a far more sophisticated analysis by British Rail (British Railways Board, 1994: 23), and lay behind the government's decision at the time not to go ahead with ATP. The figure was simply far too high, by more than a factor of ten, compared with the yardstick in use at that time for a reasonable investment for saving the life of an unknown person (the value of the baseline figure and its derivation is described later in this chapter).[4]

This approach to transport safety investment applies to all transport modes. The Department for Transport has traditionally used cost-benefit analysis in its decisions about which safety schemes to implement on the road network, and so do other agencies including the Marine and Coast Guard Agency, and the Civil Aviation Authority, but, as will be discussed later, additional factors may be brought to bear on decisions.

Healthcare and the mysterious QALY

Health and safety should obviously be about health as well as safety from injury, and so it is appropriate to look at how decisions are made in the National Health Service about which procedures and medications should be made available and which not. As noted in chapter 1, by no means all drugs nor treatments which exist are made available to patients, including some known to give real health benefits.

Just as with transport safety, healthcare is also about obtaining the maximum health gain from the resources at its disposal. Within the Health Service this is normally not a question simply of lives lost or saved as in transport,[5] but is more often about prolonging life or improving the quality of life. Therefore, the yardstick used in transport safety – the cost of avoiding a fatality is less useful – and what is frequently used instead is the Quality Adjusted Life Year (QALY). According to this measure, a year of life lived in full health would have a QALY score of unity, and this score would progressively reduce for less perfect health states down to a value of zero for death. In some extreme cases, even negative scores are conceivable for conditions regarded as worse than death. So the rational approach to deciding whether or not some health intervention should be provided would require the benefits of the treatment, measured in QALYs, to be compared with its cost, and for the modified Pareto criterion to be applied to determine if, overall, benefits exceeded cost.

This would of course require the monetary value of one QALY to be determined. A recent legal case against the National Institute for Health and Clinical Excellence (NICE), over its decision not to authorize the use of certain drugs for treating Alzheimer's disease, led to extensive discussion of NICE's decision-making procedure in the national press (Hawkes, 2008: 6). Although various articles portrayed NICE's decision-making process as 'secretive', it is far closer to the truth to say that NICE's decision process, along with that of all the above-mentioned transport agencies, and many others besides, is simply unfamiliar to most members of the public.[6] But what this case illustrated was that NICE determines whether a treatment will be made available on the NHS by weighing its cost against the benefits, and that drugs are generally approved if they cost the NHS less than £30,000 per QALY. This is tantamount to putting a value of £30,000 upon one year of life lived in full health. The advantage for the NHS of this yardstick is that it can calculate which treatments are economically efficient and should therefore go ahead, and also argue its case for their funding with central government in competition with other government departments which themselves wish to maintain or expand their own services. In this way, a level playing field is created for the allocation of public monies.

Environmental protection

Some environmentalists think that the environment should be pristine and, of course, it would be nice if it were (except for those lowly and possibly important organisms at the bottom of the food chain who thrive in mud, filth and decay). But, as with those who believe that safety is paramount, there are limits to how much it is reasonable to allocate to cleaning up the environment. HM Treasury (2003: 61) gives the example of air pollution's impact upon human health (though it could equally be the impact upon non-human species). The line taken is similar to that in healthcare and transport safety decision making. Namely, do your best to put a monetary value on the health benefits associated with the planned lower pollution level, so that you can compare it with the cost of the proposed abatement strategy and thereby decide if the strategy is a sensible investment of public money.

It is plausible that most people would automatically go through a thinking process of this kind were they faced with the following situation. Imagine that your local council has a waste incinerator and that, although it is reasonably clean and well managed, there is still some concern about residual emissions of some pollutants and their possible health effects. Bearing in mind that the council has a fixed budget which also covers schooling, police and many other services as well as the environment, which option would you vote for?

1. Addition of extra waste-gas scrubbing equipment at modest cost.
2. Addition of state-of-the-art waste-gas cleaning equipment at higher cost.
3. Relocation of the incinerator at very high cost.

It would be perfectly reasonable in these circumstances to ask, before answering the question, by what fraction each option would reduce pollution levels, what the projected health benefits might be, and what actual costs would ensue. Armed with that information it would be easier to make a judgement.

This kind of thought process can be traced back a long time, certainly to the British Alkali Inspectorate established in 1863 and the Alkali Act of 1874. This agency was set up to deal with serious industrial pollution generated by the alkali industry, but its work also covered many other of the dirtier industries. The remit of the Inspectorate was as follows:

> *to use the best practicable means for preventing the emission into the atmosphere from the premises of noxious or offensive substances and for rendering harmless and inoffensive such substances as may be emitted.*

The most important words in this statement are 'best practicable means' (BPM), in particular the word 'practicable'. This word has legal connotations which, as will be seen later, imply a balancing between the benefits of a control measure and its costs. Thus, a very expensive control measure with limited potential to reduce emissions would be unlikely to meet the requirement of being a 'practicable means'. Note that the word 'practicable' should on no account be substituted with either 'practical', which would imply that as long as something could be done it should be done, or 'possible', which would suggest total disregard for the cost element in the decision and the difficulty of its implementation. And there is a logic here, for although Victorian factories were notorious polluters, they also provided jobs and wages, and this too had to be considered in arriving at the optimum societal position.

These same concepts underpin the thinking of the present-day Environment Agency and the Environment Act of 1995. According to the Act, the Agency should, in deciding whether to exercise its power to protect the environment: 'take into account the likely costs and benefits' of its actions. The purpose of this being to demonstrate to those who are being regulated, and the public, that it is acting efficiently and that costs imposed are not disproportionate to the benefits gained (Environment Agency, circa 1998).

Health and safety at work

The landmark legislation here is the Health and Safety at Work etc. Act of 1974, which followed directly on from the work of the Robens Committee.

What Robens identified as being needed was a piece of overarching, goal-setting legislation, which described a general principle that could be applied in all circumstances. The principle was that risks, of whatever kind, should be reduced 'so far as is reasonably practicable' (SFAIRP) or, with the same meaning, until 'as low as reasonably practicable' (ALARP).[7,8] So, here again, the word 'practicable' appears, this time qualified by the adjective 'reasonable'. This will be discussed much more carefully in chapter 6, for it is crucially important in understanding the UK approach to this whole business of safety management in whatever sector.

Here, though, it is simply necessary to emphasize that the use of the words 'reasonably practicable' signifies that decisions about which safety measures should be implemented do entail consideration of the cost, as well as the effectiveness of those measures in reducing risk. This, of course, is sensible because it means that safety measures which have minimal safety benefit and which are very costly are not required by law, whereas those that do improve safety for a reasonable outlay must, by law, be implemented.

The Health and Safety Executive must itself operate within the framework provided by the HSW Act, and in so doing uses cost-benefit analysis implicitly or explicitly to inform its decisions when regulating and managing risks. According to its publication *Reducing risk: protecting people*, it does this by expressing all relevant costs and benefits in a common currency, usually money (HSE, 2001: 64).

But is it ethical to put a price on safety?

These examples from across the United Kingdom demonstrate that health, safety and environmental decision making are by no means exempt from considerations of cost and efficiency. The same is true of many international agencies with global remits, including the World Health Organization (WHO, 1987: 3). However, bearing in mind that this leads to the realization that human health and safety has, in a sense, a price tag, it is legitimate to question whether this is ethical. Should not such things as health and safety be beyond mercenary considerations? It would appear that many people, at first sight at least, believe they should.

Ethical objections typically take one or more of the following forms:

- The very thought of placing a value on a human life or health is anathema. Surely life is priceless and everything possible should be done, regardless of cost, to save an individual?
- All lives are not equal, nor all deaths. One health programme might save children and another adults. One safety measure might reduce the risk of slow, painful deaths and another sudden deaths. Even if life were valued, surely there is no single value?
- Economic methodology and cost-benefit analysis lack the sophistication to deal with these issues.
- In selecting healthcare or safety measures, society is concerned with much more than value-for-money. It is concerned with liberty, civil rights and

equity, and these are all ethical considerations which cannot be measured (Ball, 2006: 89).

The most fundamental of these objections is probably the first. Nobody would want to put a price on someone's life or their health, but this is not actually what is being done when monetary values are assigned to life and health for policy purposes. Firstly, the values are being used for forward planning and no known persons are involved. Secondly, what is normally being dealt with are small changes in the risk exposure of individuals, and not life and death situations. Even so, in a situation where there are finite resources and a range of objectives of which health and safety are but two, a line has to be drawn somewhere whether it is explicit or implicit. Failure to be explicit about a decision on the availability of a medical treatment on the NHS, or the reason for imposing a safety measure, does not mean that health and safety have not been valued, merely that the value has not been disclosed. And, importantly, failure to be explicit is not necessarily ethical or even neutral. It could mean that health and safety has been undervalued or overvalued, in both cases leading to inefficient use of public money and potentially more harm rather than less.

As for the second point, there is no fundamental reason why weighting factors could not be used to accommodate these concerns, although current evidence suggests they would not lead to very different valuations. The third point is of even more questionable validity, as there is now an abundance of international research on the valuation of safety and health of increasing sophistication (e.g. Kniesner et al, 2007; Zhang et al, 2004). The fourth point is undeniably relevant and significant, for these objections are legitimate. However, the incorporation of monetary considerations into decisions does not preclude the consideration of these wider issues in the overall decision process. Cost-benefit analysis is meant to be an aid to decision making and not a substitute for it (Arrow et al, 1996), just as assessing a risk does not tell you how it should be managed.

The economist Michael Jones-Lee has approached these ethical challenges from a different perspective, by examining the alternatives to valuing life and health. His conclusion is that all alternatives raise ethical concerns of their own (Jones-Lee, 1984). For example, to ignore estimates of the value of health and safety because this appears morally repugnant is essentially to give these zero or infinite value. Or to rely upon informal judgement on a case-by-case basis opens up the door to inconsistency and hence inefficiency. Or to rely instead upon, say, occupational safety standards actually begs the question, because these standards themselves should have been set with regard to some notion, implicit if not explicit, of the value of safety. There is, it would seem, no escape.

Value your own life

The second major difficulty with the incorporation of economic considerations, notional or otherwise, into safety is, once the ethical dilemmas have been addressed, to come up with actual valuations. It was mentioned earlier in the context of rail safety that, in 1994, £14 million far exceeded the government's going rate for preventing a fatality and, that in connection with healthcare, a quality-adjusted life year had a value somewhere in the region of £30,000 in 2008. How on earth were these valuations arrived at?

There is, in fact, a whole history of methods which have been used for this purpose (Ball, 2006: 90–96). Firstly, though, you might like to try valuing your own life. If so, try answering one or both of the questions in Box 4 using just the information provided in the question, and your own knowledge and preferences. The questions might well seem a bit strange, and you might feel you want more information on something or other, but what you should do is answer them quickly on the basis of the information provided and your own inclinations. That is, as if you were at the railway station, or about to set off for work, and had to make a quick decision. Having done that, read on.

These types of questions are known in the field of welfare economics as 'willingness-to-pay' (WTP) questions. The idea behind them is to find out how much individual consumers are willing to pay for their own safety. Questions of this type have been widely used by public bodies to help them make what they call 'resource allocative decisions'; that is, decisions about how best to spend their resources in the public interest.

Box 4 *Answer these questions to value your own life*

Q1: Imagine you are in Bristol. You wish to travel to Edinburgh by train and two train companies (A and B) offer a service. The services are identical except that the trains run by A are more likely to be involved in fatal accidents. Your risk of death on A is 1/50,000, whereas on B it is half of that (i.e. 1/100,000). The fare on train A is £100. How much more would you be prepared to pay to travel on B?

Choose one of the amounts below or just give your own figure. The choice is yours …

Zero, 1p, 5p, 10p, 50p, £1, £2, £5, £10, £50, £100, £200, £500

Q2: Imagine you live in Haringey and work full-time in Enfield. You elect to travel by car. The Mayor of London has had a new road built between Haringey and Enfield to relieve congestion. However, so far as you are concerned the ONLY advantage is that it is safer on the Mayor's new road. The risk of being in a fatal collision is 1 in 15,000 per year on the new road, compared with 1 in 10,000 by the normal route. The Mayor plans to impose a toll for users of the new road. How much would you be prepared to pay, per trip, to use the new road? Note: being in favour of public transport, the Mayor does not give discounts for regular users.

Choose one of these amounts below or just give your own figure. The choice is yours …

Zero, 1p, 5p, 10p, 50p, £1, £2, £5, £10

With respect to both questions 1 and 2, you should logically be prepared to pay something extra for the safer route because to answer zero would imply that you placed no value at all upon avoiding a risk of death. So suppose you had said in answer to question 1 that you would pay an extra £5 to go on train B. In effect, this means that you would be buying a risk reduction of:

$$1/50,000 - 1/100,000 = 2/100,000 - 1/100,000 = 1/100,000$$

This means that for £5 you have bought 1/100,000th of your life, so that the implied value of your whole life (rather than the tiny fraction 1/100,000th of it) is then £5 × 100,000.[9] In other words, the question reveals that your value of your life is £500,000 or half a million.

In the case of question 2, suppose you had decided that it was reasonable to pay 20 pence per trip to go on the new road. Then, assuming that the journey is made twice a day for 200 days per year, the annual amount paid would be £80. This would buy a risk reduction of:

$$1/10,000 - 1/15,000 = 3/30,000 - 2/30,000 = 1/30,000$$

So, as before, this means that £80 is the value of this fraction (1/30,000) of your life, so the value of your whole life is indicated to be £80 × 30,000, or £2.4 million.[10]

Researchers typically obtain answers to questions such as these from randomly selected samples, usually of 1000 or so people. Zeros and other 'strange' answers are usually discarded, and the remaining results used to find the mean or median value. Sometimes the value obtained is supplemented by

an estimate of a typical person's lost earnings, through dying prematurely, and there may be a further small addition for medical and ambulance costs.

This willingness-to-pay approach is now the favoured method for valuing safety in the UK and many other countries because it is perceived to be theoretically sound. This is because the consumers who are invited to answer the questions are essentially giving their own valuation of their own safety (whether they realize it or not), and it might well be argued: 'What could be fairer than that?'

For many people, including the authors, the methodology of WTP gives rise to a fair degree of scepticism. Can people really give meaningful answers to such questions and is the subsequent manipulation of their answers entirely above the board? Doubts linger, but it may be possible to gain some reassurance because there are other methods of valuing safety which can provide a cross-check, and the trend across a range of methodologies is that the numbers that emerge are reasonably consistent.

For example, by studying someone's behaviour (e.g. whether they buy and maintain smoke detectors in their home), it is possible to infer something about their personal value of their safety, although it requires a number of speculative if not heroic assumptions, such as the persons being studied knowing what the risk of dying in a fire is with and without detectors, and that the purchase has been made with only their own safety in mind and not the safety of others, nor the safety of their postal stamp collection in the attic or their cat. An entirely different approach has been to study the compensation awards granted by courts in the case of accidental death, although the problem with this is that it tends only to reflect the value of the lost earnings of the deceased, whereas the WTP approach is more to do with the value a person places on his/her life, which is sometimes referred to as 'the joy of living'.

Official values

So far as human safety is concerned, the Health and Safety Executive is the UK's primary source of reference for valuing safety from injury, and the figure they quote for preventing a fatality is £1 million in 2001 prices (HSE, 2001: 65).[11] This is a rounded figure based on WTP research by the Department for Transport. The Department for Transport has since published more recent valuations because these need to change each year in line with inflation and real per capita economic growth. The latest figure (updated to 2007 prices) is in the region of £1.5 million (DfT, 2004). DfT has also valued serious and slight injuries using WTP methods, although another method for doing this is to take the above value of preventing a fatality and multiply it by a factor between zero and unity, depending how serious the injury is relative to death.

Finally, it is worth noting that the value of the QALY used in healthcare, which is in the region of £30,000, would amount to a value of life of around £1.8 million for a lifespan of 60 years or so lived in good health. This is reasonably consistent with the above figure of £1.5 million, as it should be.

Afterword

Although considerations of health, safety and environment are inextricably tied up with cost of supply, there is obviously a great reluctance to talk about it publicly, and agencies tend to shy away from this admission. As Howard Margolis, late professor of social theory at the University of Chicago, has put it:

> A visitor from Mars, watching what we do, could only conclude that we do not mind trading off dollars for lives, we just do not want to be pushed into noticing it. Or, more generously: the world is such that there is often nothing we can do that does not implicitly involve trading off lives for dollars, so of course we do what we cannot avoid. But we hate to be pushed into noticing it. (Margolis, 1996: 154)

Nonetheless, it goes on all of the time and though at first sight it might seem unethical, it can be argued that it is unethical not to do so because when resources are ill-spent there is less scope to do good elsewhere. Moreover, it may be surmised that the public at large presume that agencies are allocating their taxes in rational and effective ways.

Summary

Although there is a fairly widespread belief that safety is paramount, this position is not reflected in the traditional practices of government agencies in the UK or other countries. Evidence from all sectors of society, from industry to healthcare and environmental protection, shows that the decision to adopt, or not, measures affecting health and safety is ultimately based upon considerations of the costs and the benefits of those measures; in other words, upon their 'practicability'. To aid decision makers, researchers have concluded that the current value for preventing a fatality should be in the region of £1.5 million, and within the NHS a year of life in good health is valued at about £30,000. These values are based upon consumers' own preferences as revealed by Willingness to Pay surveys, and should therefore reflect what consumers actually want. If it is accepted that this is what consumers want, then to deviate from it, without justification, could be seen as not giving them what they want.

4
Risk and Safety –
A National Philosophy

The previous chapter dealt with the fable of the paramountcy of safety and described how the concept of practicability was the real basis of our society's approach to such decisions, and how this is broadly consistent with approaches across the industrial, healthcare and environmental sectors too. There is, however, more to it than that. All systems have their limitations and it was noted in chapter 3 that there were certain ethical challenges to the use of cost-benefit analysis as an aid to decision making. One of the problems is that it pays no heed to the distribution of costs and benefits which might result either from intervention, or from a decision not to intervene. Nor, under the modified Pareto rule, are those who benefit from some decision required to compensate the losers. But there is a second issue. A decision not to implement some measure on cost-benefit (i.e. practicability) grounds might be reasonable from the perspective of society as a whole, but could still leave some people exposed to high levels of risk and this itself raises ethical issues.

Debates over the ethics of cost-benefit analysis and its underlying utilitarian ethic have been with us for centuries. The 18th century philosopher Jeremy Bentham, widely considered the founding father of the modern utilitarian ethical philosophy, contended that, within reason, the right act or policy is that which would produce the greatest happiness for the greatest number of people – also referred to as the 'greatest happiness principle'. This principle of utility would go on to be both expanded and revised by his student John Stuart Mill (Mill, 2001). Utilitarianism today manifests itself in the guise of cost-benefit analysis, which similarly contends that social policies should be arranged so as to maximize the ratio of benefits to costs, when all of the benefits and costs are measured in economic terms.

The Tolerability of Risk framework

This problem was confronted, in part at least, by the Health and Safety Executive following a Public Inquiry in the 1980s over the planning application to build the Sizewell B nuclear power station in Suffolk. The Inspector at the inquiry, Sir Frank Layfield, heard evidence from the HSE and noted its use of the concept of reasonable practicability. He was concerned that the term lacked clarity and requested that the HSE remedy the situation, which it did in 1988 when it published its groundbreaking document known as *The tolerability of risk from nuclear power stations* (HSE, 1988). Although aimed at nuclear industry issues, the document set out a philosophy which applied to occupational health and safety much more widely. This philosophy, of fundamental importance, is known as the 'Tolerability of Risk' or ToR framework.

Figure 4.1 sets out the framework as published by the HSE in 1992.[1] The diagram divides the annual level of risk of death from accident that an individual might be exposed to into three zones. As you move upwards on the diagram, the level of risk faced by an individual increases. At the top of the triangle, a level of risk is encountered which is deemed intolerable. In contrast, at the bottom of the diagram is a region where the risk is so low it is felt to be broadly acceptable. In between lies the so-called 'tolerable region', in which risks are tolerated in exchange for the benefits of the thing or the activity with which they are associated. In the tolerable region, risks must, according to the HSW Act, be reduced until as low as reasonably practicable (ALARP).

This means that whoever is responsible for the hazard generating the risk (such persons are sometimes referred to as 'duty holders') must think about what measures are available to reduce it, and apply all of those measures which are reasonably practicable; that is, all those measures which give a reasonable safety benefit at a reasonable cost. This is a very clever device, for it means that those responsible for any hazard must: a) think about the risks in advance (surely a good thing); and b) must implement all those measures which are reasonably practicable. In other words, a proactive and thoughtful approach is required. Also important is that duty holders need not, and it can be argued should not, implement measures which fail the test of reasonable practicability.[2]

The requirement is different for hazards creating risks in the top, unacceptable zone. These activities are not normally permitted and should cease, or the situation be otherwise rectified immediately. In contrast, for hazards that are associated with risk levels in the broadly acceptable zone at the bottom of Figure 4.1, further action is not normally required other than monitoring of the situation. This is because the risks are at a level that ordinary people consider insignificant or trivial in the context of their daily lives (HSE, 2001: 43). It is also worth noting that it would in addition be difficult to find measures that were reasonably practicable to apply within this zone. This is because the risk is already very low by definition as it's in the broadly acceptable zone, so any reduction in the already low risk would produce little in the way of improvement, and consequently could not justify much in the way of resource. Tinkering with already small risks also opens up the possibility of introducing some new, unintended risk, which is worse than that previously existing.

The three zones of Figure 4.1 are important and useful. As noted in chapter 3, there are some legitimate ethical criticisms of the utilitarian philosophy which underpins reasonable practicability. However, the specification of the

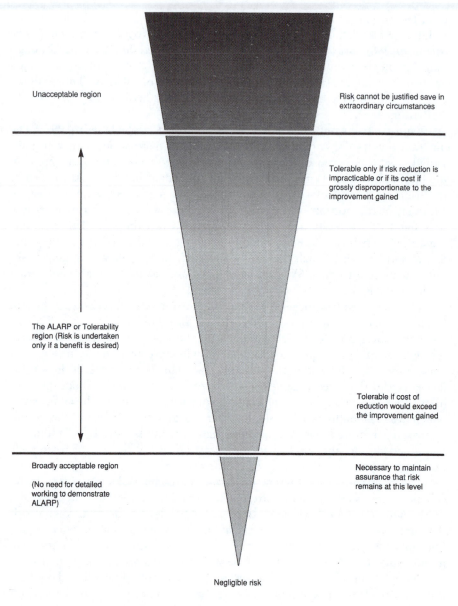

Unacceptable region

Risk cannot be justified save in extraordinary circumstances

Tolerable only if risk reduction is impracticable or if its cost if grossly disproportionate to the improvement gained

The ALARP or Tolerability region (Risk is undertaken only if a benefit is desired)

Tolerable if cost of reduction would exceed the improvement gained

Broadly acceptable region

(No need for detailed working to demonstrate ALARP)

Necessary to maintain assurance that risk remains at this level

Negligible risk

Source: Crown Copyright, HSE (1992)

Figure 4.1 *The Tolerability of Risk framework*

upper risk limit introduces at least an element of equity, for it says that all individuals have a right to protection from high levels of risk. The lower boundary, specifying broadly acceptable risk levels, is useful in another way. It helps avoid wasteful expenditure on assessing and remediating risks which are trivial.

Positioning the three zones

It is helpful to get some idea of where, in terms of risk, the zone boundaries in Figure 4.1 lie. This is neither a technical nor a scientific question. The Royal Society of London (Royal Society, 1983: 179–182) was one of the first agencies to consider this and is probably the most appropriate. The Health and Safety Executive has done likewise, with similar conclusions (HSE, 2001: 45–46).

Broadly, the position of the upper boundary, between the tolerable and unacceptable risk zones, was arrived at by considering the kind of risks that workers face in the more dangerous industries, and which society appears to just about tolerate in exchange for the benefits of those activities. The more dangerous industries include things like mining, deep-sea fishing, diving, construction, forestry and working on railway tracks. From this it was concluded that as far as workers are concerned the boundary to the unacceptable zone was in the region of 1 in a 1000 risk of dying per annum. On the other hand, it was felt that this limit should be more stringent for members of the public because they receive no wages for facing the risk, and the limit proposed for them was 1 in 10,000 per year. By way of comparison, this level of risk is in the region of the annual risk of dying in a car accident in the UK.

Very few workers, or members of the public, face imposed risks of these magnitudes, but of more interest when dealing with public safety is the position of the broadly acceptable risk boundary. According to the Royal Society:

> *There is a widely held view, though perhaps better described as speculation, that few people would commit their own resources to reduce an annual risk of death that was already as low as 1 in 100,000 and that even fewer would take action at an annual level of one in a million. (Royal Society, 1983: 180)*

The HSE has lent its support to this position, saying that an individual risk of death of one in a million per annum for either workers or the public corresponds to a very low level of risk, and should be used as a guideline for the lower boundary on Figure 4.1. It goes on to say that such a level of risk is extremely small when compared to the background level of risk which people face in going about their normal activities; for example, using gas and electricity appliances, or travelling by air or motor vehicle. Moreover, all of these activities bring huge benefits (HSE, 2001: 45–46).

Furthermore, as noted, trying to interfere with very small risks might actually increase risk overall, since the uncertainty involved with safety measures at this level is significant, and there is always the possibility that safety measures might introduce their own risks; that is, they could actually destroy more lives than they would save (Margolis, 1996: 168).

The issue of 'gross disproportion'

There is one final feature of Figure 4.1 which has yet to be described. This is the tapering of the risk triangle. This arises because of a concept known as 'gross disproportion'. This stems from a legal case in the 1940s, which is of supreme importance because it gave birth to the idea of reasonable practicability as it applies to occupational safety, and which was later enshrined in the HSW Act 1974. The case in question was Edwards v. the National Coal Board (1949).

The facts of the case are as follows. Mr Edwards was a colliery timberman in south Wales. He was killed in a mining accident in 1947 when a rare and hidden defect in the rock gave rise to a rock fall. On the evidence put to him, the presiding judge, Lord Justice Asquith, thought that it was not reasonably practicable for the employer to prop every inch of his underground tunnels and that it would have been prohibitively expensive to do so. However, the judge added a balancing perspective by saying that the greater the risk that existed, the less weight should be attached to consideration of the costs involved in reducing the risk.

The following is what he said:

> 'Reasonably practicable' is a narrower term than 'physically possible' and seems to me to imply that a computation must be made by the owner in which the quantum of risk is placed on one scale and the sacrifice involved in the measures necessary for averting a risk (whether in money, time or trouble) is placed in the other, and that, if it be shown that there is a gross disproportion between them – the risk being insignificant in relation to the sacrifice – the defendants discharge the onus on them. (Asquith, 1949)

The HSE has placed its own interpretation on this as follows:

> Although there is no authoritative case law which considers the question, we believe that it is right that the greater the risk: the higher the proportion may be before being considered 'gross'. But the disproportion must always be gross. (HSE, 2001)

And

> ... There should be transparent bias on the side of health and safety. (HSE, 2001: 67)

From this it can be discerned why the diagram in Figure 4.1 is tapered. At higher risk levels it reflects HSE's view that more emphasis should be given to reducing the risk, and less to the money, time and trouble associated with reducing the risk. That is, there should be a bias on the side of safety. This is probably a reasonable proposition and one which could possibly be argued on ethical grounds at high risk levels. However, the concluding statement by the HSE, that '... the disproportion must always be gross', could be the cause of some conflict, particularly for those managing the, usually low, risks to the public which lie towards the bottom of Figure 4.1.

The question is whether this presumption, that there should always be 'bias' in favour of safety, is legitimate if it challenges other things of value in public life, such as public health, environmental protection, sustainability and so on. It is not obvious that this is what is required either by law or by custom. But statements of this kind, if transferred from the factory floor to public life, might encourage health and safety personnel to impose a gross disproportion test upon hazards in the public domain where the risk is already low. This could lead to the adulteration and destruction of public places and activities, or prohibition of things previously enjoyed. Indeed, since 'gross' is undefined, public life could be eliminated by excessive application of this mantra.

It is also of interest to note that if a weighting factor were applied in the case of hazards which only pose a low risk, this would also be in conflict with the methodology used to arrive at a value for preventing a fatality. This is because, if a price is placed upon safety using consumers' own expressed willingness-to-pay for safety, as described in chapter 3, why then would it be reasonable to disregard that value by introducing a weighting factor?

Professor Evans of UCL (Evans, 2005) has also pointed out that, at the time of its instigation in the late 1940s, gross disproportion was a needed concept because in those days the official valuation of safety was based only on the lost earnings of fatally injured persons. There was no willingness-to-pay element to cover one's enjoyment of life, as there is now courtesy of the willingness-to-pay valuations. He argues that the courts of the day would have been aware of this, and perhaps this was what led to the genesis of 'gross disproportion'. It was a compensatory mechanism for the niggardly sums then allocated by government departments to life saving.[3]

Of course, careful study of Figure 4.1 shows, because of the taper, that the value of the gross disproportion factor diminishes as the risk level reduces, and this is sensible. The problem is not all health and safety personnel are familiar with this framework, and are more likely to be influenced by bold statements such as 'the disproportion must always be gross' which are in widespread circulation.

The ToR framework outside of the UK

It is interesting to ask if the ToR framework is a purely UK concoction, or if it has international manifestations. The answer is that its presence can be discerned in practically all countries. This is because an essentially similar framework is used for managing ionizing radiation, based on dose limits in place of risk limits and reasonable achievability in place of reasonable practicability. Because ionizing radiation is used or encountered worldwide in industry, hospitals and the natural environment, ToR is thereby essentially universal in its application. The existence of a similar framework for handling toxic chemicals in the environment also exists, though is less apparent (Ball, 2006: 101 & 125).

Summary

The national framework for making decisions about risk has been described. Although very few people are aware of it or appreciate its significance, including some health and safety professionals, it is vastly important for all with an interest in risk and safety decision making, which is pretty well everyone. This framework can also be observed to be in use internationally.

The framework contains three important features. One is that it defines a level of risk which should not be tolerated save in exceptional circumstances, and this provides a safeguard for all persons. It thus deals to some extent with issues of equity. Also defined is a broadly acceptable level of risk, which is a useful device for heading off the obsessive pursuit of safety, and which is likely to be especially important in matters of public risk.

Secondly is that the framework incorporates the notion of reasonable practicability, an immensely important instrument for ensuring that all sensible safety measures are implemented, and that those which are ineffective or unduly expensive or troublesome can be ruled out. This concept originates from case law, in particular the Edwards v. National Coal Board case of 1949, as now enshrined in the Health and Safety at Work Act 1974.

Thirdly, the idea of gross disproportion has been discussed and found to be a possible source of problems in the management of public risk.

5
What Works in Public Life?

Previous chapters have described how methods of risk assessment which developed mainly in industry and commerce have spilled over into public life, and affected decision making about public space and activities. However, it is not only the methods of risk assessment and the (incorrect) notion of risk minimization that have crossed over, but the perceived solutions. These solutions have too often not been benign, nor are they necessarily low cost, and judging by the furore which has been created, some harm has been done to the quality of the public realm and public life. However, there is an underlying issue which is that different people have different ideas, sometimes radically so, about what makes things safe.

To explore this, it is instructive to note that the philosopher David Seedhouse has proposed that when people are confronted with a problem or a decision to make, rather than review the evidence dispassionately as a basis for formulating a plan, they always start from a position anchored in their own preconceived ideas, prejudices if you like, which may actually come to dominate the decision process. To this may be added some evidence, possibly selected evidence, from which emerges a solution or a plan (Seedhouse, 2004). The Seedhouse formula looks like this:

a preconceived notion + a bit of evidence = a decision about what to do.

This may be hard to swallow for technical or professional people who believe they are being objective, but the fact is that even people like Albert Einstein had their beliefs; for instance, 'God does not play dice', which in Albert's case influenced the direction of his research on quantum mechanics.

Seedhouse's main area of work is healthcare, but there is no reason why his ideas should not be equally valid across other sectors, including public safety. Indeed, a number of schisms can be observed which seem, as his proposition suggests, to be lodged more in prior beliefs than evidence.

Ways of making things safe

The first schism revolves around what makes things safe. When it comes to injury prevention, there are broadly speaking two main schools of thought.

The HSE, for example, has set out its preferred hierarchy of risk control principles as follows (HSE, 1997):[1]

- Eliminate risks; for example, by substituting the dangerous with the less dangerous (e.g. avoid certain processes).
- Combat risks at source by the use of engineering controls; for example, separate operators from exposure to risk.
- Minimize risk; for example, by using protective clothing (as a last resort).

This hierarchy, to quote the HSE, 'reflects the fact that eliminating and controlling risk by using physical engineering controls and safeguards is more reliable than relying solely on people'.[2] In public life engineering controls might include things like barriers, gates, hand rails, traffic lights, speed cameras, rubber surfaces in playgrounds and surveillance systems.

However, this position is not without challenge. Professor John Adams, of University College London, has been writing about different perspectives on the things which work in the field of injury prevention for many years (Adams, 1985). He distinguishes between two rival schools of thought that dominate the safety community. One is anchored in finding 'engineering solutions' to problems, whilst the other believes progress can better come by addressing human behaviour. Whilst his early work is based on road safety, one could

argue that this clash of ideologies is prevalent in many other arenas, including public risk.

Adams' view is that 'safety engineers'[3] have their own psychology which tells them where to look for solutions to safety problems. Thus, they recommend, like HSE has, that safety efforts should be concentrated on tangible measures which acknowledge human fallibility and protect people from its consequences. According to this perspective, measures of an engineering nature are more cost effective, easily identifiable and implementable than those that involve behaviour.

Adams, however, believes that people naturally and instinctively engage in a process known as risk compensation. That is, they alter their behaviour in response to the implementation of new safety measures to the point that, for example, 'protecting motorists from the consequences of bad driving encourages bad driving'.[4] Moreover, as conventional engineering safety measures are now approaching their saturation point, the only way left to achieve further reductions in accidents is to improve drivers' behaviour.

Professor Kip Viscusi, of Vanderbilt University, has come to a similar conclusion. He warns that, in general, technological safety remedies may induce what he has called a 'lulling' effect on public behaviour. This has the effect of causing people to alter their behaviour, so changing the risk, and not necessarily in the hoped-for direction (Viscusi, 1992). For example, the introduction of alleged childproof caps on medicinal materials caused some parents to become so relaxed that they failed to even lock the medicine cabinet. Likewise, the fitting of children's play areas with rubber surfaces creates an impression of safety, but which may not live up to the expectation of users, either children or parents. None of these products provides total safety from injury, as some appear to imagine. This could lead them, children and parents, into a more risky situation than if they were dealing with a natural surface, like grass, sand or earth, with whose properties they would be familiar as a

---

Box 5 *The 'safe' playground – an ideological battleground*

The conventional, industry-led, approach to the design of ladders and stairs in children's playgrounds is that they should have rungs and steps which are equally spaced, and that the inclination of stairs should be constant (BSI, 1998).

In contrast, Helle Nebelong, landscape architect and designer of green space for young disabled people, and President of the Danish Playground Association, says: 'The prefabricated playground tries to live up to 100 per cent safety standards based on media horror stories. Yet standardised playgrounds can be dangerous. When the distance between ladder rungs is the same the child has no need to concentrate. Play becomes simplistic and children no longer have to think about their movement. The ability to concentrate on estimated distance, height and risks needs practice. And the playground is where that practising should begin' (Nebelong, 2008).

result of lifetime experience. Thus, children have been known to take bigger risks in situations which seem safer, and parents relax their vigilance if they believe there is less to fear.

The 'safety engineers' that Adams describes, and others who think in this way, are evident and widespread. Such engineers have their own embedded psychology that has taught them to think and see the world in a certain way, deconstructing complex problems into measurements, statistics (sometimes) and factory-style safety measures. They see an unambiguous link between cause and effect, and problem and solution. The HSE is of course well aware that there is more to making things safe than engineering measures. Personal factors and human behaviour in general are also determinants of what happens (HSE, 1997: 10). Nick Hurst, formerly of the HSE, has described how accidents are caused by one or more of the following: equipment failures, people and their behaviour, or failures in systems of working; the latter sometimes referred to as management systems or cultural attitudes to safety (Hurst, 1998). So, while the predilection is often for engineering controls, other approaches are possible; for example, warning, educating or training people to cope with risk, or even just leaving them to get on with it by themselves using their vast resources of learnt and innate ability, as will be discussed in chapter 8.

The most effective solution for any given circumstance is dependent on a number of factors. It may well be that in the world of heavy industry, engineering solutions work the best and one should favour them. Within public life, however, things are, as Oliver Letwin MP has suggested, 'complex' (chapter 1). This is because situations involving interactions between the environment, the public and objects are simply very difficult to forecast. While experience may give you some clues, there is bound to be a lot of uncertainty every time a change is made to a public place or a new activity is sanctioned.

It might be guessed that there is something of a contest between supporters of these approaches.[5] Indeed, one example of this contest can be found in road safety. The late Hans Monderman,[6] the Dutch traffic engineer who spent much time studying driver behaviour, came to the conclusion that signs and regulations could have an adverse effect on the ability of drivers to interact safely with other road users. This led him to challenge the prevailing orthodoxy that road safety can only or best be achieved by an arsenal of speed bumps, barriers, signs and segregation of people from traffic. His approach was instead to demonstrate that people, including drivers, were intelligent citizens capable of respecting each other's freedom to move around safely. From this he developed the concept of 'shared space', in which streets are seen as valuable social and economic assets, and not just as conduits for high-speed traffic to pass through communities. The impact of this thinking can be seen in places like Kensington High Street in London (*London Evening Standard*, 2009), New Road in Brighton (UDC, 2009), and in many other towns and cities where the paraphernalia of engineering solutions is being partially stripped away and replaced with softer measures which use landscape, lighting, public art, local materials and greater ambiguity to encourage a more thoughtful approach to the use of public space by all concerned.

A second example can be found in Play England's recently published *Design for Play*, which is about creating successful play spaces for children and young people. The emphasis here is far less on the now traditional, fenced-off, industrial-style play equipment located on rubber surfaces which have dominated the play scene for several decades, and more on the integration of a new generation of more interesting and challenging equipment, sensitively placed in natural landscapes which include trees, hillocks, water features and as much nature as possible (Play England, 2008a).

The shift from the engineering perspective to the softer, behavioural standpoint remains a battleground. Many agencies are worried and uncomfortable about the prospect that such a change could result in more accidents for which they could be held accountable. Others just believe that the ways of the last few decades are right and should not be challenged. Yet others make a living out of the familiar ways and are reluctant to adapt, perhaps also feeling that there would be a loss of face in making what might be described as a U-turn.

Management systems

A second contested area is that of management systems, including auditing and governance arrangements. As industrial-style health and safety has rolled out into the public sector, so have associated management systems such as that described in *Successful Health and Safety Management* (HSE, 1997), which are recommended by HSE in its Approved Code of Practice on the management of health and safety at work (HSE, 2000: para. 26). These systems are predicated upon the belief that they will bring safety benefits. It is not, however, obvious that all management systems in general are necessarily effective in every context or that they produce value for money, and this is clear on consideration of some of the crises we have endured – the banking crisis for one. There can be no doubt that banks all have had risk management (referred to in banking as internal control) systems for decades following earlier fiascos and the recommendations of the Turnbull report (ICA, 1999), but these did not prevent problems with several British banks, nor the global banking crisis. Likewise, Haringey and other councils all have childcare management systems, but these have not prevented tragedies such as Baby P; indeed, some believe that they may have contributed to them.

Even the trivia of MPs' expenses, which held public interest for a surprisingly long period in 2009, could be attributed to a defective management system. MPs, for the most part, thought that obeying the rule book (management system) was okay, but when opened up to scrutiny it was seen to lack certain things, including, some would argue, a sense of morality. The problem with that system, it could be said, is that its existence encouraged MPs to suspend their normal moral codes. A thoughtful process was replaced by box ticking.

With respect to governance – that is, the higher level processes by which strategic decisions are taken and managers are held to account – the relationship between health and safety and corporate governance styles is still a matter of research (Acona, 2006), and therefore not yet something which can be prescribed with confidence.

Nor do these management systems come cheap. In the context of regulation, Rick Haythornthwaite, former Chairman of the Better Regulation Commission, and later Director of the Risk and Regulation Advisory Council, has suggested that the nation is now spending around £100 billion a year, or between 10 per cent and 12 per cent of GDP, on regulation (Haythornthwaite, 2006), a good deal of which is likely consumed by management costs, some related to safety.[7] Yet HSE reports that over the five years to 2007/8 there had been little change in the rates of injury or ill health, and there is some evidence the trend, or lack of trend, has been around much longer than that (HSE, 2004a and 2009).

This lack of a trend is also observed in public leisure accident data which was collected by the Department of Trade and Industry from 1988 to 2002 (Fig 5.1).[8] During that period the number of leisure accidents remained in the region of 3.1 million cases per year in the UK, never deviating by more than 10 per cent and without any obvious trend. Historically, other researchers have similarly reported a lack of trends in, for example, child accidents in England and Wales, and expressed concern over the apparent inability to find solutions that worked (Jarvis et al, 1995: 110), a position reaffirmed by

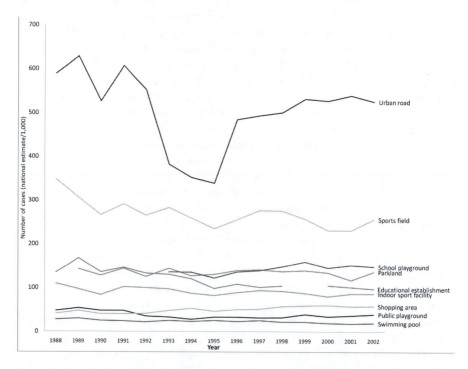

Source: Based on DTI Leisure Accident Surveillance System (LASS) data, which was operated from 1988 to 2002.

Figure 5.1 *Trend in leisure accidents by accident location, as measured by hospital accident and emergency attendances*

NICE as recently as November 2010 (NICE, 2010). This should, of course, be of interest to exponents of management systems. With all the resources which have been poured in, some evidence of a return on investment should be expected.

Professor Michael Power, now of the London School of Economics, has himself posed a number of questions about internal control with respect mainly to finance, but which have wider resonance:

> *Internal control systems are also highly problematic. Not only is it difficult to define their effectiveness, but, more crucially, a growing obsession with internal control (a mutation of the earlier audit explosion) may itself be a source of risk. First, internal control systems are organizational projections of controllability which may be misplaced; such systems are only as good as the imaginations of those who designed them. Second, internal control systems are essentially inward-looking and may embody mistaken assumptions of what the public really wants reassurance about. (Power, 2004)*

Power identifies here the possibility that management systems can increase risk. This can happen in a variety of ways. One is by bringing about subtle changes in how individuals perceive their responsibility, which can operate from the institutional level right down to the individual level. One harrowing example is the 2008 case of a woman who fell into a mine shaft in Ayrshire. According to reports, firefighters were hindered in their rescue attempts by a Fire Service safety memorandum which had banned the use of rope equipment for lifting members of the public to safety. The consequence was that her rescue was severely delayed, during which time the injured woman's condition is believed to have deteriorated. She later died.

Other cases have been reported whereby 'systems' have prevented agencies from responding to crises, or have led them to respond in a way which causes more harm than good. The initial blanket closure of UK airspace in 2010 because of volcanic ash is a case in point. It is inevitable that when there is massive disruption to public life there are casualties, particularly among those less able to cope with the problems which these measures bring, although these may be dispersed and thereby hidden from view. The danger is that systems thinking and blanket-rules can inhibit people from using their initiative in situations where the system designer had not thought out all of the possible eventualities, what some people have called the 'unintended consequences' (Graham and Wiener, 1995; RRAC, 2009).

Professor Hood, at Oxford University, and colleagues have written a thoughtful, research-based book about what they describe as 'regulatory regimes', by which they mean the approach to regulation taken by different agencies (Hood et al, 2004). Their book describes a wide range of regulatory positions adopted by different regulators in Britain, over things as diverse as exposure to chemicals, pesticide residues in food, road safety, paedophiles and dangerous dogs. They paint a picture of a mosaic of different approaches which are largely experimental, in the sense that it is not known for sure how effective they will be. They conclude as follows:

> *At a time when public sector organizations are being urged to take on board private-sector-sourced business risk-management ideas, some of the basic policy trade-offs between collective and organizational risk management merit more attention. Indiscriminate or inappropriate application of corporate risk management approaches could detract from, rather than augment, the quality of government of risk by putting more emphasis on existing bureaucratic tendencies to blame-avoidance. What seems to be needed is an approach to business risk management in government that is neither an unreflective adoption of private business practice nor based on an unrealistic view of organizational behaviour in the public sector. Such an approach would need to include several ways of regulating the regulators of risk ... (Hood et al, 2004)*

Thus, it can be inferred that the transfer of corporate management systems into public sector organizations is best described as an experiment, and experiments may or may not work. The above statement also identifies the tendency for agencies of all kinds to become more focused upon a kind of 'secondary risk management' or blame-avoidance, rather than the primary focus, which should be taking reasonable care of those for whom they are responsible. The same critique can sometimes be made of regulators whose definition of 'the public interest' deviates from what was originally intended and is socially desirable.

In a similar vein, Power has also critiqued the 'explosion of auditing', which has manifested itself in multiple fields from medicine to education and local government. As he says, the spread of audit constitutes a major shift in

---

Box 6 *Council staff worry about regulators not public*

A council chief executive has claimed that her own local authority is geared to please regulators rather than meet local needs.

Asking members of Suffolk County Council to approve plans to spend up to £122,000 on employing consultants to improve management, Andrea Hill said: 'Our structures have responded to new central government requirements, an ever-growing regulatory culture and ring-fenced funding opportunities. We have an overly complex organisation. Inspection, performance management and audit have begun to dominate the local government culture to such an extent that our council is more focused on the regulator than the consumer.'

The Times, 4 May 2010, p16

power, from the public to professionals, and from teachers and local government officers to managers and overseers. This is not a passive practice, but one which strongly influences the environment in which it operates, and not necessarily for the better (Power, 1994).[9]

In search of evidence of things that really work

There are many situations where there is good evidence that engineering solutions to safety do work, just as there are examples of management systems that do not. There are also many situations where the effectiveness, and practicability, of systems has been questionable, especially in public life. It should not be too readily presumed that measures which are traditional, fashionable or come with strong recommendations necessarily work. Constant vigilance, and questioning, is necessary if the goal is truly to manage public safety, along with other public aspirations, in the most beneficial way.

One example of this can be found in debates over the safety of cycling and, in particular, the use of cycle helmets. It is commonly taken for granted that helmet-wearing is good practice, and on the face of it, it appears an obvious and common sense thing to do. This has led some agencies to seek legislation to require cyclists to wear helmets. But the fact is that this, as reported by the National Children's Bureau, is another contested territory with as yet no clear answers (NCB, 2005). One of the problems of helmets is that users very often do not understand their design limitations (Walker, 2005), as with rubber surfacing in playgrounds, and expect to be safer when wearing them than they actually are. This can lead to a false sense of security, as with Viscusi's medicine cabinets, and a greater propensity to take risks, both by cyclists and the motorists around them. As the 'Why Cycle?' website says:

> The truth is that there is no simple answer. Certainly, in some accidents a helmet can reduce the risk of severe head injury but every accident is different and therefore the outcome can never be judged before the incident. Indeed the majority of head injuries which result in death are caused by collision with other vehicles, travelling at comparative high speed, something which a bicycle helmet is not designed to cope with. In reality, the numbers of these serious head injuries is extremely low and it is felt that the overall health benefits offered by regular cycling far outweigh the small amount of risk involved.[10]

If that is not enough, an additional word of caution is also due. For many years a popular approach to road safety has been for road traffic engineers to identify and treat 'accident black spots' – places where accidents have historically occurred – with engineering solutions. Numerous evaluation studies have been carried out of such schemes and at first sight there often appear to be large accident reductions, suggesting the measures are effective. However, critical examination has shown that this is often untrue. For one thing, a

---

Box 7 *What works? Views from far and near*

Judith Green (1997: 7) describes how anthropologist Margaret Mead's study of the Manus tribe, of the Admiralty Islands of Papua New Guinea, led to the supposition that Manus children, who lived on a 'slight framework of narrow boards above the changing tides of the lagoon', had no room for costly mistakes, but learned to cope through a combination of early parental discipline and refusal to sympathize with the accidental outcomes of childhood clumsiness. By this means, Mead claimed, the children of the Manus grew up 'physically dextrous, sure footed, clear-eyed, quick-handed'.

David Peat (1995: 59) describes an experience with the Blackfoot in North America. A young Blackfoot boy was steering a motor fishing boat with his father on board. The boy was observed to be heading towards dangerous submerged rocks, but the father gave no warning. At the last moment the boy saw the danger and cut the motor. How, mused Peat, could the father's behaviour be explained? Only, he surmised, if you accept that: 'you cannot give a person knowledge in the way a doctor gives a shot for measles. Rather, each person learns for himself or herself through the process of growing up in contact with nature and society; by observing, watching, listening, and dreaming.'

Judith Hackitt (2008), chair of HSE, has said with directness and realism: 'If we don't allow children to experience managed risk I have grave concerns about the future for workplace health and safety. If the next generation enter the workplace having been protected from all risk they will not be so much risk averse as completely risk naïve – creating an enormous task and dilemma for their employers – how to start that health and safety education process *or* to continue to try to protect them from all risk which is of course impractical and impossible.'

---

phenomenon known as 'regression to the mean' is likely to be in play. This refers to the fact that any extreme situation, whether high or low, is likely to gravitate as time passes towards the centre of the range of possible values. Secondly, in the case of road traffic accidents, the remedial measures may simply cause the black spot to migrate to some other place. There are many ways in which this can happen. For example, the safety measure might cause some drivers to take another route which could have a higher or lower risk, or it could modify their perception in some way and alter their vigilance further along the road. Rune Elvik, of the Institute of Transport Economics in Norway, has concluded that the more these factors are taken into account, the less likely are these kinds of safety programmes to show beneficial effects (Elvik, 1997). The same is likely true of other public safety hazards.

So it is not going to be easy to prejudge the effectiveness of interventions, of whatever kind, in public life, and this is largely down to the complexity of life. This suggests, as will be discussed in chapter 10, the need for an alternative strategy.

The advent of risk-benefit assessment

Ten years ago one of us (DJB) was commissioned by the HSE to research the safety of children's playgrounds, then and still a hot topic, and to interpret this in terms of the UK's philosophy of control, the 'Tolerability of Risk' framework, as described in chapter 4. It turned out that the risk of serious injury on playgrounds was in fact very small, but what emerged as far more important was that children and young people were being deprived of important developmental opportunities. This was because the aims of play provision had been pushed aside amid a scramble to minimize risk of injury, a history which has been documented by a number of authors, prominent among whom are Tim Gill (2007) and Helene Guldberg (2009).

To quote from the report for the HSE:

> *In marked contrast to the concern over safety on the playground, the evidence gathered here suggests that the crucial societal problem of playgrounds and their provision relates less to safety of playgrounds per se, than to the issue of how to realise for children the full range of social, physical, emotional and cognitive benefits associated with play. Second to this is the issue of how to balance these positive attributes against the inevitable risk of injury which any activity, including play, generates. (Ball, 2002)*

There is no reason why this conclusion should not apply equally to public space. It can easily be adapted as follows:

> *In marked contrast to the concern over public safety, evidence suggests that the crucial societal problem of public activities and public space relates less to safety from injury per se, than to the issue of how to realize the full range of social, physical, emotional and cognitive benefits associated with public life. Second to this is the issue of how to balance these positive attributes against the inevitable risk of injury which any public activity generates.*

The implications of this, however, are potentially far-reaching. Inter alia, it would seem that risk assessment should, in the public domain, be replaced by risk-benefit assessment (RBA). This is not quite such a revolutionary step as it might at first appear, for, as will be seen in chapter 10, RBA is in fact very much used in other sectors. But before going on to discuss RBA, and how it might apply to public activities in more detail, it is time to consider, in the next chapter, the legal position and the attitudes of the courts.

Summary

As industry-style risk assessment procedures have encroached upon public life, they have tended to bring with them industry-style remedial measures for combating risk. Typically, these include engineering-style solutions like crash barriers, handrails and rigid adherence with industry protocols, specifications and the like. However, it is arguable and there is some evidence that these measures are less effective or even ineffective in the public sphere, because they take little account of the complexity of human behaviour and their interactions with their surroundings. Alternative, behavioural approaches are beginning to find their place in public life and many believe that they are also better able to accommodate wider public interests.

Questions are also being raised about management systems, and rightly so. These come in a variety of forms and it is not true that there is a single form which is appropriate in all circumstances. These systems can take on a life of their own, consuming vast resources and deflecting attention from the true objectives of public service provision.

A further issue of crucial importance is that industry-style risk assessments pay little heed to the benefits of space and activities, and if followed to the letter would logically eliminate numerous things which are valued. This leads to the proposition that, in public life, the correct procedure is to carry out risk-benefit assessment, as opposed to conventional risk assessment.

6
Legal Matters

Earlier chapters have drawn attention to several issues which could be regarded as controversial. These include the position that society does not in general aim to minimize risk, that things like the cost and effectiveness of risk control strategies should be considered when contemplating new injury reduction measures, and that the benefits of public life should be factored into those decisions. None of these could survive for long were they in some sense unlawful. So this chapter will describe the extent to which the law currently provides support for these ideas. There is another reason for doing this too. Judges, and other members of the legal profession, have put an immense amount of effort into thinking about how risk should be managed in our society, and this is an invaluable source of wisdom.

Of course, many persons are also rightly concerned about their legal responsibilities with regard to risk and safety. So it is doubly important to identify key elements of the legal background as it relates to safety, and show how it links up with the philosophical and ethical positions arrived at in the preceding chapters. This can be done by considering in particular the HSW Act, and the Occupiers' Liability Acts of 1957 and 1984,[1] the common law, and some recent developments and pronouncements. Duty holders, in this context people with responsibility for public space, have general duties under all of this legislation to ensure that risks to people's health and safety are properly controlled.

The Health and Safety at Work etc. Act (1974)

One might fairly ask: what has the HSW Act got to do with public space and activities, since these are not obvious workplaces? This is a good question, and one which is being considered under the auspices of the review commenced by Lord Young (HM Government, 2010) and now being taken forward by a number of parties including, notably, Professor Ragnar Löfstedt of King's College London. Those who ask it will frequently be directed to section 3 of the Act, which describes the general duties of employers and the self-employed to persons other than their employees. In particular, section 3.1 of the Act says as follows:

> *It shall be the duty of every employer to conduct his undertaking in such a way as to ensure, so far as is reasonably*

> *practicable, that persons not in his employment who may be*
> *affected thereby are not thereby exposed to risks to their health*
> *or safety.*

The consequence of section 3.1 is that those responsible for public space have a duty of care for the health and safety of members of the public visiting that space. The way it is interpreted is that this applies not just when workers are actually present (e.g. cutting the grass or doing maintenance), but even when people are visiting the space and no work is being carried out. Little Suzie, playing in the sandpit in the local authority-owned public playground, is thereby covered by the HSW Act. This seepage of the HSW Act into the management of public space and activities is assisted by the wording of the Management of Health and Safety at Work Regulations 1999, which say, under Regulation 3 (1b):

> *Every employer shall make a suitable and sufficient assessment*
> *of the risks to the health and safety of persons not in his employ-*
> *ment arising out of or in connection with the conduct by him of*
> *his undertaking. (HSE, 2000)*

The words 'arising out of or in connection with the conduct by him of his undertaking' have potential for broad inclusiveness. It was not, however, always like this. Prior to 1974 and the HSW Act, this situation did not pertain. As the HSE itself has said:

> *Those affected by work activities were brought under the legisla-*
> *tive umbrella for the first time. In the mid-1970s, this latter*
> *provision provoked widespread astonishment. (HSE, 2004a)*

As can be observed from section 3.1 of the HSW Act, employers are required to *ensure* the health and safety of employees and those affected. This means that if an accident occurs, on the face of it, the duty holder has failed to ensure safety and has thereby breached this requirement. However, section 3.1 qualifies this responsibility to ensure safety by inserting the words 'reasonable practicability'. This means that if the duty holder can demonstrate that everything that was reasonably practicable to ensure health and safety had been done, his/her duty would be seen as satisfied.

The meaning of 'reasonable practicability' was set out in chapter 4. It may be recalled that Lord Asquith provided the definition during the Edwards' case, and it is worth repeating because it is so central to the proper understanding of health and safety:

> *'Reasonably practicable' is a narrower term than 'physically*
> *possible', and seems to me to imply that a computation must be*
> *made by the owner in which the quantum of risk is placed on*
> *one scale and the sacrifice involved in the measures necessary for*
> *averting the risk (whether in money, time or trouble) is placed*

in the other, and that, if it be shown that there is a gross dispro-
portion between them – the risk being insignificant in relation to
the sacrifice – the defendants discharge the onus upon them.
Moreover, this computation falls to be made by the owner at a
point of time anterior to the accident. (Asquith, 1949)

This concept, of weighing the costs and the benefits of safety measures, was reinforced in another important legal case in 1954, this time involving a roof collapse in a gypsum mine. In summing up this case the presiding judge, Lord Reid, said:

If a precaution is practicable it must be taken, unless in the
whole circumstances that would be unreasonable. And, as men's
lives may be at stake, it should not lightly be held that to take
a practicable precaution is unreasonable ... the danger was a
very rare one. The trouble and expense involved in the use
of the precaution, while not prohibitive, would have been
considerable. The precautions would not have afforded any-
thing like complete protection against the danger, and their
adoption would have had the disadvantage of giving a false
sense of security. (Reid, 1954)

From these early days the concept of reasonable practicability became the central plank of the HSW Act.[2] This was not without some political resistance, for it was feared that employers would be too easily let off the hook of seeking further safety improvements if they could simply claim that improvements were not reasonably practicable, when perhaps they just didn't want to bother. However, properly applied, this condition actually pressures employers to be proactive; that is, to make them think ahead, to do a suitable and sufficient risk assessment, and then to apply all measures which meet the criterion.

Notwithstanding this, the European Commission brought a case against the UK in the European Court of Justice (ECJ) in 2005, specifically in relation to the use of the phrase 'so far as is reasonably practicable'. It too had reservations about this qualification of the employers' responsibilities to safeguard employees, but in 2007 the ECJ dismissed the objection and there is no procedure for launching an appeal (HSE, 2007a).

From this, it can be seen that reasonable practicability is the guiding principle in Britain's health and safety law, and that this entails a balanced approach to deciding what safety measures should be implemented, with the balance comprising on the one hand the risk reduction benefit which a measure might bring, and, on the other, the time, cost and difficulty of implementing the measure. This, of course, is an eminently sensible approach because it does not require immensely expensive interventions to be made which have little actual safety benefit. In contrast, it does require, by law, cost-effective measures to be implemented. Reasonable practicability is, of course, not consistent with risk minimization or risk elimination, which has no legal basis (except perhaps in some very special situations).

There is, though, a contested area which is important in the context of public life. This revolves around the issue of the benefits of public space and public life. When talking about benefits in the context of reasonable practicability, the benefits referred to are usually the 'safety-from-injury' benefits of the measure being contemplated. But in public life, where the Act is being applied, one encounters a different class of benefits which might include things like the enjoyment of public activities or places, the health-giving benefits of leisure activities, or the intellectual stimulation of some architectural feature. Does the Act permit consideration of these factors in reaching a decision about what is, or is not, reasonably practicable?

To some of us, it would seem that it should, and if it doesn't, we might then be tempted to say the HSW Act is therefore inappropriate legislation for making decisions about public space and activities, at least as it is currently

---

Box 8 *Right to swim in Hampstead Heath ponds*

In the context of civil law, Lord Hoffmann, in a speech in Philadelphia in 2005, referred to the possibility that the idea of 'cost' embedded in 'reasonable practicability' might itself include the notion of benefits. The following quote by him refers to a well-known legal case involving swimming in Hampstead Heath ponds. Hampstead Heath Winter Swimming Club had brought a High Court challenge against a ruling by the Corporation of the City of London to ban self-regulated swimming. The Corporation felt it would be liable under health and safety laws if there were an accident. In this hearing, the swimmers triumphed.

Lord Hoffmann said as follows:

> But, unless you stretch the meaning of the cost of taking precautions, it leaves out of account what I might call the social cost of the precautions necessary to avoid risk; the effect they have on the lives of other citizens. In the pond case, that effect was particularly striking, because, as I have said, it made it necessary to prevent people enjoying themselves in a way they had being doing perfectly legitimately for many years. And people suddenly began to notice other ways in which activities which they used to enjoy were disappearing because authorities responsible for those activities were afraid that it might be said that they had not taken sufficient steps to avoid an accident. School outings under the supervision of teachers became rarities because educational authorities were concerned that they might be sued for taking insufficient care to prevent some child from having an accident. Country parks were becoming disfigured with notices warning people against obvious dangers. Old gravel paths were being replaced with ugly non-slip resin compounds. Even the worn flagstones in the 15thC church of the Cotswold village where we have a country cottage had to be replaced in case someone slipped and we were asked to contribute to the cost of the stone. (Hoffmann, 2005)

interpreted. As Lord Hoffmann has put it, in a speech in Philadelphia about a legal case involving the right to swim in Hampstead Heath ponds in London (see Box 8 for more details):

> *But, unless you stretch the meaning of the cost of taking precautions, it leaves out of account what I might call the social cost of the precautions necessary to avoid the risk; the effect they have on the lives of other citizens. (Hoffmann, 2005)*

After all, the fundamental approach to public policy decisions should be about balancing a range of considerations, of which safety from injury is but one. There is overwhelming evidence that the public is concerned about more than just safety, and this should be reflected in how society sets its priorities. This is fully recognized by government agencies that have a broader remit than the narrow focus of safety from injury; for example, HM Treasury (2003, 2005) and the National Audit Office (2001). Others, though, who confine themselves to a more restricted brief, may take a harder line. The Act is then interpreted more narrowly, strictly in line with the letter of Lord Asquith's 1949 definition such that one may only take account of 'money, time or trouble', but with no allusion to the social benefits which might be impacted upon by the safety measure. Agencies who are in this position have opinions upon this, of course, but they are not more than that. The answer lies, as it should, with the courts.

In passing, it is of interest to note that in 1956 Lord Reid, in a civil law context, gave a slightly different definition of employers' duties when he said:

> *It is the duty of an employer, in considering whether some precaution should be taken against foreseeable risk, to weigh, on the one hand, the magnitude of the risk, the likelihood of an accident happening and the possible seriousness of the consequences if an accident does happen, and, on the other hand, the difficulty and expense and any other disadvantage of taking the precaution. (Lord Reid, 1956, in Morris v. West Hartlepool Steam Navigation Co. Ltd quoted in Charlesworth and Percy, 1997: 442)*

The reference here to 'any other disadvantage of taking the precaution' seemingly opens the door to the consideration of these other benefits which are the essence of public life.

The Occupiers' Liability Acts

While the HSW Act provides the starting point for criminal prosecutions, the Occupiers' Liability Acts provide the basis for civil claims. These Acts are the result of a re-examination and consolidation of previous common law cases relating to occupiers' liability, with the aim, somewhat like the HSW Act, of simplification.

The Occupiers' Liability Act (1957), which is of most importance here, states as follows:

> *The common duty of care is to see that the visitor will be reason-ably safe in using the premises.*

The crucial point is that a duty holder with premises which are frequented by visitors – your country park, for instance – is required to see that visitors are 'reasonably safe'. Again, the word 'reasonable' is there, and there is no mention of a requirement for absolute safety, that is, to either eliminate or minimize risk.

An obvious follow-up question is whether 'reasonable' and 'reasonable practicability' are the same. Legal opinion seems to be that in most circum-stances they are much the same (Charlesworth and Percy, 1997: 849), and the case law described below shows that in making decisions about what is either reasonable, or reasonably practicable, similar considerations apply with one exception, and that is that the importance of the social benefits of public space and activities is much more clearly registered in civil law than is the case with the HSW Act.

The following historical cases provide insight into the factors which are likely to be taken into account by courts in deciding whether reasonable care was taken, and hence on liability in the case of accidents. They also show how, below the surface, the law is deeply fascinating.

Some historical cases of influence

From Lord Reid's 1956 statement in Morris v. West Hartlepool Steam Navigation Company, it can be seen that there are four factors of potential importance in deciding liability. These are:

- the level of risk (i.e. the probability of harm) to which someone might be exposed;
- the seriousness of the potential consequences;
- the difficulty and expense of preventative measures; and
- any other disadvantages of taking the precaution.

These factors did not emerge overnight – they can be traced back to earlier case law.

Thus, in 1951 the quintessentially English game of cricket became the focus of the case known as Bolton v. Stone, and was heard in the Appeal Court. This owed its origins to a 1947 game of cricket at Cheetham Cricket Ground in Manchester, during which a batsman from the visiting team struck the ball so hard that it sailed out of the ground. As luck would have it, the ball hit the claimant-to-be, Miss Stone, who was standing on the road outside her house some 100 yards away.

The facts of the case were that the club had been playing cricket at the ground since 1864, long before the neighbouring road was built. The ground was surrounded by a 12-foot fence, which itself was high above the level of the pitch, being on a slope. There was evidence that balls had been hit out of the ground before, though only rarely; in all, about six times in the previous 30 years. The claimant argued that the ball being hit so far, even once, was sufficient to give the club warning that there was a risk of injuring a passer-by, such that it should be liable for her injuries. The court decided, however, that the club was not liable because, although the possibility of this happening was foreseeable, such a colossal hit had so rarely been recorded. The risk was thereby too low to qualify as unreasonable.

However, the 1951 case of Paris v. Stepney Borough Council shows that a court's interpretations are not purely based on risk, but can be qualified according to a second factor: the potential seriousness of the consequences. In this example, Mr Paris was a welder who worked for the Council and who had lost an eye during the war. Unfortunately, Mr Paris was totally blinded during his work when a metal fragment damaged his good eye while he was trying to loosen a bolt with a hammer (not, we think, something to be recommended). At that time there was not a requirement to wear goggles;[3] nonetheless, after working its way up through the courts, the House of Lords eventually ruled in favour of Mr Paris on the grounds of the potential gravity of the consequences for a man who was starting out with only one good eye. The moral is that the more serious the possible damage, the greater the precautions that should be taken.

The third factor, the difficulty and expense and hence practicability of preventative measures, is of course central to the Edwards v. NCB case as already described. It also figured in another well-known case, that of a Mr Latimer v. AEC Ltd in 1953. Mr Latimer, an employee, slipped and injured himself on the factory floor, which was still slippery after having been flooded the previous day. AEC had done their best to clean up the flood with sawdust and other measures. The trial judge found in favour of Mr Latimer, but the Court of Appeal reversed the decision because it considered that the employer had taken all reasonable steps in the circumstances, short of closing the factory down, and in so doing had negated any possible allegation of negligence. Thus, a defendant does not have to totally eliminate a risk, but must do as much as the reasonable person in the circumstances.

This leaves the final factor, of special interest here: any other disadvantage of taking the precaution. There are many cases to choose from. In Daborn v. Bath Tramways Motor Company Ltd (1946), Lord Justice Asquith said this:

> In determining whether a party is negligent, the standard of reasonable care is that which is reasonably to be demanded in the circumstances. A relevant circumstance to take into account may be the importance of the end to be served by behaving in this way or in that. As has often been pointed out, if all the trains in this country were restricted to a speed of five miles an hour, there would be fewer accidents, but our national life would be intolerably slowed down. The purpose to be served, if sufficiently important, justifies the assumption of abnormal risk. (Asquith, 1946: 449)

This statement clearly identifies the 'social utility' of activities as a consideration in deciding what is reasonable.

Some recent events

Barrister Simon Wheatley has recently produced a useful summary of the current position with regard to occupiers' liability, including social utility considerations (Wheatley, 2008). Although his review pertains specifically to ancient monuments and places of historical interest, the primary point which

---

Box 9 *Optimal levels of protection*

The analogy used by Lord Asquith in Daborn v. Bath Tramways Motor Company Ltd was used recently in modified form by Rick Haythornthwaite, former Chair of the Government's Better Regulation Commission (BRC), who said as follows in a speech, regarding what he called *optimal levels of protection*:

I said at the outset, and I think few would disagree, that it is neither possible nor desirable to eliminate all risk from our lives. Regulators recognise that there is a point beyond which further risk reduction is impractical or unacceptable. But how do they determine where that point lies? There is a road safety advertisement on television at the moment. You may have seen it. It starts with a young girl's body lying crumpled and lifeless at the side of the road. The film rewinds and the child is gradually restored to life. The commentary tells us that a child hit by a car travelling at 40 mph has an 80 percent chance of being killed while a child hit by a car travelling at 30 mph has an 80 percent chance of survival. The closing message is that the urban speed limit is 30 mph for a reason. Let us analyse this. I am not a highway engineer, but it is reasonable to assume a fairly close correlation between speed of impact and rates of death. So what is the reason for the 30 mph speed limit? It represents some sort of balance – moderated by public acceptability between the costs to the economy of further slowing down travel times and the benefits of saving the lives of more children. The advertisement implies that 20 percent of children struck by a car travelling quite legally at the urban speed limit are likely to be killed. In effect, it is saying that this is the optimal level of protection that child pedestrians should enjoy and that any lower speed limit would be subject to the law of diminishing returns. This is a particularly telling – if inadvertent – example of the tradeoffs and judgments that our policy makers are obliged to make in regulating to control risk. Regulators frequently talk about the need to provide 'proper' protection, to avoid 'excessive' risk aversion and to 'balance' benefits and risks. But these terms are undefined, value laden and mean different things to different people.
(Haythornthwaite, 2006)

---

is made, which is about the 'social value', or *benefits*, of such locations, also has manifest resonance for public places and activities more widely. Wheatley points out that based on consideration of a number of recent personal injury cases brought under the Occupiers' Liability Act, and involving premises offering a social value, the courts are likely to consider, inter alia, the following factors:

- whether the visitor had unrealistic expectations given the nature of the premises (in that case, ancient buildings);
- that the occupier is not under a duty to warn visitors of risks that should be obvious to the reasonable observer;
- the four test criteria of risk of injury, likely severity, cost of preventative measures and social value of an activity.[4]

In considering social value, Wheatley suggests that the courts would contemplate the purpose of the activity, numbers of persons involved, what the actual benefits were, and the extent of the benefit to society as a whole. From this it can be seen that the civil courts are well aware of the benefits of public space and activities, and their social importance.

One particularly influential case highlighting the benefits of public space and activities is that known as Tomlinson v. Congleton Borough Council and others (House of Lords, 2003). This involved a very serious accident to a young man, Tomlinson, while visiting a publicly owned lake which had previously been a quarry. The lake is popular and attracts many visitors, some of whom swim there. In 1995, Mr Tomlinson waded into the lake and launched himself forward into the water. Unfortunately he dived deeper than he intended and his head hit the sandy bottom, resulting in a severely damaged spine. Mr Tomlinson initially lost the case against the occupier in the lower court, but this decision was later overturned in the Court of Appeal, only to be finally rejected in the House of Lords. In his summing up, Lord Hoffmann said this of the Court of Appeal's decision:

> *My Lords, the majority of the Court of Appeal appear to have proceeded on the basis that if there was a foreseeable risk of serious injury, the Council was under a duty to do what was necessary to prevent it. But this in my opinion is an oversimplification. Even in the case of the duty owed to a lawful visitor under section 2(2) of the 1957 Act[5] and even if the risk had been attributable to the state of the premises rather than the acts of Mr Tomlinson, the question of what amounts to 'such care as in all the circumstances is reasonable' depends upon assessing, as in the case of common law negligence, not only the likelihood that someone may be injured and the seriousness of the injury which may occur, but also the social value of the activity which gives rise to the risk and the cost of preventative measures. These factors have to be balanced against each other. (House of Lords, 2003, para. 34)*

Lord Hoffmann went on to say:

> *The Court of Appeal made no reference at all to the social value of the activities which were to be prohibited. The majority of people who went to the beaches to sunbathe, paddle and play with their children were enjoying themselves in a way which gave them pleasure and caused no risk to themselves or anyone else. This must be something to be taken into account in deciding whether it was reasonable to expect the Council to destroy the beaches. (House of Lords, 2003, para. 42)*

Lord Hoffmann also referred to the case of Bolton v. Stone. His comment was that the cricket club were carrying on a lawful and socially useful activity (para. 36), suggesting he might also have liked cricket.[6]

The Compensation Act 2006

Since the Tomlinson case, the Compensation Act has been passed in response to concerns expressed by the Better Regulation Task Force (2004) over disproportionate fear of litigation and subsequent risk-averse behaviour by

> ### **Box 10** *Safety measures do not guarantee safety*
>
> In 2002 a fit young man, Mr Gary Poppleton, went low-level climbing without ropes at an activity centre run by the Portsmouth Youth Activities Committee. He was given no explanation of risks, nor was he asked about his ability as a climber. He had been there three or four times before, but was not an experienced climber. Mr Poppleton attempted to jump from the climbing wall, as he had seen other climbers do, and grab a girder. He failed to achieve this and landed awkwardly, sustaining severe spinal injuries, despite the presence of matting on the floor.
>
> There were rules posted on a board which inter alia prohibited jumping, but Mr Poppleton's attention had not been drawn to them. His solicitors pursued a claim based, amongst other things, on a breach of the Occupiers' Liability Act. They claimed there was a duty of care which extended to carrying out induction, training, assessment and supervision.
>
> In March 2007 a High Court judge disagreed and ruled that Mr Poppleton was largely responsible for his own well-being. In June 2008 the Court of Appeal went further and ruled that he was wholly responsible. This court decided that there was also no duty of care to warn Mr Poppleton about the risks or that the mat did not make the climbing facility safe. In a landmark ruling, Lord Justice May said: 'Adults who choose to engage in physical activities, which obviously give rise to a degree of unavoidable risk, may find that they have no means of recompense if the risk materialises so that they are injured.'
>
> In this case, Mr Poppleton's decision to make the jump meant that the accident was, most unfortunately for him, deemed to be his fault as opposed to being someone else's. This is a strong signal from the Court of Appeal that they do not embrace what some have described as the nanny state.

those responsible, in particular, for public activities. The Act places a statutory requirement on courts as follows:

> *A court considering a claim in negligence or breach of statutory duty may, in determining whether the defendant should have taken particular steps to meet a standard of care (whether by taking precautions against a risk or otherwise), have regard to whether a requirement to take those steps might:*
>
> 1. *prevent a desirable activity from being undertaken at all, to a particular extent or in a particular way, or*
> 2. *discourage persons from undertaking functions in connection with a desirable activity.*

Although some regard this new legislation as unnecessary because, they maintain, the courts always took the wider social implications of claims into account (Copnall, 2008), the unequivocal identification of the importance of the benefits of public places and activities is to be welcomed, particularly if it can help in stemming the tide of risk averse behaviour which originates beyond the courts by offering reassurance to those public and private agencies who provide these opportunities.

Uncertainty of court decisions

Despite the above account of factors which courts consider in making judgments about liability in relation to public space, and the consistency with the approaches described in the preceding chapters 3 and 4, there is no escaping the fact that court decisions are sometimes surprising. They may even be reversed one or more times if and when cases are referred to higher courts, as happened with both the Tomlinson v. Congleton Borough Council and other cases such as R v. Porter.

Barrister Jerome Mayhew has proposed that judges have been interpreting with increasing stringency situations which would previously have been interpreted as one of voluntarily accepted risk, while not taking account of the cumulative impact upon society of this approach to awards of compensation (Mayhew, 2007). There are some signs, though, that this trend, if it existed, might be reversing. Luke Bennett, of Sheffield Hallam University, has also offered an alternative explanation, namely that the lower courts cannot always be relied upon to apply the law consistently, and a return to a more balanced position may in some cases be required by the Court of Appeal (Bennett and Crowe, 2008), or even the House of Lords. One possible explanation for the apparent failure of lower courts (sometimes referred to as the courts of first instance), on occasion, to be consistent, is that they tend to be more influenced by expert testimony and published advice which can be a mixed bag, whereas the appeal courts are far more concerned with basic principles of law and the intent of the original law-makers (Ball, Maggs and Barrett, 2009).

The fact is, however, that taking cases to the higher courts is an expensive and traumatic business for all those involved and this is a route seldom pursued.

Summary

The courts and the legal profession have made a major contribution to the approach taken in the UK to the management of risk, in particular through defining and fleshing out the meaning of key terms such as 'reasonable practicability' and 'reasonableness' which have been referred to in earlier chapters. It has been shown here that under civil law the courts, in deciding whether reasonable measures have been taken by a responsible person to protect the public, are likely to consider four factors: the prior level of risk; the potential seriousness of any harm; the cost and difficulty of applying further safety measures; and the effect upon the benefits or social utility of the place or activity.

So far as the HSW Act is concerned, the situation is murkier. Issues of the prior level of risk, the potential seriousness of harm, and the cost and difficulty of applying remedial measures, are clearly identified in law, even if sometimes ignored by professionals who might know better. The role of social utility, though, in determining what measures are reasonably practicable, still retains an air of uncharted territory. Different views exist and the courts will decide.

Anomalies have been noted in some court decisions, and there is a series of cases in which decisions of lower courts have been overturned by appeal courts. However, a gradual change may be underway in which greater recognition is being given to the benefits or social utility of public space and activities. This change may be encouraged by the Compensation Act 2006, which authorizes courts to consider whether any requirements to take precautions against a risk might prevent or discourage desirable activities from taking place. Lord Young's report, and its acceptance by government, gives further impetus to this development.

7
Advice – *Whose Advice?*

The previous chapter has described how the courts, key thinkers and decision makers within society have given recognition to the need to take into account, amongst other things, the benefits of public space and activities when deciding what is reasonable. However, decisions about safety are influenced by many other agencies long before the courts are involved, if ever they are. These include insurers, people who write advisory documents including standards, assorted experts, campaign groups, professional bodies and regulators. Experience has shown that these agencies or individuals can hold partial, different and conflicting positions over what exactly is meant by the concept of 'safety', and how to approach it. While some might interpret it as zero or minimal risk, others think of it as compliance with some standard, and yet others interpret it as doing what is reasonable, or maybe something else entirely, as indicated in Table 7.1. The fallout from this non-commonality of purpose can of itself lead to many unintended consequences for public life.

Layered on top of this is the issue of benefits and how, if at all, they are factored in to decisions. Apparent failures to consider benefits are not necessarily attributable to some lack of awareness, but may be because agencies are adhering to some form of compartmentalized thinking or 'bounded rationality',[1] which is consistent with their interpretation of policy, or fits in with some imposed management system, or is simply what they believe to be right, based upon their education and background.

Various positions

To illustrate the conundrum, consider factors influencing the behaviours of the above agencies e.g. insurers. Generally speaking, insurers would not see it as their role to either encourage or discourage public activities. This is simply not their job. Their job is to provide insurance cover in the event that something untoward happens, as it will from time to time, and they reasonably expect to charge a premium reflecting the likely level of claims, including occasional claims for negligence through the courts. Naturally, therefore, insurance companies would wish insured parties to take as many steps as were available to avoid legal claims, as these can be very expensive; millions of pounds in some cases.[2]

Table 7.1 *An analysis of six different concepts of 'safety' (based on Ball, 2000).*

Safety criterion	Zero or minimal risk	Safety targets	Compliance with standards, CoPs and advice	Risk assessment	Cost-benefit	Risk tolerability and ALARP
Typical adherents	Campaign groups	National and international agencies	Traditional industries, courts of first instance, accident investigators	Actuarial sciences, health and safety profession	Economists, national agencies	Regulatory bodies, higher courts, international agencies and major industries
Motivation or basis of approach	Worldview, commitment	Political desire	Belief in expertise	Realistic approach to business; legal requirement	To get the maximum benefit from given resources	Basis in law; concept of 'reasonableness'
Strengths	Simplicity, clear statement of intent	Clarity of mission; measurability of achievement	Reflects expert opinion. Evolved over time	Analytic tool; forecasts future; may be evidence-based	A rational approach to decision making	Logic
Limitations	Achievability, cost, unintended consequences	Top-down approach of uncertain achievability by reasonable means	Validity and motivation of expert judgements. A bottom-up approach which may be inconsistent with policy goals	Data availability and uncertainties; assumptions and predisposition of assessor	Requires lots of data; difficulty of valuing non-traded goods; externalities	Requires data and intellectual effort
Examples	'Vision zero' for road safety; Greenpeace on nuclear waste	Public Service Agreement targets; Injury reduction targets	Product safety standards; use as a substitute for risk assessment	Setting insurance premiums; occupational safety assessment	Road safety (normally); use of the QALY by the NHS	Radiation protection; major hazard control; recognition that prior medical advice to 'stay out of the sun' is counter-productive

Brokers provide the principal link between the public and insurance companies who underwrite the risks, and although there is a trend to greater specialization, brokers frequently do not claim expertise in public activities, preferring to rely upon guides, standards or codes of practice, produced by regulators, governing bodies, trade associations and so on (Barrett and Ball, 2009a). It would be common, therefore, for insurers to expect their clients to maintain an audit trail of documentation showing how they have complied with any published advice as a defence against potential claims.

In a study for the Home Office of the impact of insurance practices upon the Voluntary and Community Sector (VCS), Alison Millward Associates and colleagues observed as follows:

> *Risk management has become the major focus of attention in the Insurance Industry. Insurers are attracted to business where Health and Safety and Risk Management are maintained to a very high standard. Good working practices and effective training and supervision are considered to be of paramount importance. It was clear that the VCS suffers from the perception that the people involved tend to be well meaning volunteers with a lack of understanding regarding risk assessments, health and safety responsibilities and the management of risk. Evidence suggests this perception to be without justification ... Larger organisations, within the VCS, will be considered for cover by most insurers as they are perceived to have the organisational structure and skills to ensure compliance with legislation and risk management practices. (Millward et al, 2003)*

From these passages it may be deduced that auditable management practices, and compliance with codes and standards are the watchword. This, indeed, is apparently what many safety professionals now believe to be the primary requirement for managing risk. Others, though, as noted earlier, are more sceptical (Power, 1994, 2004 and 2009). For one thing, the strength of the relationship between accident rates and what are described as 'good management systems' is open to question; and, secondly, the subtle shift of emphasis from decision making by 'front line professionals' to 'back room management systems' is itself a prospective source of risk. Professor Michael Power, of the Centre for the Analysis of Risk and Regulation (CARR) at the London School of Economics, put it like this:

> *... the risk management of everything poses a different agenda of concern, namely that the experts who are being made increasingly accountable for what they do are now becoming more preoccupied with managing their own risks. Specifically, secondary risks to their reputation are becoming as significant as the primary risks for which experts have knowledge and training. This trend is resulting in a dangerous flight from judgement and a culture of defensiveness that create their own risks for*

organisations in preparing for, and responding to, a future they
cannot know. (Power, 2004)

We ourselves are also aware of the difficulties of identifying what truly is good practice from the swathe of documentation which has been churned out in its name. As the American policy analyst, Harvey Sapolsky, Professor of Public Policy and Organization at Massachusetts Institute of Technology, has summed it up:

> *There is no shortage of advice about risks. Let a potential risk*
> *be identified and soon all possibly relevant professions, agencies,*
> *and trade groups will offer public positions in order to protect*
> *established interests or proclaim new ones. Add the news appeal*
> *of risk stories, the availability of advertising dollars to defend*
> *and promote products, and the ongoing flood of scientific*
> *reports and there is a flood of guidance for the concerned.*
> *(Sapolsky, 1990)*

Apart from the problem of sifting through the deluge of advice, difficulties arise in other ways too. For example, in the case of the many public activities or situations for which specific advisory documents, despite the deluge, do not exist, there is a tendency to shoehorn the activity into something similar, however vaguely so, so that advice concocted for another purpose can be used. This can be misleading, absurdly so in some cases. It was recently alleged in court, for example, that an inflatable paddling pool, because it contained some water, should comply with diving standards for swimming pools.

Documents may also be interpreted too literally or narrowly to the detriment of some activity (Barrett and Ball, 2009b). And, with more subtlety, but nonetheless important, the underlying philosophy upon which advisory documents rely in making their recommendations is all too often unexpressed or hidden, yet there is no shortage of contending philosophies, as indicated in Table 7.1. Thus, there is no way of checking whether recommendations are consistent with the national philosophy of reasonableness and reasonable practicability and, ultimately, the law. This should not be surprising. Apart from the widespread lack of awareness and comprehension of these concepts, authors of advisory documents may have other axes to grind.

Personal injury barrister Jerome Mayhew recounts his own experience of dealing with the British Standards Institution (BSI) on discovering that there was a proposal to produce a European standard on outdoor adventure activities, using what are known as 'high ropes'. These comprise aerial rope courses, often suspended between trees, with zip wires, trapezes, towers and other fun features:

> *We contacted the BSI, only to be told that such a committee did*
> *not exist. In the end, it took six months, an uninvited arrival at*
> *a meeting in Antwerp, and numerous conversations with BSI to*
> *receive acknowledgement that the process was underway, and*
> *then to be affiliated to the committee as a national member.*

The makeup of both the national and European committees was very surprising. The national committee was dominated by a particular section of the industry that happened to know of its existence. Both were dominated by representatives of manufacturers, and were not truly representative of the industry that they were supposed to regulate.

In our experience, the quality of the draft standard was massively affected by the quality and objectives of the committee members. We felt that some committee members were seeking to use the standard to stifle competition and restrict innovation within the industry.

By grasping the nettle and forcing the system to allow us to get involved, we were able to radically alter the composition of the draft standard. As with all products of committees, there are still parts of the final version with which we are unhappy. However, during the course of our involvement we were able to change what would have been a deeply restricting and damaging document into what should be a positive contribution to the design and operation process. (Mayhew, 2007)

This experience, as recounted by Mayhew, has some similarities with the attempt to introduce a standard on tree maintenance, as recounted in chapter 1. A difficulty for many, particularly smaller, public organizations that are affected by the promulgation of such advice is that they do not have the resources to get involved with these processes and thus their legitimate interests may be sidelined.

The above discussion has also identified once again the presence of contrasting belief systems, similar to the schism described in chapter 5 over the relative efficacy of either environmental or behavioural controls for managing public risk. Just as some people prefer engineered (environmental) solutions such as barriers and surveillance systems, some lay heavy stress on management systems, the more autocratic varieties of which may have the unintended consequence of disenfranchising front-line professionals who are at the sharp end of the provision of public space and activities.

Another apparent schism revolves around the extent to which published advice, even advice of marginal relevance, is preferred over intuitive, on the spot, risk assessment. Many supposed experts in risk assessment are in fact loath to carry out their own personal risk assessment, and prefer to rely upon comparison of a situation with some published standard, code or advisory document. The intellectual exercise of doing a risk assessment can thus be avoided and replaced with the less onerous task of making physical measurements, and comparing them against written specifications. This also shields the 'expert' from having to give an opinion for which s/he might be held liable. This approach is often deemed, including by some courts of the first instance, to be a suitable way to demonstrate the reasonableness of some feature of a public place. Ironically, though, much published advice is not based on anything even faintly resembling risk assessment, let alone the concept of reasonableness. For example, a primary motivation behind the production of European Standards is to do with restraints on trade and the free movement of goods. This may apply even in the case of some standards which are ostensibly about safety. A further difficulty with these generic documents is that they are written in remote places, often by committees, and involve persons with unknown motivations, and who may, for instance, have no awareness of the benefits of some public activity or place which you are trying to organize.[3]

The impact on public life can be particularly severe where single-issue campaign groups are involved, or where key stakeholders have a narrow remit. The central argument of this book is that public safety is not paramount and is something which has to sit alongside other objectives such as user-friendliness, social benefits, environmental attributes, and even beauty. This is not something which campaign groups readily acknowledge. One would not expect to make much headway, for example, in trying to discuss the potential environmental and other benefits of nuclear-generated electricity with Greenpeace. Likewise, RoSPA (Royal Society for Prevention of Accidents) has traditionally acted as a campaign group seeking, as its name implies, to prevent accidents. On the face of it, the cause is noble and to be respected, and automatically conceded to RoSPA apparent ownership of the high moral ground. But the mantra of *accident prevention*, in the absence of frank acknowledgement of the existence of other factors which are important in public life, can lead to one-sided decision making.[4]

To what extent should, for example, natural water bodies be fenced or somehow made inaccessible to the public? Should the public be deterred from swimming in natural waters unless a qualified lifesaver is present? Should children in the care of teachers or activity leaders be allowed in water at all unless their leader is a qualified lifesaver? Should children's playgrounds be fenced off? From a narrow, injury prevention perspective, the answers might be affirmative, but from a broader perspective they could be very different, and one reason for this is that activities provided by these spaces have health and social benefits!

Safety versus health

This consideration exposes yet another schism. The debate over safety is normally couched in terms of being about both 'health' *and* 'safety', and in this way we often talk of 'health and safety' professionals. Most health and safety professionals, however, have a narrow remit in relation to health. 'Health' within the health and safety world is largely about ill health, associated with exposure to chemicals in the workplace, occupational disease, and musculoskeletal problems associated with lifting or, say, incorrect posture at computer terminals. It is not about the *health benefits* of public activities, and it is likely true that most health and safety experts know no more about this than members of the public, yet it is of such obvious importance.[5]

The increasing incidence of obesity in Britain alone should flag up a stern warning that anything that inhibits public activities involving physical exercise ought to be viewed from a broad perspective and not solely one of reduction of injury risk. The health implications of obesity can be just as dramatic as the injuries which campaigners seek to prevent, including increased risk of diabetes and other life-threatening conditions, such as heart attacks, strokes, blindness and kidney disease. Lack of physical exercise is of course not the sole cause of this, but most health experts believe it is contributory.

Public places and activities also yield immense psychological benefits for both individuals and wider communities. Though less easy to quantify, these may be of even greater importance from a societal perspective, yet they get no mention in standard health and safety management procedures. It's as if some-one has decided, or presumed, that all else should play second fiddle to safety from injury. A much-needed, broader perspective has been taken by the courts. As Lord Hoffmann said in 2003, in his summing up of the Tomlinson case:

> *It is of course understandable that organisations like the Royal Society for the Prevention of Accidents should favour policies*

> *which require people to be prevented from taking risks. Their*
> *function is to prevent accidents and that is one way of doing so.*
> *But they do not have to consider the cost, not only in money but*
> *also in deprivation of liberty, which such restrictions entail. The*
> *courts will naturally respect the technical expertise of such*
> *organisations in drawing attention to what can be done to*
> *prevent accidents. But the balance between risk on the one hand*
> *and individual autonomy on the other is not a matter of expert*
> *opinion. It is a judgment which the courts must make and which*
> *in England reflects the individualist values of the common law.*
> *(House of Lords, 2003)*

To be fair to some safety agencies, such as RoSPA, there is clear evidence that they have been thinking very hard about their philosophy, and they have of late started to talk about the need to consider benefits of public activities when offering safety advice.[6] At times they now go so far as to say: 'As safe as necessary not as safe as possible.' How this is achieved, though, is another matter. If your raison d'être has been accident prevention, then it requires something of an intellectual paradigm shift. More portentous still, perhaps, is Lord Hoffmann's proposition, which is mirrored by the discussion in chapter 2 about the separation between risk assessment, which is essentially technical, and decision making, which goes far beyond technical issues, that the decision about the proper balance between risk and autonomy is *not* a matter of technical expertise at all. If accepted, where does this leave health and safety experts who venture beyond the workplace and into the public domain? This issue, which could be said to be partially one of competence, will be revisited in later chapters.

Regulatory stances

There is no shortage of agencies in Britain fulfilling regulatory roles and issuing advice. Arguably the most powerful of these is the Health and Safety Executive (HSE), and the one which, with much justification, is most respected. Until recently the HSE was responsible for the executive function, with its policy dimension being overseen by the Health and Safety Commission (HSC). For good or ill, these bodies were merged on 1 April 2008.

The HSE draws its authority from the HSW Act of 1974, and therein, too, lies the source of its underlying principles and philosophy of safety, crucial amongst which is to see that risk is reduced according to the dictum of reasonable practicability. More simply this has been described as 'managing risk properly', with 'properly' presumably being synonymous with reasonable practicability, and all of that eminently good sense which went into the drafting of the 1974 Act. This philosophy is of course quite distinct from that of risk minimization or risk elimination with which it is inherently at odds, because the latter pay no obvious heed to opportunity costs such as the cost-effectiveness of safety interventions, the time and difficulty of their implementation, or any unintended consequences.

From time to time HSE publishes important documents describing its decision-making processes. In 2001 it published the invaluable *Reducing risk: protecting people* (HSE, 2001).[7] As would be expected, this includes a description of the ALARP concept and the Tolerability of Risk framework, as described in chapter 4. In other HSE documents, though, HSE has afforded less prominence to these important concepts. Thus, readers of some versions of widely disseminated HSE publications like *Five steps to risk assessment*, and of its best-selling, *Successful Health and Safety Management* (also known as HSG65), might occasionally get a different impression.

The current version of *Five steps ...*, for example, while at least referring to the concept of reasonable practicability,[8] does not explain its meaning (HSE, 2006a). It says: 'You can work this out for yourself, but the easiest way is to compare what you are doing with good practice.' Further on it says that you need to be able to show that 'the remaining risk is low', without reference to reasonable practicability, or risk tolerability in exchange for benefits, leaving an impression that the one and only aim is risk minimization. This notion is strongly reinforced by *Successful Health and Safety Management*, which includes messages and examples of health and safety philosophies of the following kind:

- Organisations that want to behave ethically and responsibly ... show that they are concerned not simply with preventing accidents and ill health (as required by health and safety legislation) but also with positive health promotion.
- ... minimising risk to people, plant and products is inseparable from all other company objectives.
- In the field of health and safety [we] seek to achieve the highest standards. We do not pursue this aim simply to achieve compliance with current legislation, but because it is in our best interests.
- All accidents and ill health are preventable. (HSE, 1997)

Given the kind of impression that these statements create, coupled with the parallel belief in management systems and engineering controls which has been fostered in the workplace (where it might have some legitimacy), the subsequent emergence of problems in public life, as this ethos has spread beyond the workplace, should provoke little surprise.

Indeed, the HSC/HSE has itself been very aware that health and safety was getting a bad name. In 2006, Bill Callaghan, then Chair of the HSC, delivered the following oft-quoted proclamation:

> *I am sick and tired of hearing about petty health and safety stopping people doing worthwhile and enjoyable things, when at the same time others are suffering harm and even death due to poor management and complacency. That is why today we are launching a set of principles of sensible risk management.* (Callaghan, 2006)

The principles of 'sensible risk management', which will be examined shortly, were duly launched by the Health and Safety Commission in August 2006 (HSE, 2006b). Despite this, the media reporting of a stream of seemingly overzealous, disproportionate, or whatever, safety interventions has not dried up.

To further combat the bad press generated in connection with health and safety anecdotes, the HSE initiated a 'Myth of the month' item on its website. The following 'myths' were recorded there in 2009:

- You can't throw out sweets at pantomimes.
- Health and safety rules stop classroom experiments.
- Graduates are banned from throwing mortar boards.
- Health and safety bans traditional school ties.
- Health and safety laws mean concert-goers have to wear earplugs.
- Health and safety is a threat to village fêtes.
- You can't wear flip-flops to work.
- Ice-cream toppings have been banned for safety reasons.
- People don't have to take any responsibility for their own health and safety.
- Health and safety rules take the adventure out of playgrounds.
- Pancake races are banned!

But, one might ask, in what way were these stories mythical? And what is implied by use of the word 'myth'? In current usage, a myth is regarded as something which is unfounded. Traditionally, though, a myth would be seen as a 'truth-bearing story', and indeed many of the reported 'myths' have seeds of truth within them.[9] Many, if not all, have been reported by the national broadsheet press, the BBC, and other reputable agencies, and some at least must have some validity unless the media is totally unreliable. The HSE itself confirmed on its website that something lay behind these stories. In respect of the pancake race, for example, it noted that health and safety requirements *were* given as the reason that a pancake race couldn't take place. Its response then being that a risk assessment, albeit a simple one, was *all that was needed*. Likewise, it said that health and safety rules *were* blamed when a pantomime stopped throwing out sweets to the audience, but that the real concern was not the actual risk of harm but the liability should there be a claim. The cheery advice this time being '*consult your insurer*'.

Thus, it is perhaps no wonder that public activities are suffering. The mere thought of having to produce a documented risk assessment for a pancake race, or of needing to consult one's insurer over the trivia of pantomime sweets, is sufficient to drive most people, trying to bring some pleasure into others' lives, often at their own time and expense, to despair.

Nor should it be forgotten that too much control can also do harm by delegitimizing front-line people who deal directly with hazards. The number of these cases is uncounted, but there have been several harrowing stories, some recounted in this book, which seemingly paint a picture of death at the hands of what has been called 'spreadsheet management', 'box ticking' and 'managerial proceduralism' (*Spectator*, 2003). As journalist Libby Purves has expressed it: 'Personal responsibility is lost in the red stop-lights of an over-regulated world. We must start thinking for ourselves again' (*The Times*, 2009).

Safety, philosophy and politics

'What', some students of health and safety enquire, 'has philosophy and politics got to do with us?' To which the correct answer is 'A great deal'. The healthcare professor and philosopher, David Seedhouse, whose work was introduced in chapter 5, has with great clarity outlined why, in the context of health service provision, an understanding of philosophy is essential at the policy level, if consistent goals are to be set (Seedhouse, 2004). At the moment, according to his analysis, healthcare provision is driven by a mixture of competing philosophies. It is well worthwhile to contemplate his analysis as an aid to understanding some of the deeper issues troubling health and safety.

To use Seedhouse's terminology, on the one hand there exists a way of thinking which he describes, for want of a better term, as 'medical health promotion'. This seeks to treat disease, injury and ill health because these things are inherently bad, and it does this by firstly targeting individuals and, secondly, by using interventions that can be justified on both scientific and economic grounds. In this way the approach subscribes to an essentially utilitarian ethic, seeking to produce the greatest benefit to the population with the resources at its disposal. Thus, an important tool in helping decide which drugs and medical procedures should be available on the National Health Service is cost-benefit analysis.[10] This, in a clear application of the Kaldor-Hicks rule described in chapter 3, weighs on the one hand the benefits to health of an intervention and compares it against the costs. As a rule of thumb, if benefits outweigh costs, then the intervention is supported; if not, and there are no other influential considerations, then it may not be. The parallels with the world of health and safety, particularly the concept of reasonable practicability, are obvious. Reasonable practicability can be seen to be an essentially utilitarian ethic.

In contrast to this philosophy, however, is what Seedhouse calls 'Social health promotion'. This also seeks to deal with disease, injury and ill health, but sees the causes of these conditions as attributable to group dynamics, as opposed to individual behaviour with the cause ultimately lying in social inequality in the population. It therefore seeks to bring about improvement by social change and thereby pursues a more socialist agenda.

Thirdly, a new and fashionable philosophy has been identified, which he describes as 'Good life promotion'. This goes beyond the treatment of injuries and illness, and tries to 'improve' people's lives, some would say, whether they like it or not (Berger et al, 1991). As can be imagined, this is a hotly contested arena because it first requires an agreement about what constitutes a 'good life'.

At this point it is informative to consider the internal consistency of statements appearing in some HSE publications, and made to the media by their spokespersons, as well as their conformity with the stipulations of the HSW Act and other important legislation such as the Occupiers' Liability Acts. A good starting point is the *Principles of sensible risk management*, published by the HSE in 2006 in response to its growing concerns about health and safety 'myths'. Table 7.2 gives an analysis, commentary and some suggested alternative wording.

The left hand column of the table merely repeats HSE's principles as they set them out. Helpfully, HSE grouped them into those which 'Sensible risk management' *is* about, and then what it *is not* about. In the principles there is quite a lot of emphasis on the workforce, unsurprisingly given this is the HSE's primary area of responsibility, although it is likely that the principles were generated mainly in response to issues arising in the public domain. The general tenor of them is helpful and certainly a step in the right direction, but maybe some opportunity to set the record straight has been lost. The word 'reasonable', for instance, the now familiar cornerstone of the HSW Act and the Occupiers' Liability Acts, is absent, while there is plenty of emphasis on 'ensuring' and 'managing', and 'responsibility.' This could perhaps give the impression that in this area of public safety, one is dealing with absolute facts which good managers would easily recognize and cope with, so providing a safe world, rather than the reality of complex trade-offs between safety and the healthy enjoyment of public space, and the huge and unavoidable uncertainties which eternally dog the assessment and management of risk. In truth, many safety decisions are shadowy shades of grey rather than black and white. They are frequently judgemental and anything but absolute. Nonetheless, the principles helpfully acknowledge that a risk-free society is beyond the pale, that risks and benefits are interconnected and have to be balanced, and that recreational activities should be encouraged. Column two of the table gives our more detailed commentary and the third column suggests alternative wording, which the authors of this book believe might sit even more comfortably in public life.

Potentially less helpful in public life though, as already mentioned, is some of the wording in *Five steps to risk assessment*, and more so in *Successful health and safety management*. While freely acknowledging that these were originally written for the workplace, and that both are advisory, they are deeply embedded in Britain's health and safety culture, and are widely used by people whose job is now to make decisions about public life, space and activities. The HSE indeed encourages their use in the public sector.

Successful health and safety management also deploys ethical arguments, while occasionally lapsing into the contention that health and safety is about minimising risks. As noted earlier in this chapter, it proposes the following as an example of an approach to be adopted by good organizations:

> *Organisations that want to behave ethically and responsibly ...*
> *show that they are concerned not simply with preventing accidents and ill health (as required by health and safety legislation)*
> *but also with positive health promotion. (HSE, 1997)*

Table 7.2 *Analysis and commentary on HSE's Principles of sensible risk management*

Sensible risk management is about:	Commentary	Suggested alternative wording for the public domain
Ensuring that workers and the public are properly protected	This is consistent with the HSW Act providing 'properly' is properly defined; i.e. a) that risks are reduced so far as is reasonably practicable b) that in the public sphere wider benefits, including health and other forms of social utility, are incorporated into the definition	Ensuring that all reasonable measures are taken for the safety of the public in public places and during public activities
Providing overall benefit to society by balancing benefits and risks, with a focus on reducing real risks – both those which arise more often and those with serious consequences	The opening clauses are admirable. Modest reflection is warranted over the second half. 'Real' risks certainly deserve to be prioritized, but defining 'real' risks is not that easy and there are many different ways of prioritizing those identified	Taking a balanced view of the health and other benefits of public places and activities versus the risks of harm
Enabling innovation and learning, not stifling them	This is manna from heaven	Enabling pleasure, enjoyment and healthy activity, not stifling them
Ensuring that those who create risks manage them responsibly and understand that failure to manage risks responsibly is likely to lead to robust action	Outwardly reasonable, but what is reasonable and responsible is frequently open to interpretation, particularly in the public realm. Is it therefore appropriate to intone a veiled threat to persons where there is, except in circumstances of obvious negligence, no absolute truth and where decisions are necessarily based more on judgement than scientific evidence?	Taking a broad view of the aims of public life, and then acting thoughtfully and proactively
Enabling individuals to understand that as well as the right to protection, they also have to exercise responsibility	If this is targeted at the public as beneficiaries of public places and organized activities, it is largely true with the exception to some degree of younger or incapacitated persons	Encouraging the public to accept that, in exchange for the freedom and enjoyment of public places and activities made available, they should exercise some personal responsibility for the safety of themselves and others to whom care is owed

Sensible risk management *is not about:*	Commentary	Suggested alternative wording for the public domain
Creating a totally risk-free society	Absolutely true, and fully in accord with the law of the land and the nation's evolved philosophy	Creating a totally risk-free society
Generating useless paperwork mountains	If only this were true. Unfortunately, most responsible agencies feel obliged to do this for fear of the consequences should there be an accident	Generating useless paperwork mountains
Scaring people by exaggerating or publicizing trivial risks	Unarguable	Scaring people by exaggerating or publicizing trivial risks
Stopping important recreational and learning activities for individuals where the risks are managed	The degree and kind of management referred to will be open to interpretation, otherwise the sentiment is sound	Stopping important recreational and learning activities for individuals where reasonable precautions have been taken
Reducing protection of people from risks that cause real harm and suffering	Unarguable	Reducing protection of people from risks that cause real harm and suffering

While on first reading this may seem quite reasonable, it reveals a number of subtle and problematic viewpoints:

- Firstly, it presupposes that there is somewhere an absolute set of ethical rules. Were it true, life might be easier, but the fact is that there is no such rule book.
- Secondly, it presumes that ethical behaviour is synonymous with preventing accidents and ill health, yet society has multiple goals ranging from environmental protection to leading fulfilling lives. Their relative importance is a matter for debate.
- Thirdly, health and safety's primary legislation does not require that accidents and ill health be prevented.
- Fourthly, it is intoned that ethical behaviour is about 'positive health promotion'.

The latter, with reference to the earlier discussion of the work of David Seedhouse, enters a new domain entirely, the one which Seedhouse called 'Good life promotion'. What could be wrong with 'Good life promotion'? As Seedhouse has put it:

> The philosophical foundation of this form (of philosophy) depends essentially upon the way in which 'the good life' is characterised ... (Seedhouse, 2004)

Thus, it could range from a deeply conservative perspective to a Marxist one. From the former perspective, it could, as Seedhouse says: 'seek to protect the status quo as the best possible social organisation, support capitalism, and claim that many social inequalities are unavoidable – indeed acceptable. However, the range of alternative founding philosophies of good life promotion is as broad as the range of possible descriptions of the good life itself.'

Seedhouse's conclusion is that 'Good life promotion' is an *illegitimate* extension of health care. We might similarly ask: where lies the legitimation for this pursuit of the 'good life' into health and safety, whose brand of 'good life' is it, who pays for it, and where does it stop?

Of course, it could be argued that HSG65, and other HSE documents which stimulate similar ideas, are not more than advisory documents giving guidance, and that is so, but duty holders often find it hard to distinguish between what is a legal requirement and what is merely HSE's opinion on how the world should be run. This distinction, between HSE's opinion and the interpretation of the law by the courts, was explored in R (HSE) v. North Yorkshire County Council (2010), as will be described later.

Judith Hackitt, HSE's current Chair, has also taken up the cudgels to try and reassure the public that health and safety was not behaving badly. In 2007 the following three statements were made at the Royal Society for the encouragement of Arts, Manufactures and Commerce (RSA, 2007), largely in the context of children and young people, though the message has obvious parallels with public activities:

It is a simple statement of the obvious that we are all exposed to risk all of the time – people in work, people at home and children. What I believe we as adults are charged with doing is helping children to understand that risks are there and how to deal with them NOT how to avoid them.

There can be no question but that adventure is good for children – it keeps them fit, helps them learn and develops social skills and a sense of responsibility. But it is also beyond question that we all have a moral obligation to protect them from very obvious and foreseeable dangers. The difficulty we all face, and we as regulators in particular, is how to strike that balance between enabling activities to go ahead but ensuring that the risks are managed. This is especially difficult when we are actually removed from the decisions themselves and much depends on how others interpret – or misinterpret – our guidance. The process of risk assessment is a perfect example of this. Risk assessment is something that all of us do all the time mostly without even knowing consciously that we're doing it – whether it's driving a car in poor weather conditions or gardening and taking care of our dodgy backs. But 'risk assessment' becomes a dirty word when it gets translated into a bureaucratic mountain of paper or a valueless 'tick-box' exercise.

Debates such as this taking place here today are important to make it clear that the Health and Safety Executive/Commission are absolutely not about risk elimination but we are about risk management and enabling things to go ahead safely – so that people don't get hurt or injured or killed. And that applies to everything whether it's adults at work or children in school or at play in public places. Our role is to ensure that risks are considered, managed as best they can be and then the activity should continue.

Of these three statements, the first is no less than refreshing. The lament, if any is warranted, is that in a well-functioning society such a statement would be unnecessary.

The second, too, provides welcome recognition, of which in this era there cannot be enough, of the benefits of public activities. It also acknowledges the difficulty of striking a balance between the benefits of public life and the risks they unavoidably entrain. An issue which lurks there, however, is whose responsibility it is to set this balance. The statement implies that it might be HSE's, by issuing guidance for others to follow, but a question which this generates is how far the guidance should go, and whether HSE is indeed the right agency to weigh up both the risks *and* the benefits of public life. In other areas of its activity, such as the management of hazardous industries, HSE has not seen itself as the adjudicator, but has handed this task to the local planning authority. And this seems reasonable because HSE does not lay claim to expertise in the economic and social welfare benefits to a community of an industrial presence. Lord Hoffmann too, as mentioned earlier, did not see decisions about these broader trade-offs as a mere 'technical matter'.

The third statement also raises an issue in its opening sentence. If the HSE/C is not about risk elimination, then safety, usually taken in common parlance as meaning zero risk, cannot be guaranteed, and it has to be expected that people will at times get hurt, injured and killed. Hard though it is for regulators in particular, and anyone in general, to be upfront about this, it is a fact of life that most risks cannot be eliminated, and one day it will perhaps come as a great relief when people feel able to say those words and explain frankly what the implication of living in a 'risk-based society' really is.[11] Indeed, in other notable HSE pronouncements, such as expressed in *Reducing risk: protecting people*, HSE meticulously describes the difference between risks which are broadly accepted and those which are tolerated, even putting numbers to them (as has been described in chapter 4).

At a meeting in the House of Lords in 2008 Judith Hackitt said:

> But we all have a duty to walk the talk when it comes to the common sense approach. Given the wealth of 'evidence' in the media of 'health and safety gone mad', we must all ensure that our professional advice and guidance doesn't add to the burden of bureaucracy and red tape. We have to lead the way in demonstrating that proportionate common sense approach and I can promise you that this is one theme that will feature in HSE's new strategy for Health and Safety in Great Britain when we publish it later this year. (HSE, 2008)

The frankness here is likewise welcoming, including the acknowledgement of the media 'evidence' that something actually is awry and the way to approach the problem. But what of this new strategy, and how might it be implemented? Although not ostensibly about public space, it will obviously be read by and influence people who are involved with its provision, so it is worthy of scrutiny.

The health and safety of Great Britain

This 2009 strategy is introduced on the HSE's website with these words:

> We believe this strategy represents a clear statement of core principles and a sensible approach to health and safety in Great Britain. Whilst the economic climate is difficult and the temptation for some may be to cut corners, HSE, and its partners and businesses must resolve to continue to strive to improve health and safety performance. Good health and safety is good business. (HSE, 2009)

The opening paragraph of the document then reaffirms that the HSW Act provides the legitimation for HSE's activities: 'The 1974 Health and Safety at Work etc. Act and its underlying principles and philosophy provide us with a legislative framework that is adaptable and remains fit for purpose today.'

The document, however, contains a variety of statements with variable degrees of justification. On the one hand, there are several references to a 'common sense', 'practical' and 'proportionate' approach to health and safety, all of which are of course eminently reasonable and consistent with the government's commendable 'Principles of managing risk to the public' (HM Treasury, 2005 – see Box 11). On the other hand, a strong motivation is expressed firstly, to generate renewed momentum in a drive for lower rates of injury and ill health; and, secondly, to deal with 'trivial or ill-informed' criticism of health and safety.

The former appears to be predicated on the fact that workplace rates of injury and ill health in Britain had been static for the five years to 2008, despite the substantial efforts by HSE, and others, to bring them down.[12] HSE points out that the cost to the economy of these accidents could be as high as £20 billion per annum (approximately 2 per cent of GDP), and that: 'Clearly, maintaining the status quo is morally, legally and financially unacceptable.' HSE's recipe for this state of affairs includes an extension and invigoration of its earlier drive to ensure that health and safety is championed at board level, the instigation of a further round of 'cultural change' to alter the corporate ethos, even of SMEs, and to regard legislative compliance as the minimum acceptable standard. There is an additional reference to ill health which may be partly aimed at non-workplace activities, presumably personal lifestyle, and how this should be managed.

These statements raise many issues. There is no direct mention of the notion of reasonable practicability or reasonableness in the document, nor that this legal requirement has been an invaluable mainstay of the national philosophy for centuries. Indeed, the document actually says, albeit in a section on competence, that the HSE sees legal compliance as a *minimum acceptable standard*. This could give the impression that it requires duty holders to do more than required by law. As noted in chapter 6, the logic of this kind of thinking, if transferred to public life, warrants at the very least careful scrutiny lest it do more harm than good. It would appear to come under the heading of what the Risk and Regulation Advisory Council called 'regulatory creep'; that is, putting constraints on people that 'go beyond what law-makers originally intended' (RRAC, 2009: 21).

The law, as discussed in chapter 6, is all about reasonable decision making, which involves taking a balanced position on the safety benefits of prospective risk-control measures versus the cost, difficulty and time involved in their implementation, and, logically, other consequences. To suggest, therefore, that one should go beyond the law, by seeing it as a *minimum* requirement, would be tantamount to adopting a political position disturbing the essence of the legislative intent (and the composure of the man on the Clapham omnibus[13]). This is because it is favouring one commodity, health

Box 11 *Government's principles of managing risks to the public*

- **Openness and transparency**

Government will be open and transparent about its understanding of the nature of risks to the public, and about the process it is following in handling them.

Government will make available its assessment of risks that affect the public, how it has reached its decisions and how it will handle the risk. Where facts are uncertain or unknown, government will seek to make clear what the gaps in its knowledge are and, where relevant, what is being done to address them. It will be open about where it has made mistakes, and what it is doing to rectify them.

- **Involvement**

Government will seek wide involvement of those concerned in the decision process.

Government will actively involve significant stakeholders, including members of the public, throughout the risk identification, assessment and management process. It will seek to balance conflicting views in a way that best serves the wider public interest.

- **Proportionality and consistency**

Government will act proportionately and consistently in dealing with risks to the public.

Government will base all decisions about risks on what best serves the public interest. Action taken to target risks to the public will be proportionate to the level of protection needed and targeted to the risk.

- **Evidence**

Government will seek to base decisions on relevant evidence.

Government will aim to ensure that all relevant evidence has been considered and, where possible, quantified before it takes decisions on risk. It will consider evidence from a range of perspectives, including the public as well as experts. It will make clear how evidence has informed its decisions and will keep them under review as new evidence comes to light.

- **Responsibility**

Government will seek to allocate responsibility for managing risks to those best placed to control them.

Government, where possible, will ensure that those who impose risks on others also bear responsibility for controlling them. It will aim to give individuals a choice in how to manage risks that affect them, where it is feasible and in their interest to do so, and where this does not expose others to disproportionate risk or cost.

HM Treasury (2005) (Abridged)

and safety, over others (e.g. resources which could, for example, be used to buy health and welfare improvements in other sectors, or environmental improvements), and so the list of opportunity costs goes on.

One can, of course, understand HSE's frustration over non-declining incident rates, given all its efforts. This frustration is probably enhanced by HSE's acceptance of injury target levels in June 2000 in a joint promotion by the government and the HSC, referred to as 'Revitalising targets' (HSE, 2004b). According to this, there should have been a 20 per cent reduction in the rate of work-related ill health, a 10 per cent reduction in fatalities and major injuries, and a 30 per cent reduction in the rate of working days lost, by 2010. Setting targets of this kind is, of course, a risky thing to do. In this case it was doubly so because the targets have no obvious legal basis, could promote disproportionate or narrowly focused behaviour by regulatory agents, and lack parity with the stipulation of the HSW Act that risk should be reduced until as low as reasonably practicable.

The proposition that the cost to the economy of workplace accidents could be as high as £20 billion per annum is also only a part of the picture. It is plausible that the cost of the existing control regime, were all costs considered, already exceeds that figure. As Haythornthwaite (2006) has rightly reminded us (chapter 5): 'Regulation is not a free good, although governments often behave as though it is. Based on international comparisons, we estimate the cost of regulation to be around £100 billion a year or between 10% and 12% of GDP. To put that into perspective, the total amount of income tax collected each year is about 10.9% of GDP.' Lord Young also expressed concern over the burden of regulatory costs upon, in particular, small and medium-sized enterprises (HM Government, 2010: 28).

Therefore, in thinking about the appropriateness of the balance of control, it is much preferable to consider the marginal cost of control. That is, if the amount of regulation is changed, up or down, what is the marginal change in cost and the marginal change in benefit?

Furthermore, the existing regime is, according to HSE's statistics, not obviously delivering. Should not the appropriate action be to find out why, rather than requesting more of the same overtly managerial approach?

HSE's references in 'The Health and Safety of Great Britain' to 'cultural change', and hints about beyond-the-workplace lifestyles, are also disputatious because, depending upon what exactly is meant, these might conceivably lie beyond HSE's remit and outside its areas of professional competence. Such endeavours might also fall under Seedhouse's 'Social health promotion' or maybe even 'Good life promotion'. Towards the end, in a section entitled 'Taking a wider perspective', there is, however, welcome acknowledgement that 'Health and safety does not and cannot exist in a vacuum'.

Summary

The pursuit of health and safety is influenced by many bodies whose motivations and goals are diverse. Some believe their needs are best satisfied by high-level management structures and auditable paper trails. In some situations they may be correct. Others suspect that health and safety itself is less well served by these procedures, partly because they shift emphasis away from the front line where risk is encountered, and that it inhibits front-line decision makers. The final truth is unknown, although there may be indications that the managerial approach, which has been much in evidence over the last decade, is faltering, as accident rates have not declined as had been hoped and costs are mounting.

Issues to do with the quality of advice on health and safety are also noted. Standards and codes are in no short supply, are often relied upon by safety 'experts' as substitutes for risk assessment, but may not reveal their underpinning logic, leaving open the question of reasonableness, the legitimacy of the evidence base and consistency with the law. There is a variety of ways in which advice can be inappropriately used.

For public risk, in particular, another important issue is the benefits of public space and activities. It is noted that although safety 'experts' often come under the banner of 'health *and* safety', the 'health' component is largely about ill health from exposure to hazards, and not about health gains – physical, psychological and emotional – of public life. The latter may be greater than the health risks and the injury risks with which health and safety practitioners are concerned. Health and safety practitioners who lack knowledge, awareness or interest in these issues may thus be poorly placed to make balancing judgements about the risk-benefit trade-off associated with public activities.

Recent examination of position statements by the HSE finds less prominence being given to the core philosophy of reasonable practicability, even though this is central to the HSW Act from which it derives its authority. One might even begin to wonder if risk minimization is replacing reasonableness, which, if true, would be a departure from the statute, and might contribute to the spate of anecdotes which have challenged the credibility of health and safety. The HSE has recognized the seriousness of the latter challenge, conceded it has some modest legitimacy and has taken steps to remedy the situation. Unfortunately, the steps are only partially convincing, though they are helpful, and expose seemingly divergent ideologies embedded within the organization.

In 2009, HSE published a new Health and Safety Strategy for Great Britain which proposes the stepping up of its campaign against workplace accidents and ill health using similar methods to those already tried. The primary motivation appears to be some anxiety over the existing campaign to reduce accidental injury rates, although other arguments are deployed. The document raises further questions about the path being taken.

8
A Closer Look at Decision Making

While the legal system is in general well aware of and sensitive to the benefits of public space and activities when considering how safe these should be, the same is not necessarily true of the many other agencies who are somehow involved in this provision. In particular, those using work-based risk assessment techniques in the public arena, which make little or no reference to benefits, will be prone to undervalue or disregard benefits. Alternatively, some may not be actually assessing risk, but falling back on proxies such as protocols, standards and advice promulgated by a variety of interests, potentially with quite different purposes in mind, and which themselves may take no account of benefits.

The implication of this is that different mental strategies and different decision criteria are being applied to decisions about public space. From experience it would appear that this issue, fundamental though it is, has not been fully acknowledged and often has passed unrecognized. In the interests of good and consistent decision making, this should not be so, even though reluctance to concede that there are other viable perspectives out there is understandable. And as concluded at the end of chapter 5, the issue of the benefits dimension of public sector decision making suggests that risk assessors should be using an alternative decision process, with the one proposed going by the name of risk-benefit assessment, or RBA.[1] This, however, could appear somewhat shocking, given how well-established the terminology of risk assessment has become, so the primary purpose of this chapter is to consider the following questions:

- How radical a proposal is a switch to RBA?
- Why aren't we doing it already?
- How do people make decisions?
- What kind of expertise is relevant?

Rebirth or radical?

Earlier chapters have revealed that there is, in reality, nothing new about risk-benefit assessment. For instance, the courts have long been familiar with the unavoidability of these trade-offs, in which something bad is accepted in exchange for something good. Indeed, as Lord Hoffmann has said (chapter 7), the courts are the ultimate arbiters of these decisions:

> *It is a judgment which the courts must make and which in England reflects the individualist values of the common law. (Hoffmann, 2005)*

Even so, in 2008, much more than a frisson of interest was created when Play England, and the Departments for Culture, Media and Sport (DCMS), and Children, Schools and Families (DCSF), jointly published an implementation guide which recommended the use of RBA when assessing children's and young people's play environments (Play England, 2008b). This sector had been particularly active in getting the benefits of activities back on the agenda of play through the efforts of the Play Safety Forum. The motivation had been that the PSF had for some years been trying to wrest play from the strictures of what some had come to see as an overemphasis on safety, resulting in a perceived proliferation of sterile play environments which were unfit for any child, and certainly not for most self-respecting ten-year-olds, let alone teenagers who rightly demanded something with a bit of fun and challenge.

Although there are obvious parallels between the provision of outdoor space for the young and for the public in general, there is at least one key difference. This is because, in play, some level of risk is seen as a positive benefit, it having been accepted by a broadly based coalition of leaders in the sector that children enjoy exposure to risk,[2] want it and learn from the experience (Play Safety Forum, 2002). In public life more widely, however, it is not usually the case that some risk is a benefit, with the likely exception of adventure activities, as will be discussed in the next chapter. But apart from this detail, it is clear that both play provision and public activities have much common ground, including the need to accept some risk in exchange for the benefits, or, in other words, to make trade-offs. Importantly, the Play England document was endorsed by many agencies with interests in child safety and child welfare, and more recently Lord Young has also added his support, specifically lending it to the proposition that there should be a shift from risk assessment to RBA in the context of education (HM Government, 2010: 16). The HSE itself was particularly supportive of RBA in the Play England document, boldly stating, at the outset, that:

> *(the) application of risk-benefit assessments is a sensible approach to the health and safety management of play provision.*

This report was by no means, however, the genesis of RBA as some of its readers, for good reasons, seemed to think. In fact, for anyone working more widely within the risk arena, it had long been taken for granted that risk-benefit trade-offs were an inevitable way of life. As described in chapter 2, for example, hospitals regularly use procedures that are not risk-free in an attempt to improve their patients' quality of life. Thus, any X-ray exposure is harmful in that it poses a risk of cell damage and cancer, but the diagnostic power it provides has health benefits which are judged, up to a certain level of dose, to outweigh the risks. For that reason it is accepted that a certain number of X-rays per year is tolerable. Likewise, most medicinal compounds – aspirin being one which has recently been in the news – and operations have undesirable side effects of varying degrees, and in deciding whether or not to take them, one has to weigh these against the benefits. The fact is, even when we are not making these decisions ourselves, they are going on around us all of the time, and, as research has shown, this way of thinking and doing can be traced back over thousands of years, even to ancient Mesopotamia (Covello and Mumpower, 1985) and, as one may reasonably speculate, to the dawn of the human race.

In 2009 postgraduates at Middlesex University investigated the extent to which RBA was in current use in modern society, and also its potential utility, compared with conventional workplace risk assessment, in making public sector decisions. They concluded as follows:

> *We find that the core legislation in the UK is for the most part adequate for application to public risk decisions, although there is a danger of misinterpretation, especially of some of the guidance documents which disseminate the legislation into wider society. The comparison of traditional risk assessment with Decision Analysis exposes some flaws of the former, in particular that it frequently fails to appreciate the multidimensional nature of public risk decisions. We find that what has been termed 'Risk-benefit assessment' is being used widely in a multitude of different fields, suggesting that it is a viable option for replacing the standard risk assessment that is currently used for public risk. (Elmontsri et al, 2009)*

By way of explanation, and using the definition provided by the Australian Government Department of Health and Ageing, Decision Analysis is 'a technique that formally identifies the options in a decision-making process, quantifies the probable outcomes (and costs) of each, determines the option that best meets the objectives of the decision maker and assesses the robustness of this conclusion'. The crux of the matter here is that Decision Analysis is a technique that looks at *all* the factors impacted upon by a decision, as opposed to, say, the single dimension of safety, as in conventional workplace risk assessment as currently practised.[3]

There is nothing novel about making choices where several factors have to be considered and weighed. Suppose, for example, that you were thinking of buying a car and you had a choice of several models. You might well be interested in the relative safety of each model and you could make the choice on that basis alone if you wished, and in effect you would be treating safety as paramount. Alternatively, you might also be interested in some of the following: fuel economy, carbon emissions, road tax, insurability, purchase price, performance, number of passenger seats, load-carrying capacity, longevity, off-road capability, appearance and so on. If so, then you will be performing some sort of Decision Analysis in your head in order to make the best choice, based upon the factors which interest you and how you view their relative importance.

By scanning the academic literature, Elmonstri et al (2009) rapidly confirmed that RBA, and its variants, constituted a widely used tool. Applications ranged from the analysis of the risks and benefits of hands-free cell phone use while driving, to studies of avalanche protection measures, the optimal arsenic content of drinking water, and the lifetime of space satellites in orbit. It was abundantly clear that RBA was being applied in all sectors, from environmental to public health, fire protection, technological innovation, natural hazards and many more. Within the healthcare sector RBA was found to be particularly well established, whereby medical interventions, including drugs and new medical procedures, were routinely subject to risk-benefit assessment. Why this should be so is already established. Almost all health interventions have risks and side effects which need to be weighed against the benefits before patients are given recommendations, or asked to make their own choice. In support of this, the International Society for Pharmacoeconomics and Outcomes Research (ISPOR) has, for example, established a risk-benefit working group whose mission is to conduct risk assessments of new drugs, assess medical efficacy, and develop a framework for balancing risks and benefits.[4]

Another sector found to be heavily involved in risk-benefit assessment is that dealing with food safety. For example, the European Food Safety Authority recently published a risk-benefit assessment of nitrate in vegetables (Bottex et al, 2008). And in April 2009, Deirdre Hutton, Chair of the UK Food Standards Agency, gave a speech on 'The risk and benefit assessment landscape', in which she stressed a number of issues, including the importance of science and the use of an evidence-based approach to decision making, the need for consumer involvement, and the consideration of ethical, social and environmental factors in food policy decision making. A highly pertinent quote from her presentation, which could be adopted immediately in decision making about public space and activities, is as follows:

> *Essentially: risk assessment belongs to science but does not give the answer as to the 'right' level of risk – that judgement belongs to society and involves trade-offs between risk and benefit ... (Hutton, 2009)*

It is worth noting that this statement, in fact, reiterates the important message of the Cabinet Office contained in Figure 2.1, namely, that risk assessment of itself does not provide answers; it is one step in a process of deciding what to do, and moreover the final stage involves many wider considerations which lie beyond the sphere of mere technical competence.

From the examples given above, however, it can only be concluded that within society as a whole the need to make trade-offs between the risks and benefits of public goods is of little, if any, novelty. The strange thing is not that this is going on, but that within public life, when issues of safety from accidental injury arise, it is not. This suggests that the original question, of whether the introduction of RBA to decision making about public space and activities was radical, should be replaced with a different question. That question is: Why has decision making about the safety of public space and activities departed from the norm?

Dawkins' memes

There are various ways of approaching this question. One makes use of the thinking of evolutionary biologist Richard Dawkins, who coined the term 'meme' to describe how and why some ideas propagate rapidly and pervasively in society, while others wither and die. In this respect, a meme is some form of cultural unit (Dawkins, 1976). It could be a new musical score which almost overnight gains popularity around the world, or this year's clothing fashion, the type of plants people put in their gardens, or some new way of thinking about a topic. Memes can be seen to behave in some ways like viruses. They spread from one person to another, sometimes like a contagion, then often die out. In some cases they can lie dormant for a time, only to re-emerge later. They may also mutate in order to survive, say, when confronted by competing memes.

It is proposed here that the present-day culture of workplace health and safety, or to be more precise the ideas which underpin it, could be regarded as a Dawkinsian meme. If so, this meme was probably released into the public sphere sometime after 1974, after the passage of the HSW Act, but much more so during the subsequent period when other regulations were being passed to operationalize the Act. As the HSC has itself said:

> HSC's current responsibilities are spread across almost all risks arising from workplace activity, ranging from nuclear and offshore installations through to schools, farms and factories. In the early 1970s the picture was very different, with large numbers of British workers falling outside the protection offered by sector-specific regulations. An immediate effect of the HSW Act was to extend protection to a further 8 million workers – including employees working in local government, hospitals, education and other services. It also imposed duties on self-employed people and on the designers, manufacturers and suppliers of equipment and materials. Those 'affected by work activities' were brought under the legislative umbrella for the first time. (HSE, 2004a)

As we have argued earlier, the meme embodied in the HSW Act – primarily the notion of managing risks in a way which was reasonably practicable – was entirely consistent with historical thinking in the UK about hazard management and was eminently rational. Therefore, although the extension of the HSW Act to the public sphere provoked surprise, it was still about reasonableness, as were the Occupiers' Liability Acts, and should not have brought with it much that was alien. However, in the following years the meme was modified, in a sense making it more inflexible and more virulent.

This probably happened because, in the decade or so from the mid-1980s, there was a stream of new regulation and guidance issued, including the Management of Health and Safety at Work Regulations of 1992 and 1999 (HSE, 2000), and the first edition in 1991 of HSE's best-selling *Successful Health and Safety Management* (HSE, 1997). These documents, written primarily for the workplace, said comparatively little about reasonable practicability, and started talking more in terms of eliminating or minimizing risk, management cultures, and 'positive health promotion'. Some of these developments were influenced by European legislation; for example, European Council Directive 89/391/EEC which was passed in 1989, and which is specifically about the safety and health of workers at work (EU, 1989). This Directive is not couched in terms of reasonable practicability, but more in terms of avoiding risks if possible or otherwise combating them. It is unclear from this Directive about how one decides whether measures are reasonable or not. Interestingly, there is no mention of 'persons affected by work activities' in the Directive, which suggests its authors never intended it to apply to public life beyond the workplace.

Nevertheless, this trend to combating risk was further reinforced in the UK post-2000 when HSE launched its aforementioned strategy for 'Securing health together', which incorporated an intention to deliver a 20 per cent reduction in the rate of ill health by 2010, a pattern which has resurfaced in 2009 with the publication of *The health and safety of Great Britain*. The present day intention of HSE appears to be to apply yet more robustly its ideas on injury prevention and health promotion.

Of course, memes, like viruses, need to have something going for them – a fertile environment – if they are to survive and proliferate. In this regard, memes which are seemingly true or have the aura of ethical wholesomeness will generally attract supporters without much difficulty. Hence groups that campaign for the paramountcy of safety and against accidents can expect to make some easy progress, at least for a time, until either the penny drops with the realization that 'there is no such thing as a free lunch'; or the proclaimed objectives are found to be unachievable, with or without bankrupting the nation; or even that they start to conflict with the legitimate interests of some other stakeholders.

Some memes may also survive and spread for motivational reasons, where motivational here refers to some kind of self-interest. Recalling the words of Rick Haythornthwaite of the RRAC, it is easy to spot the potential for self-interest:

> *Regulation is not a free good, although governments often behave as though it is. Based on international comparisons, we estimate the cost of regulation to be around £100 billion a year or between 10% and 12% of GDP. To put that into perspective, the total amount of income tax collected each year is about 10.9% of GDP. (Haythornthwaite, 2006)*

Whereas taxpayers, parliamentarians, companies, and the Risk and Regulation Advisory Council, may be concerned about such expenditure, it is obvious that others who belong or are connected to the regulatory industry, of which health and safety is a part, have some interest here for which to fight.

It remains to be seen how the risk-benefit concept, which may itself be described as a meme, will be accommodated by the entrenched health and safety meme. It could result in a Darwinian war of ideas, with the fittest surviving. Or it may be that the existing health and safety meme will adjust itself, superficially or otherwise, to swallow and absorb the new pretender, with the intention either of adapting itself for change or, also possible, of giving no more than the semblance of doing that while maintaining the status quo at all costs. Hints of such behaviours have been observed.

From risk assessment to risk-benefit assessment

There is a legal requirement to carry out a risk assessment of work activities and, courtesy of the Management of Health and Safety at Work Regulations 1999, to write it down if your agency has five or more employees (see Box 12). Even if it has less, in the current regulatory climate, it would probably be advisable to write it down anyway, though this is said here with reluctance through concern over the proliferation of paperwork and administration which thereby results, and which has helped create a whole new industry devoted to the storage of documents.[5]

As noted in chapter 2, there are many ways of assessing risks, but for public places simpler, less resource intensive methods, of the kind described in HSE's *Five steps to risk assessment* or its *Adventure Activities Centres: Five Steps to Risk Assessment*, are normally favoured, and this is consistent with HSE's *Principles of sensible risk management*, which, it says, are not about 'Generating useless paperwork mountains'. This, however, does give rise to some further feeling of unease. This is because risks in public life are not actually that simple. They are not just about 'things' or 'hazards', natural or manufactured, as is conceivably more nearly the case in the workplace, but more about interactions between people, objects and environmental conditions. A proper risk assessment of canals and waterways, historic buildings, statues in city squares, cobbled streets, shade-giving trees, car boot sales, and the like, would need to factor in knowledge of people, with all their behaviours, and the weather, also notable for its vagaries. A dry cobbled street on a sunny afternoon may be quite different in terms of risk from the same street on a damp evening when the theatres are emptying.

In actuality, this kind of complexity is probably less of an issue in the workplace, where people are there to do a specified job, are not simply enjoying themselves howsoever they please and the environment is controlled. So while it may be useful in a workplace risk assessment to produce a list of hazards along the lines of 'falls from height', 'slipping and tripping', and 'chemical inventory', and it may even be possible to assign some quantitative or semi-quantitative level of risk posed by each based on past experience in order to prioritize them, the meaningfulness of the same type of descriptors

---

Box 12 *The MHSWR – obligations, advice and guidance*

These regulations were first published in 1992 and revised in 1999. The Regulations have been published in tandem with an Approved Code of Practice (ACoP) and other material which is simply guidance. The ACoP, while not itself the law, is introduced in this way:

> *It gives practical advice on how to comply with the law. If you follow the advice you will be doing enough to comply with the law in respect of those specific matters on which the Code gives advice. You may use alternative methods to those set out in the Code in order to comply with the law.*
>
> *However, the Code has a special legal status. If you are prosecuted for breach of health and safety law, and it is proved you did not follow the relevant provisions of the Code, you will need to show that you have complied with the law in some other way or a court will find you at fault.*
>
> *This document also includes other, more general guidance not having this special status. This guidance is issued by the Health and Safety Commission. Following the guidance is not compulsory and you are free to take other action. But if you do follow the guidance you will normally be doing enough to comply with the law. Health and safety inspectors seek to secure compliance with the law and may refer to this guidance as illustrating good practice. (HSE, 2000)*

So from this it can be seen that there are things which must be done under the regulations, and things which are advised, the latter coming with varying levels of associated warning if you do not, or otherwise elect to go your own way.

Thus, you are *required* to make a suitable and sufficient risk assessment which includes persons not in your employment who might be affected by your undertaking, *and* to record the significant findings. The ACoP *advises* that the significant findings should be retrievable and should cover a) a record of preventive and protective measures in place to control risks b) whether further action is needed to reduce risk and c) proof that a suitable and sufficient assessment has been made. The ACoP also *advises* that HSE's *Successful Health and Safety Management* provides sound guidance on good practice.

---

for a public setting is less clear, and any associated risk estimate open to far greater uncertainty.

In HSE's document *Adventure Activities Centres: Five Steps to Risk Assessment* (HSE, 2003a,) a case-study risk assessment of an adventure activities centre is given. Under hazards, this lists drowning (during canoeing), falls from height (while rock climbing), impact with something solid (causes unspecified), slipping and tripping (causes unspecified), poisoning (stored chemicals), and thermal extremes (the weather). There is a question as to how useful, let alone cost-effective, this kind of procedure is for front-line staff who lead adventure activities, involving as it does the production of a written down, generic risk assessment. It is inconceivable that anyone qualified to lead a canoeing trip would not know of the existence of a risk of drowning, that a climbing instructor would be unaware of the ever-present danger of falling, or a mountain leader that the ground is rough and in some places a remorseless tripping hazard, and that you need to watch the weather. If they were unaware, they would not be qualified to do that job, nor would they have survived to do it. It could be surmised that this documentation seems to serve a different purpose, one of an auditing nature which has little directly to do with public safety. This may not have been the original intention, but as behaviours have evolved the original intent may have been lost or diluted.[6]

It could of course be said that these lists of hazardous things are there to generate thoughts about risk controls, like taking a suitable buoyancy aid, a climbing rope and chocks, or wearing proper shoes, all of which is more banal than thought provoking. Yet the point of Lord Robens' recommendations, which laid the groundwork for the HSW Act, was to engender a more thoughtful approach by duty holders – those responsible for safety – in managing risk by giving them ownership and to get away from the tendency of people, when hemmed in by too many imposed protocols, to go through the motions.

An alternative approach to management has been described by Peter Holbrook, Chief Executive Officer of the Social Enterprise Coalition, regarding Central Surrey Health, which is the first of a new kind of not-for-profit organisation providing community nursing and therapy services. In a letter to the *Guardian* (16 March 2010) he says of the empowerment of front-line staff:

> *Central Surrey Health is owned and run by its nursing team and has been able to make decisions based on experience and the needs of customers, rather than the directives of a top-down bureaucracy. Its ownership structure is not about profit, but about giving control to frontline professionals ...*

The struggle over the empowerment or disempowerment of front-line professionals has been going on for some time, and seems to be gathering momentum. The journalist Simon Jenkins, for example, has proposed that the death of Baby P was a product of a system which did not get the balance right between enfranchised professionals and bureaucracy (The *Guardian*, 2010):

> *In the case of the death of Baby P, the real scandal appears to be not so much the failure of the family – families 'fail' every day – nor the failure of supervision. The scandal seems to lie in why that supervision failed. A local agency of government was so hard pressed by regulation and monitoring that its social workers spent 60% of every day in front of a computer safeguarding their information trails, rather than doing the job of looking after children.*

Jenkins attributes the situation to a modern-day political orientation which does not trust professionals, preferring protocols, targets and what some refer to as 'managerial proceduralism'.

However, it can be argued that what matters far more is the competency of the front-line staff, and their ability to adapt to complex and ever-changing situations. In the case of adventure activities, the weather, the dynamics and emerging capabilities or incapacities of the group, the infinitely varied nature of the environment, and most of all the interactions between these variables, need constant observation, and this is what they get, instinctively, from these professionals. This ability, one of continually thinking and adapting to circumstances, is sometimes referred to as dynamic risk assessment, although in earlier days it might simply have been called 'thinking on your feet' or 'experience' even, before the area was colonized and captured by those would-be experts in health and safety or management systems. It could even be no more than 'normal life', as in the normal survival skills which we learn as toddlers and develop during our lives, although for outdoor adventure leaders we can imagine that the ability to make these decisions is much more highly refined.

The relative importance of ongoing awareness, as opposed to written-down, office-based assessments, has occasionally been recognized by regulatory agencies. For example, the Adventure Activities Licensing Authority (2001), now absorbed into the HSE, has said that the amount of detail warranted in formal, written risk assessments of adventure activities depends upon the training and experience of expedition leaders. The less experience, the more the detail, they say, with the implication that if you are experienced less needs to be documented. It also says that within the outdoor sector the availability of competent individuals as leaders (experienced, well-trained, highly qualified) may permit these to take 'a more autonomous approach to how they operate'. In this way, the emphasis is refocused on the front-line person's competence and less on the on-paper risk assessment system, which, interestingly, is described by AALA in that publication as follows:

> However perhaps the best way of thinking of a written risk assessment is as a checklist of things you would mention to new activity leaders during their induction period.[7] (AALA, 2001: 18)

But for the diehard health and safety professional, less is likely not more, and the view expressed here by AALA in 2001 may be unwelcome.[8] If anything, there has been a tendency in some quarters for risk assessments to become more onerous. For instance, a three-tier system is sometimes demanded, such that in-between the above dynamic risk assessment and generic risk assessment, another category of assessment, known as site-specific risk assessment, appears. Logical though this may be in some circumstances, the vision of a 'simple' risk assessment is once again to be found receding into the distance. This leads to a further proliferation of office routines and an apparent shift of emphasis away from front-line decision makers.

Tim Gill (2010), writing in a new publication of the English Outdoor Council, arrives at similar conclusions regarding this trend:

However, in recent years the trend has been to conduct ever more detailed risk assessments, because of fear of litigation. The trend has become so pronounced that it has even troubled the HSE, which states bluntly on its website that 'sensible risk management is not about generating useless paperwork mountains'. There is a clear call for local authorities and other agencies to reduce the bureaucratic burden imposed on those involved in visits and activities, focusing on people and processes, not paper.

Gill also has something to say about the proliferation of guidance, strikingly reminiscent of Lord Robens' pre-1974 advice on the need for general guiding principles rather than detailed prescription:

Such materials should be helpful and supportive. However, guidance can only go so far, and can never deal fully with all the possible circumstances and situations that may arise on a visit or during an activity. Indeed too much guidance, at too great a level of detail, can be counterproductive, because it can reinforce a distorted approach to risk management that focuses on technical compliance rather than critical thinking and proactive problem solving.

So it can only be concluded that apart from the unresolved technical problems associated with risk assessment, as described in chapter 2, there are other issues at a deeper level which arise when it is applied to public space and activities. On the face of it, risk-benefit assessment is yet more demanding because it conflates consideration of risk with consideration of the benefits of public space and public activities, so adding another dimension. Before going on to consider this challenge in chapter 10, it may be fruitful to contemplate some recent work on the psychology of decision making and on expertise itself.

Psychology and decision making

When confronted with some hazard, a decision has to be made about what, if anything, to do. Within the world of heavy engineering and more recently the National Health Service, for example, such decisions have come to rest substantially upon scientific evidence. Even within the financial sector there is now a much greater use of scientific models which project the consequences of investment decisions, though their effectiveness in preventing disasters is obviously now receiving close scrutiny.

This evidence-based approach to decision making is regarded as a rational reasoning process based on explicit assumptions. Counter to this, there exists an emerging body of research which emphasizes the importance of the emotions and tacit assumptions which help people decide what to do when confronted with several options. This thinking is particularly relevant in the case of the safety of the public, where facts are sparse and complexity reigns.

The general aim of this research has been to try and explain how experts and laypeople make decisions. Recent years have seen a resurgence in theories that see what goes on as involving far more than strict analytic reasoning. Thus, it has been said that whilst experts are ubiquitous, they appear to have almost zero insight into human motivation. Moreover, what these experts '... studiously ignore, deny the existence of, or maybe feel is far too vague to take into consideration, is the unconscious' (*The Independent*, 1997.)

Professor Gerd Gigerenzer (2007), of Humboldt University Berlin, sees this as symptomatic of a fixation we have witnessed for decades on analytic techniques of decision making. Whilst this rationalist paradigm proposes the surveying of all alternatives, the weighing and ranking of them using statistics and formula, as in Decision Analysis, 'this does not describe how actual people reason'. Experts in economics, psychology and other fields, as well as the public, readily accept the idea of a perfect being with infinite knowledge and time. But in reality we are all partially ignorant and our time is limited. Enter 'gut feelings', as Gigerenzer puts it. In an uncertain world, we often have to forgo the detailed processing of information and rely instead on our brain's ability to use 'short cuts'. Paul Slovic, the American psychologist who specializes in the perception of risk, has come to the same conclusion. He refers to short cuts made by the brain to cope with ever-changing risk situations as 'heuristics', and to 'gut feelings' as 'affect', affect being a feeling that something is good or bad (Slovic, 2000).

From this work it emerges that experts and laypeople alike rely heavily and constantly on 'gut feelings' and 'affect', whether caring to admit it or not. The mind adapts and economizes by relying on unconscious rules of thumb, and on what Gigerenzer terms 'evolved capacities'. These are the learned capacities of humans which heuristics exploit and they should not be devalued. As he notes, seemingly simple evolved capacities such as running, or tracking moving objects through flight (e.g. catching a ball), have proved extremely difficult to replicate in the most advanced of robots. The simplicity that underlies this 'gaze heuristic' is not only a characteristic of beauty; it also enables 'fast, frugal, transparent and robust judgements'. And who can deny that this way of making decisions is essential in a public life full of the requirement to make near-instantaneous decisions while coping with a multitude of hazards?

Gigerenzer goes on to challenge us to imagine a world in which more information is not always better, in which weighing the pros and cons of activities does not make us happier than following our intuition, and in which gut feelings can act as the steering wheel through life. Moreover, he notes that expert judgement is also generally of an intuitive nature: a police detective spotting drug couriers in an airport, if questioned, would not necessarily be able to articulate exactly what made the courier stand out of a crowd of several hundred. Instead, she may well talk of 'instincts' or 'hunches'; something which would look far out of place on a risk assessment, but is the reality of numerous judgements!

Paul Slovic and colleagues (2000) have summarized the properties of the 'analytic' way of thinking, and its basis in rules and complex formulae, such as probability calculus and formal logic. This system, thought to be associated with part of the brain known as the prefrontal cortex (PFC), is slow, methodical and deliberate – the sort of thing that goes on perhaps when a risk assessment is being written out. The 'experiential system', in contrast, is intuitive, rapid, mostly automatic, and is not subject to what we might term conscious awareness or control, and in this sense is akin to Gigerenzer's gut feelings and Slovic's affect.

It is obvious that this experiential system has been the mainstay of human existence throughout evolution and, ultimately has ensured survival through providing a quick and effective way to avoid danger. To this day it remains the most natural and common way to respond to risk; for example, in deciding when and where to cross the street, or how close to go to the cliff's edge. It relies on image and association, linked by experience to emotion and affect, all of which have been accumulated through life's experiences and some of which may even be coded in our genes. It presents risk as a feeling that tells us whether it is safe to swing on a rope swing or to paddle at the seaside.

Some proponents of formal analysis techniques reject affective risk responses because they see them as not rational and thereby unreliable, if not useless. Others contend that current wisdom disputes this view. Good decision making, they say, depends on both the rational and affect systems, operating in parallel, as each seems to depend on the other for guidance. Studies have indeed demonstrated that analytic reasoning cannot be effective unless it is guided by emotion and 'affect' (Slovic, 2000: 390–412).

David Seedhouse, as described in chapter 5, goes a step further with his bold contention that when decisions are being made, such as those about public risk, the experiential, affective system in the form of personal beliefs invariably intrudes, even *before* consideration of the evidence. In this way, practice is necessarily based more on the assessors values and 'untestable beliefs' than on facts (Seedhouse, 2004).

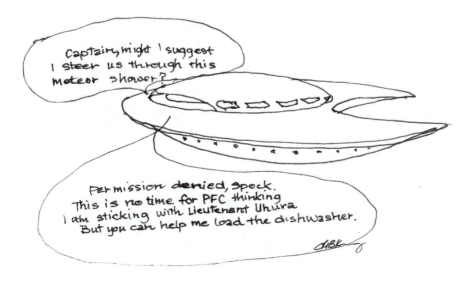

Such an assertion greatly weakens the perceived detached and objective status of the external expert, as they too are approaching problems from the bias of their own beliefs. As discussed in chapter 5, some experts believe, for example, that public safety is best served by engineering solutions rather than behavioural solutions. Evidence for this position is generally not provided – it is, as Seedhouse says, a prior belief, which is just accepted by them as obvious and not requiring justification. Likewise, some experts believe in particular management styles without necessarily providing any evidence to substantiate their position. Even Albert Einstein, as mentioned earlier, had his prior beliefs when he averred 'God does not play dice', a position he adopted because he so disliked the randomness that lies at the heart of the theory of quantum mechanics to which he contributed so much. In this way, prior beliefs, or values, come to dominate supposedly rational decisions.

It could be argued that the old way, pre-1980s, of deciding about safety was largely based on gut feelings, intuition, experiential thinking, affect and beliefs, and that we now have a better, expert-driven, analytic approach. This might be true in some circumstances. Managing nuclear reactors, flying modern passenger aircraft, or running a factory, for example, should be and are heavily reliant, though not totally, upon scientific and engineering solutions. But this would be less true in the domain of public life in towns and the countryside. Indeed, what appears to have happened in public life is that a new form of quasi-expertise has edged in, where common sense and the accumulated wisdom and experience of front-line professionals used to prevail.

Of some significance here is the concept of 'fungibility', as has been highlighted by Howard Margolis (1996). Fungibility is defined as 'one's willingness to consider the full panoply of trade-offs when facing a risk decision'. For example, considering the benefits of taking a risk, the drawbacks of taking a risk, the drawbacks of not taking a risk, and the benefits of not taking a risk. Margolis has tended to see lack of fungibility as a problem of laypeople, with experts coming to the rescue. Sometimes this may be true. But in the case of the safety of public activities, a case can be made that there has been a tendency for some health and safety practitioners to lack this characteristic, through seeking to minimize risk without reference to other things of social value.

Not only that, we may be playing a dangerous game by substituting age-old intuitive thinking with formal analytic procedures of the kind described in chapter 2, which are unproven in public life, not truly analytic but only superficially so, and which, through lack of fungibility, may give rise to all manner of unintended consequences.

The nature of expertise

Even while recognizing the above difficulties of decision making about the safety of public space, decisions still have to be made. How can this be done and who has the answers? Help along this road can be found in academic research by Harry Collins and Robert Evans (2007) of Cardiff University, whose aim is to classify the nature of different kinds of expertise. This is important here because, along with the general trend in society to be sceptical about expertise, there are clearly grounds for doubt over the way in which public risks specifically are currently being handled. We need to understand what is the appropriate kind of expertise for that job and to be able to recognize it.

To this effect, Collins and Evans have developed a categorization of expertise in an attempt to classify those kinds that might be used when individuals make judgements. A key component of knowledge is what Collins and Evans call 'tacit knowledge'. This refers to those things that humans can do without being able to explain exactly how. It would not be possible, for example, for a concert pianist to write down everything she knew such that others could read the book and replicate her performance. Tacit knowledge, though, is not just held by people we might regard as extraordinarily gifted. We all have it, in droves, and we constantly apply it in daily life. Even in holding a conversation, one has to know somehow when to speak and when to be silent. The fleeting signals which determine when to speak are constantly observed and interpreted, but could not be written down. Even if they could be written down, they would serve no purpose because the pace of conversation is such that a need to make reference to any compilation of written rules would destroy its fluidity.

How is this 'tacit knowledge' acquired? As the authors say, the route is through social immersion in groups who possess it. And despite the ubiquity of this knowledge, people are often unaware that they possess it, as it often consists of habits and culture that we do not think about. This is a shame because, as they say, it is a fact that: 'we know (far) more than we can tell'.

A common example of tacit knowledge is natural language, which is acquired, maintained and evolves through societal rather than individual forces. Humans learn a natural language by immersing themselves in the social group to which the language belongs. Within the realm of the safety of public space, we know how to negotiate a pedestrianized street even though it often has slow-moving service vehicles present, and fewer hard and fast rules than on the public highway.

Collins has noted that the balance of reward and risk in the case of most public leisure activities is understood by ordinary people as an element of their existing knowledge, what is here described as their ubiquitous tacit knowledge. Only more unusual public space activities, like, say, canoeing on a river with rapids or hot-air ballooning, may render the ordinary person out of their realm in terms of useful specialist knowledge. For these kinds of activities, a different kind of tacit knowledge, referred to as *specialist* tacit knowledge, is needed. This knowledge is held by persons with 'contributory expertise'. Contributory expertise is what is needed to conduct a more specialized activity with competence, and is acquired through personal immersion in the activity; that is, through practising it yourself and by close interaction with the relevant community of practitioners.

There is a well-known, five-stage model of how persons acquire contributory expertise, exemplified by the process of learning to drive a car (based on Dreyfus, Dreyfus and Athanasiou (1986: 21–36), cited in Collins and Evans (2007: 24)):

Stage 1 is the novice. The novice driver will try to follow explicit rules and as a result performance will be laboured and even kangaroo-like. The skill will be exercised 'mechanically', following such rules as 'change gear when the car reaches 20mph'. These types of rule are 'context-free', because in applying them the learner ignores changes of context, such as the gradient of the road.

Stage 2 is the advanced beginner. As more and more of the skill is mastered, more subtle features of the situation start to play their part in the performance, such as using the sound of the engine to indicate the need to change gear on a hill.

Stage 3 is competence. Here the number of situational signals becomes overwhelming, and expertise becomes much more intuitive rather than calculating. Analysis is no longer the predominant mode of decision making, which is now being superseded by intuitive, experiential response mechanisms.

Stage 4 is proficiency. Here the driver recognises whole problem situations 'holistically' so that indicators like engine sound will be just one of many indicators of how to negotiate the traffic environment.

Stage 5 is expertise. At this level, complete contexts are unselfconsciously recognised and performance is related to them in a fluid way using cues that it is impossible to articulate and might even contradict the rules explained to novices. At this level, actions are carried out by the unself-conscious self.

This example, of learning to drive, also shows clearly how analytic thinking and emotional thinking (gut feelings or effect) both contribute and complement each other in everyday living. It can easily be extended to public activities. Walking through a crowded city square, for example, with people, prams, steps and other hazardous features, is not something one normally thinks consciously about – you get to the other side while possibly thinking about other things altogether, or even conversing on your mobile. Yet imagine if you were presented with a manual on how to cross the square safely and had to follow it. Reverting to this self-conscious way of thinking would assuredly impede your progress. If you followed it literally you would be virtually guaranteed never to arrive.

So what this means is that skills practised by individuals have to be internalized if they are to be used efficiently, and these skills, by their nature, cannot be written out on pieces of paper, nor would doing so, if it could be done, serve a useful purpose for that individual. This is, of course, fully supportive of the AALA proposition that within the outdoor sector the availability of competent individuals as leaders may permit them to take 'a more autonomous approach to how they operate' (AALA, 2001: 7). It might also explain the tendency of some to demand ever more sophisticated risk assessments; because there is a tacit realization that risk assessment is not after all simple and that capturing on paper what actually is done routinely by the human brain is very demanding! And worse, it could be tantamount to imposing Collins and Evans' Stage 1 thinking upon those persons instinctively operating at higher levels of competence, gained through immersion and experience; not, we think, the way to enhance safety.

For the purposes of public safety, it may suffice to recognize three kinds of expertise. First is the tacit knowledge which is held by every person in copious quantities. This wealth of knowledge has been encroached upon in recent years by alleged 'experts', some of whom have inadvertently or otherwise trivialized these essential life skills, sometimes for their own ends and sometimes through lack of awareness of their importance. Evidence that this is going on is provided by the proliferation of warnings over every conceivable consumer product and public activity. Collins and Evans see this trend to post warnings on everything as patronizing, being akin to 'treating the public as incapable of learning the rules of ordinary living through the normal process of socialisation'.

Second is true specialist tacit knowledge which is held only by persons immersed in particular activities. This knowledge too is immensely valuable, but like popular tacit knowledge suffers from lack of appreciation in the present age. Its role and contribution is under threat from those whose emphasis is upon formal risk assessment, engineering-type solutions, management systems, the uncontrolled proliferation of documented procedures, and the invasion of quasi-experts who may lack true contributory expertise.

The third kind of expertise is managerial. For this to be beneficial in the perhaps surprisingly complex arena of public safety, it obviously needs to be cognizant of all the issues involved.

Summary

The proposition that risk-benefit assessment should replace conventional risk assessment for assessing risks in public life is found to be far less radical than at first it might appear. RBA is already widely used in society, and it would appear anomalous that it is not also used for assessing the safety of public places and activities. It could be said that it no more than codifies pre-existing intuitive processes which were already in use.

Why has this occurred? One way of looking at it is that the mode of practising health and safety in the workplace has spread like one of Richard Dawkins' memes (ideologies which spread like viruses), and established itself in numerous managerial systems where it has proved initially resilient to challenge.

However, there are good reasons why a challenge should be mounted. On the one hand it lacks a property sometimes referred to as 'fungibility'. That is, it fails to properly consider the broad spectrum of benefits derived from public activities and space, and thereby has a predisposition to ride roughshod over them.

Secondly, there is a tendency to think that managing safety in public life is a relatively straightforward managerial exercise. This is wrong. Risks in public life are complex because they are not just about static hazards, but about interactions between hazards, people with all their behaviours and the ever-changing environment.

Thirdly, some of the current approaches to public safety have the unintended consequence of demoting front-line professionals, and of undervaluing the public's own ability to handle what in reality are everyday hazards. The first can be seen as churlish and could conceivably increase rather than diminish risk. The second is patronizing and undermines public respect for health and safety, which itself is a dangerous path to tread.

9
Adventure Activities –
A Hard Case

Adventure sports are both interesting and informative from the point of view of public risk. Firstly, these sports, which include activities like mountaineering, mountain biking, mountain marathons, orienteering, snow and ice climbing, kayaking and caving, provide a real and sometimes extreme example of the risk-benefit debate, being activities that involve significant levels of risk with potentially very serious consequences. Yet their followers, of whom in the UK alone there may be hundreds of thousands, voluntarily and wilfully engage in them, even though access to suitable venues often means travelling long distances to remote areas. These pastimes are all the more unusual because the risk itself is such an integral part of the activity, and indeed some have claimed it is even the key reason why people take part. Consequently, the kind of risk-minimization perspective, described elsewhere in this book, is on a patent collision course with activities such as these, leaving one to wonder how they have survived in the current era.

The other side of the coin is that, for many, adventure sports have in recent years come to symbolize the wider pursuit of freedom, providing an escape from a world which is found to be humdrum and organized to the extent that one no longer has liberty to find one's own trail, but is required to tread the same way-marked path as everyone else. Interestingly, many eminent people have stood up for the right of individuals to take part in these activities,[1] and the public generally appear to hold those who do, and are successful, in very high esteem, although when things go wrong, as sometimes happens, the mood may change. The 2008 Original Mountain Marathon (OMM), described later, provides an interesting example of the vulnerability of these activities to mood swings and media condemnation.

So the scene is set for a contest between those seeking the freedom to engage with risk, either deliberately or in passing, and those wishing to control and minimize it. This contest has been acted out in the UK most notably over the last two decades, during which there have been a number of incidents, some ending in regulatory initiatives and others in court cases. These events provide a second reason for including consideration of adventure sports here; namely, because they shed valuable light on the entire risk-benefit debate.

What are adventure sports and why participate?

Definitions of adventure sport centre around an escape from what might be termed 'pre-determined outcomes', towards uncertain, physically challenging environments in which the difference between success and failure lies solely with the efforts, judgement and commitment of the participant.[2] Moreover, the traditional human opponent is to some extent of lesser importance, in favour of a competition more against oneself or one's surroundings.

It is certainly true that one of the most distinguishing traits of adventure sports is the level and type of risk when participating in them. It is not so much the frequency of injuries that is noteworthy – sports like hockey and soccer have much higher injury rates – but rather the possibility of serious consequences that is seemingly ever-present. A simple mistake can lead to serious injury and even death. Furthermore, the inaccessible locations which adventure sports typically frequent, coupled with the characteristic presence of factors beyond the control of the participant, mean that it is impossible to remove such risks from the activities. This has led many commentators to claim that putting oneself at risk is the point of adventure sport; participants are explicitly *seeking* risk. If this were not the case, they claim, surely one would opt instead for any of the other numerous recreations that do not involve such extreme hazards. Consequently, the media have been known to coin phrases such as 'thrill-seeker' and 'adrenaline junkie', and apply them to adventure sport participants, seemingly adding a degree of glamour and marketing gloss in the process.

While few would deny that risk is an inherent and inseparable feature of adventure sports,[3] Kevin Krein, outdoor studies and philosophy professor at the University of Alaska Southeast, points out it does not necessarily follow that it is the main point of such sports, or that this is the sole reason why people participate in them (Krein, 2007). And Viviane Seigneur, social anthropologist and risk consultant in Chamonix, argues that adventure sports acquire the element of adventure not from individuals exposing themselves to risk or danger per se, but because the participant is moving towards the unknown. She illustrates her point with reference to mountaineers, saying that they stand out because of their ability to make decisions and carry them through despite a high level of uncertainty, rather than because of a willingness to take risks. Thus, she concludes that the idea of adventure, the key motivation for adventure athletes, is much more closely linked to uncertainty than it is to risk (Seigneur, 2006).

Apart from enabling participants to pit themselves against the unknown, adventure sports also bring considerable health benefits, both physical and psychological, and this is now fairly common knowledge. Even in relation to children, the educational benefits of adventure activities are coming to be widely accepted. This is unsurprising given some of the key attributes needed to succeed in these activities, which include focus, commitment, bouncing back from failure, controlling fear, and calmly thinking out the moves ahead and translating them into physical action. Thus, participation in outdoor adventure education has long been linked with a rise in self-esteem through

Box 13 *Risk and adventure – thoughts of climbers on managing risk*

Lito Tejada-Flores (1967, 1990), one of the most widely referenced essayists in the climbing world, gives an interesting pre-postmodernist insight into what he terms the 'climbing game', and which further challenges the mind on the relationship of such sports with risk, from the perspective of advanced practitioners of the sport. He notes firstly that climbing can be considered a game because one does not climb *for* something or *to* something; it is more a case of embracing the now. He then contends that climbing is both asocial and arbitrary, with a 'delicious pointlessness' in devoting the amount of time, energy, strength, talent, cunning and courage to a task that does not need to be done. Moreover, it is a creative act: climbers are not just following routes or dotted lines up cliffs as drawn in magazines, but 'are busy creating their own personas and personalities, their own lives, as they climb'. The act of climbing is its own definition, its own reason and motivation – 'a self-justifying feedback loop that never looked outside itself to society for validation'.

This 'game' is accomplished through a finely tuned balance of natural and self-imposed challenges, brought about through self-imposed climbing rules: the harder the climb, the fewer rules climbers will impose on themselves in order to preserve the inner uncertainty and adventure. Easier climbs will result in more radical and restrictive rules in order to conserve the climber's feeling of personal accomplishment against 'the meaninglessness of a success which represents merely technological victory'.

Akin to Viviane Seigneur, Tejada-Flores sees the adventure and personal satisfaction of climbing as stemming directly from the uncertainty of climbing outcomes. This has interesting implications for the idea of regulating such activities, since it identifies an area of possible contradiction. Using this framework, removing elements of uncertainty through increased regulation and concern for safety would result in climbers imposing more restrictive rules on the equipment they could use in order to preserve the uncertainty of the eventual outcome. Ultimately, therefore, it is the climbers themselves, and no one else, who will set 'the rules of the game'.

The question of how the benefits of risky adventure activities can be traded off against their danger is therefore central, and such decisions are hard to make. This sentiment is echoed by Professor Michael Thompson, experienced mountaineer and Cultural Theorist, who notes that there has always been a conflict between 'the establishment', including the government and regulators, and climbers. He sees a key facet of climbing as that of a 'self-organising system' that tends to reassert itself. This resonates with Tejada-Flores' view that ultimately it can only be the climbers themselves who define the rules of this activity, and not some external agency.

achievement and risk-taking (Kimball and Bacon, 1993), a greater appreciation of the physical body through physical activities (Mortlock, 1984), a
greater sense of control as self-sufficiency (Ewart, 1989), and a challenge to
traditional gender roles (Humberstone, 1990).

The fluctuating fortunes of adventure activities in the UK

In 2005 the English Outdoor Council published a briefing paper summarizing
evidence of the value of outdoor learning for children and the action needed
to make it a reality for all young people (EOC, 2005). It states that there is
now clear evidence that outdoor learning:

- raises education standards;
- develops resilience and contributes to physical, psychological and social
  well-being;
- helps to reduce disengagement from education, antisocial behaviour and
  crime;
- helps young people to manage risk and encourages them to welcome
  challenge.

Gathering evidence, of course, is usually a good thing, especially if you want
to justify an action or a policy. But one is tempted to ask why it is necessary
at this time to justify the obvious; say, the legions of clearly apparent benefits
of being in the natural environment? In its review of outdoor education, the
Select Committee on Education and Skills accumulated much evidence about
the state of outdoor education in Britain (SCES, 2004). In particular, it found
that many countries, both in Europe and elsewhere, achieved a significantly
higher level of outdoor learning in their schools than in the UK. Curiously,
though, this good practice, which had originated in the UK and been taken up
abroad, was now languishing in its birthplace! The SCES quotes Dr Peter
Higgins of the University of Edinburgh, himself an experienced outdoor
instructor, as follows:

> ... in many cases the countries we are familiar with developed
> their national approach to outdoor learning after detailed
> consideration of the approach taken in the UK in the 1960s and
> 1970s. In particular the carefully constructed and wide-scale
> provision in the Lothian Region of Scotland was widely
> regarded as the ideal model. Several decades of erosion have left
> such provision in a poor state, not dissimilar to the rest of the
> UK, whilst several of those countries which adapted the model
> to suit their own situation now have extensive curricula provi-
> sion. (Higgins, as quoted in SCES, 2004)

So it would seem that just as the Play Safety Forum and Play England (and
Play Scotland, Play Wales and Playboard Northern Ireland) have felt it necessary to champion the benefits of children's play, so too has the English

Outdoor Council (EOC) felt the need to do so in the context of outdoor activities in general. In the case of children's play, the main reason for doing this was the inroads made into play value by the way in which safety was being addressed. Under a section of its report headed 'Barriers – risks and bureaucracy', the SCES came to a similar conclusion regarding outdoor educational activities:

> *Many of the organisations and individuals who submitted evidence to our inquiry cited the fear of accidents and the possibility of litigation as one of the main reasons for the apparent decline in school trips. It is the view of this Committee that this fear is entirely out of proportion to the real risks. High-profile reporting of isolated incidents and some tabloid journalism misrepresents the incidence of serious accidents on school trips, which is actually very low indeed. There have been 57 fatal accidents on school visits since 1985 (this figure includes adults accompanying visits and road traffic accidents en route to or from off-site visits). In England in 2003, there were between seven and ten million 'pupil visits' involving educational or recreational activity, but only one fatality. Whilst every fatality is clearly tragic for those involved, these statistics compare extremely favourably with other routine activities such as driving or being driven in a car, or simply the likelihood of an accident at home or in school. (SCES, 2004)*

The additional threat posed by poorly informed journalism

Despite all of their positive attributes, provision of adventure activities is not, as the SCES found, something for those who enjoy 'plain sailing'. For some people the positive features of adventure sports remain a profound mystery. The media themselves, though providing extensive coverage of traditional, injury-laden sports like soccer, motorsport and downhill skiing, have been known to create controversy in the wake of adventure sport events which, from time to time, they portray as deviant and reckless.

One such instance occurred with the 2008 Original Mountain Marathon – one of the largest and most prestigious mountain marathon events in the world. Held annually either in northern England, Scotland or Wales, and attracting several thousand competitors each year, it is billed as the premier UK event to test teamwork, self-reliance, endurance, outdoor and navigational skills. Competing in pairs over two days, competitors test their mettle against some of Britain's harshest terrain, with the longest elite class amounting to two consecutive marathon-length days (53 miles) with around 2500m of ascent.

The 2008 episode proved especially challenging, with one month's rain falling on the day of the event, coupled with gale-force winds and flooding, such that it became known as: 'One of the great bad-weather nightmares in mountain running's history.' Four hours into the event, with no sign of the weather abating, the organizers reluctantly decided to call it off. Worse was to follow, for during the course of the day the OMM rapidly became a 'break-ing story' on all kinds of news stations, radio and even international news networks. The media opted for dramatic headlines such as: '1700 runners stranded in the mountains/missing/unaccounted for'; 'Race to rescue runners'; and 'Rescue drama unfolds'. This quickly changed into blame and finger-pointing at those involved, and there was widespread outrage that the event had ever been allowed to go ahead. A local landowner added unneeded drama by claiming that the situation had come close to turning the hillsides into 'a morgue'.

At the event site itself, the media swiftly arrived in force with micro-phones, recorders, cameras and satellite trucks. They had come looking for a big news story of the aftermath of a major emergency, but instead found that most competitors had already set off home, and those arriving in from the hills were generally in good spirits, sitting around chatting about the event. One competitor observed: 'They'd expected hundreds to be missing and complete chaos, and found instead that the situation had been dealt with efficiently and effectively.'

What the media failed to appreciate was that participants in this event, being keen outdoor enthusiasts, were well-accustomed to adverse weather as part and parcel of participation in adventure sports. They were well prepared with the necessary equipment, including waterproofs, warm clothing, rations and first aid kits. They were not, as was portrayed by some reporters, completely unprepared for the conditions, but rather had the specialized knowledge and experience of the risks borne from adverse weather in moun-tain marathon events. And yet 'irresponsible' was one of the first and most persistent labels used to describe the participants, as well as the organizers, for allowing the event to go ahead.

However, the event is specifically designed such that those taking part in the race are primarily responsible for their own safety. As was stated on the OMM website: 'In these days of 24/7 contact and total support this is an event to test and indeed help develop teamwork and self-reliance.' Selwyn Wright, organizer of the Three Shires Mountain Race, gives a further insight into the matter, stating that: '... if you make it the organiser's responsibility to make the race as safe as possible, you take individual responsibility away from the person on the hill' (quoted in *The Independent*, 2008). He goes on to say that he is not advocating that organizers be gung-ho, but rather he does not want people to think that, if the conditions are bad, they should not worry. Instead, he says: 'I want them to worry, and to take responsibility for themselves.'

It is clear that given that the intent of events such as the OMM is to test and develop self-reliance, this does not square with an imposed control philos-ophy of little or no risk. The unprecedented weather conditions which blighted the 2008 event could indeed have led to serious incident. However, whilst some of the media and wider public were outraged and severely critical of the organizers, the vast majority of the competitors themselves were praising the way those in charge had reacted to the unfolding events and used their judge-ment to make the correct decisions in exceptional circumstances.

The 2008 OMM highlighted the extent to which 'news' can be no more than uninformed speculation, unless it happens to coincide with something the media has direct experience of or is interested in. In the case of less familiar pursuits such as adventure sports, there is a constant danger that stories will be sensationalized. The effect of this media game, and the subsequent negative publicity, should not be understated. By, in effect, 'amplifying the risk' out of proportion (Kasperson et al, 1988), severe secondary consequences can be generated for outdoor pursuits and the livelihoods of those involved in them, as well as denying participants the experiences they seek. It can discourage future organizers, create more red tape, or even stop activities altogether.

Adventure sports and risk

From afar the risk of injury associated with adventure activities might be expected to be very high indeed when compared with the risks of ordinary life. The nature of the terrain which is typically visited would alone seem to dictate that this be so. However, what seems dangerous may not be, and what seems safe in contrast can be hazardous. The reason is that the risk is not just a product of the terrain, but of the interaction between it and individuals, and the environmental conditions. As Adams and Viscusi have said (chapter 5), people are not unthinking automatons – they adjust their behaviours to accommodate the circumstances as they perceive them. Thus, and consistent with the adage 'familiarity breeds contempt', more attention is paid in challenging situations than in those which are routine.

The reality of the risk of adventure activities is thereby most reliably discerned from accident statistics, coupled with information on participation rates over a representative period of time. Unfortunately, there is no centralized database which provides this information for adventure activities, and the best that can be done is to construct a partial picture based on those pieces of information which are available. Figures 9.1 and 9.2 summarize some such information for the UK, based on analyses published by Ball (1998) and extended by British caver Peter Mohr (2000). Figure 9.1 shows a statistic called the fatal accident rate (FAR) for selected adventure and some conventional sporting activities.[4] The FAR is an estimate of the number of fatal accidents per 100 million hours of participation in the activity. Participation is worked out by multiplying the number of active participants by the average duration in hours of the activity, and the number of times the activity is engaged in over the same period as the fatality data are collected. This makes it possible to compare the risk of very popular sports with those which have fewer participants. Although the data in Figure 9.1 are no more than crude estimates because of the uncertainties in the underlying information used in the calculations and various definitional problems, the pattern which emerges looks plausible. Activities such as air sports (which include hang-gliding and the like), caving and climbing have the highest risk of fatality, followed by water sports (because of the ever-present risk of drowning), with the more popular sports of soccer, rugby and badminton coming in at a FAR of about 1 or 2.

As a means of putting these numbers in perspective, they can be compared with hazards of everyday life. The Department for Transport, for example, reports FARs for different modes of travel in Britain, based on annual numbers of fatalities and the total time spent travelling by each mode. The FARs work out as follows: travel by car 9.8; by motorcycle 430; pedal cycle 38; pedestrian 15; bus or coach 0.63; and rail 1.5 (DfT, 2008). This means, for example, that the risk per hour of activities like caving and climbing, when averaged out, are in the region of three to 16 times higher than riding in a car, but are less than that of travelling by motorcycle.

So far as non-fatal injuries are concerned, these are dominated by sports such as rugby and soccer, which hugely outstrip the rates in adventure activities even after participation rates have been accounted for (Figure 9.2). Rugby and soccer have been estimated to have non-fatal accident rates (NFARs) of around 290 and 130 respectively, compared with figures of around 2.5 for caving, and 4 for climbing and sailing. NFARs are most-commonly measured by hospital Accident and Emergency attendances, and are the numbers of cases per 100,000 hours of activity. Surprisingly, perhaps, NFARs for adventure sports are generally low as far as can be discerned from the available data which is sparse, and not much different from those of people who stay at home, which are in the range of about 2 to 4 depending upon age.

To summarize, these estimates point to heightened risks of fatalities from some adventure activities over other more conventional sports, but less so for non-fatal injuries, which do not differ significantly from those of everyday life at home. In the case of fatal injuries, the rates can be similar to or higher than

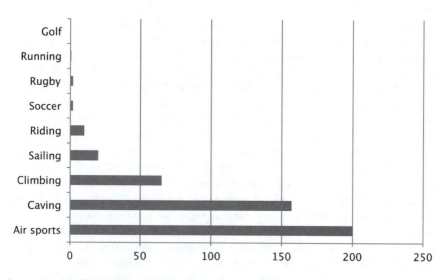

Sources: include Ball (1998); Mohr (2000); Scottish Sports Council (2007)

Figure 9.1 *Fatal accident rates for selected sports (estimated rates are per 100 million hours of participation)*

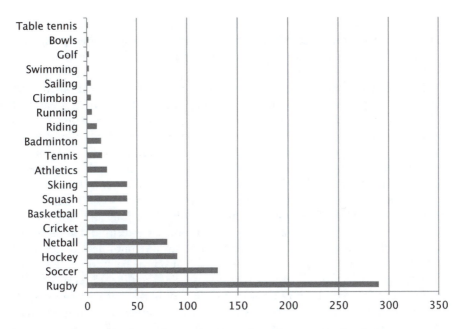

Figure 9.2 *Non-fatal accident rates for selected sports (estimated rates are per 100,000 hours of participation)*

those experienced in familiar activities such as travelling by car or bicycle, but mainly are less than those of riding a motorcycle.[5]

Changing regulatory positions

As with all human activities there are occasional tragedies with serious consequences, and these are likely to provoke harsh inquiry, particularly from those sectors which do not understand or appreciate the nature of these pastimes.

In Britain there has been a series of high-profile incidents involving adventure sports, including one at Lyme Bay in 1993 in which four teenagers drowned whilst kayaking. The subsequent trial resulted in the owner of the centre where the incident occurred and the centre itself being convicted of corporate manslaughter over the deaths, the first conviction for this offence in the UK. The event also sparked a major public debate on the safety of outdoor pursuits, and there were calls for tighter regulation of outdoor activity centres and for a statutory national system of accreditation and inspection. Ultimately, this resulted in new legislation and significant changes in the way adventure activities were controlled in the UK.

Thus, the Activity Centres (Young Persons' Safety) Act 1995 was passed through Parliament at the instigation of the then Department for Education and Skills, and an independent licensing authority, the Adventure Activities Licensing Authority (AALA), was ultimately created. There was further reorganization when, in 2007, AALA was subsumed into the HSE. AALA's main function continued to be the inspection and licensing of providers, with the aim of ensuring that, so far as reasonably practicable, participants' and employees' safety were assured.

The passage of the 1995 Act was not without serious implications for the sector, and despite the gravity of the Lyme Bay episode, there was a great deal of debate over the need for a new regulatory regime, and not everyone, including the HSE, was in favour. In retrospect, there is now little doubt that the Act was an overreaction: the response being disproportionate to the scale of the problem, leading many to criticize the legislation as a 'knee-jerk' response to an emotive media campaign. Estimates of the number of operators who went out of business as a direct result of the Act vary from zero to 600, depending on who you believe. The best estimate is probably 'some, but not many'. However, the real damage was to the reputation, self-esteem and consequential self-confidence of the sector, which some argue continues to this day. Certainly, the result was to put much of the sector on the back foot over safety issues. Exponents of solid regimes which existed at the time, in terms of risk-benefit, were in effect disenfranchised, and they didn't like it. No one would. Even then, however, the question was raised of whether the pendulum had swung too far and whether society's aversion to risk, and the threat of legal culpability, had become counterproductive. What, for instance, it was asked, might be the impact of the new measures on downstream risks such as childhood obesity (BRC, 2006)? Quantitatively, these downstream arguments are much more significant than the self-esteem of those who felt unfairly treated at the time, or even since.[6]

The impact of AALA

Prior to the Lyme Bay incident, outdoor activity centres were able to opt in to a variety of voluntary codes of practice drawn up by the appropriate National Governing Body for each activity. Centres offering caving, for example, would follow codes established by the British Caving Association (BCA), which would have, to borrow from Collins and Evans (chapter 8), the highest level of contributory and interactional expertise. For multi-activity centres there was also the British Activity Holiday Association (BAHA).

The situation now is that, under The Adventure Activities Licensing Regulations 2004, any business providing, for payment, any of the listed adventure activities to under-18-year-olds, without their parents or guardians present, is required to hold a valid licence from the Adventure Activities Licensing Service (AALS). At present the Activity Centres Act 1995 only applies to this one sub-sector of adventure sport provision in the UK – namely centres, companies or individuals who make a charge for providing adventurous activities for under-18-year-olds. The Act does not apply to voluntary organizations as long as they are only providing activities to their own members, schools providing for their own pupils, or Her Majesty's forces when on duty. Nonetheless, whilst many providers fall outside the legal remit of AALA, the standards are widely regarded as applying to any organization providing outdoor activities, and would probably, according to head of inspection services Marcus Bailie, be used as the standard in any court case. Guidance from HSE about the licensing scheme states that its aim is to 'give assurance that good safety management is being followed so that young people can continue to have opportunities to experience exciting and stimulating activities outdoors while not being exposed to the avoidable risk of death and disabling injury' (HSE, 2007b). Unusually, and as some would say, to its credit, this dual mandate allows AALA to take upon itself the task of representing the benefits of adventure activities within HSE and government departments such as DCSF, as well as helping providers identify and manage the risks inherent in the activities.

In order to determine what had been the consequences, either intended or unintended, of the regulation of adventure sports through AALA, an investigation was carried out in 2008 of the views of those in the sector who were affected by the new regulatory regime (Ball-King, 2009b). The method used was to interview members of the Association of Heads of Outdoor Education Centres (AHOEC). Full membership of AHOEC is open to those who are employed as heads and managers of established outdoor education centres and organizations, and thus represent professionals whose daily work is directly affected by the legislation, whilst being detached from the regulators and unaffiliated with AALA.

Seven members of the AHOEC were asked the following questions:

- What do you think about the regulatory regime, and how it has changed and affected the adventure activities sector?
- In what ways do you think the regulation has changed things for the better?
- Do you see any adverse consequences of the regulation? For example, do you ever find that it is obstructive to your work or to increasing participation in adventure activities, or is it balanced?
- You can only justify exposing people to risk by taking account of the benefits of the activities you promote – is there an overt, formal way in which you do this, or is it more informal/subconscious?
- Do you feel that the benefits are given adequate recognition?

Respondents were also invited to supply any other information they wished. Their responses to key questions have been recorded in Figure 9.3. An overall assessment of each respondents' attitude to AALA appears in the bottom line. As can be seen, this was overwhelmingly positive.

One likely reason for this positive attitude to AALA was that all its inspectors, including the head of inspections, had come from the adventure activity sector and thereby had extensive experience in the field of outdoor education through immersion, and were characteristically well respected within the outdoor community. In the terminology of Collins and Evans, they would have had high levels of 'specialist tacit knowledge' through years of interactional experience. Typically, they constituted former centre managers, development officers and training officers for various National Governing

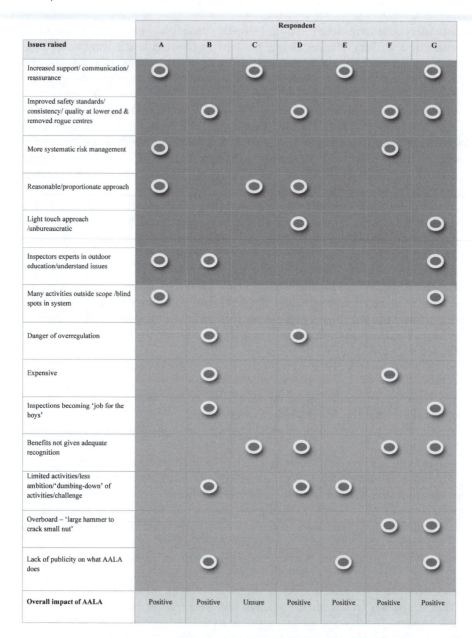

Issues raised	Respondent						
	A	B	C	D	E	F	G
Increased support/ communication/ reassurance	O		O		O		O
Improved safety standards/ consistency/ quality at lower end & removed rogue centres		O		O		O	O
More systematic risk management	O					O	
Reasonable/proportionate approach	O		O	O			
Light touch approach /unbureaucratic				O			O
Inspectors experts in outdoor education/understand issues	O	O					O
Many activities outside scope /blind spots in system	O						O
Danger of overregulation		O		O			
Expensive		O				O	
Inspections becoming 'job for the boys'		O					O
Benefits not given adequate recognition			O	O		O	O
Limited activities/less ambition/'dumbing-down' of activities/challenge		O		O	O		
Overboard – 'large hammer to crack small nut'						O	O
Lack of publicity on what AALA does		O			O		O
Overall impact of AALA	Positive	Positive	Unsure	Positive	Positive	Positive	Positive

Figure 9.3 *Respondents' views of AALA's regulatory regime (Ball-King, 2009b)*

Bodies, instructors at National Centres, school-based and local authority-based providers of adventure activities for young people, owners of commercial adventure activity centres, and so on. This, the respondents felt, had been the fundamental reason that a very helpful process for assessing activity centres had emerged. As all inspectors understood the issues and difficulties faced, the process was supportive rather than threatening. As a consequence, virtually all the respondents were in agreement that the quality of centres, particularly at the lower end, had 'unquestionably improved' as a direct result of licensing. The few 'rogue', unsafe centres that had previously existed had since been refused licenses. Thus, respondents pointed to a more consistent safety level.

Several respondents also conceded that there had been considerable concern initially that the legislation had been reflex reaction[7] and would be detrimental to the industry. However, the reality was that licensing had been introduced in such a way that it had maximized the upside and minimized the downside, and consequently staff were now very supportive of its operations. Concern had more recently arisen over the separation of AALA and the inspection service into two separate entities, and the absorption of AALA into the HSE in 2007. When this occurred, many believed that this would change the approach of inspectors, but in 2008 respondents were of the view that this did not seem to have been the case. However, clearly this did not rule out the possibility of future changes: any shifts in approach would likely occur slowly. An empathetic overseer now does not guarantee an empathetic overseer for all time: things can change.

Further incidents shed light on thinking

As noted earlier, there have been a number of serious incidents involving young people on adventure activities since the new legislation came into being. That incidents have occurred should not in itself be surprising, with there being in the region of 7 to 10 million pupil days of out-of-school activities every year (Bailie, 2003; SCES, 2004) and the admission that risk cannot be eliminated especially when venturing into the wild.[8]

One incident involved the deaths of two teenage girls who, in 2000, were swept down a fast-flowing stream, Stainforth Beck near Settle, while on a school trip involving 'river walking'. Although a Coroner's Court established that the deaths were accidental, the HSE brought what proved to be a successful prosecution against Leeds County Council on the grounds that they failed to ensure the safety of the pupils.[9] This followed a rigorous investigation of Leeds Local Education Authority's risk management procedures. Another incident occurred in 2002 when a ten-year-old boy drowned in a flooded river near Glenridding in Cumbria. In that case the HSE's prosecution resulted in a conviction of manslaughter against the teacher responsible. A further attempted prosecution by HSE, of North Yorkshire County Council, over the 2005 death by drowning of a teenage boy while on a potholing trip in Nidderdale, was unsuccessful, being rejected by the jury.

The conduct of these cases provides insights into the HSE's thinking on adventure activities, as does the advisory literature which they publish. From these experiences it is evident that despite the positive views expressed by AHOEC members in 2007 about the role of AALA in regulating the sector, there is an underlying concern that the regime could easily change. Were it, for example, to take on a more 'industrial' approach to the management of risk, the consequences for providers and provision could be significant. The NYCC case, for example, was ultimately largely fought on the grounds of beliefs about the role of risk in adventure, the adequacy of NYCC's risk assessment procedures and the suitability of their management system, all of which exposed patterns of thinking of the kind described in chapter 5.

It is informative to consider these three issues a little more closely. To take them in order, there would firstly appear to be a noticeable vagueness about the relationship between risk and adventure in some HSE literature. This can immediately be discerned in the opening to HSE's document *Adventure Activities Centres: Five Steps to Risk Assessment*, where it says:

> *Adventure activities aim to allow young people to develop by meeting challenges they do not necessarily face every day and to experience a sense of achievement in overcoming them. Some degree of risk is unavoidable if the sense of adventure and excitement is to be achieved. However, it is important to remember that adventure activities should only create a **sense** of adventure and excitement and **not cause harm**. (HSE, 2003a; the emphases in this quotation are the HSE's)*

To concur with this statement it is necessary to hold the following beliefs: a) young people need to meet real challenges; b) that in so doing some risk is inevitable; c) that the adventure should be fake (only sensed); and d) not cause harm. This, of course, is both illogical and a recipe for turning adventure activities into a Disneyesque experience. The moment you go into the wild, risk is unavoidably real. Therefore, it is necessary to accept that some harm will from time-to-time occur. What should be done is to manage it to the best of one's ability and as the circumstances demand.

But even after crossing this difficult bridge, which acknowledges the possibility of harm, one is inexorably faced with a second challenge. If there is a risk of going out there into the wild, how can its acceptance by society be justified? The answer, of course, is to reap the benefits, and in this respect it is fortunate that there is a growing recognition of the fact that children and young people, and probably older people too, get benefits from the activities which expose them to risk, as well as all the other benefits which are acquired through venturing into the natural environment (e.g. Play Safety Forum, 2002; SCES, 2004; Ogilvie, 2005; Gill, 2010; Hackitt, 2010).

However, in the NYCC case this notion of benefits seemed also a largely alien concept for the prosecution. As was drawn out by the defending barrister, Robert Smith QC, in cross-examination of witnesses, the notion of any consideration of benefits was barely alluded to in the prosecution's case. The case itself thereby provided a stark exposé of one way of thinking versus another, and of the kinds of issues raised in chapter 5 by Seedhouse and others over the parallel existence of competing world views.

Other systems of belief were also exposed by the trial. The prosecution placed heavy emphasis on the suitability and sufficiency of risk assessments carried out by NYCC, and on NYCC's management system. In this particular trial, however, these beliefs did not go unchallenged. There is, of course, a legal requirement to do a risk assessment, but there is more than one way of doing this, and probably this is the way it should be since one size seldom fits all.[10] Here one may recall that a primary aim of the Robens Commission was to encourage duty holders to think, and thinkers tend to devise their own systems rather than simply follow someone else's formula. NYCC had, in fact, devised their own system which, evidently, some in HSE did not like or maybe did not understand, but a considerable number of independent defence witnesses from the outdoor activity world were far more supportive of NYCC's approach than of HSE's. One of the reasons for this was perhaps that the HSE system was heavily into the language of management through trying to invoke a need for multiple layers of assessment from generic risk assessment, through site-specific assessment to dynamic assessment, with additional reference to go/no-go criteria, triangulation and the like. It all sounded very fine, but was a far cry from the 'risk assessment is simple and not to be overcomplicated' message proclaimed in other HSE literature (HSE, 2006a). Another reason for dislike of this approach was the likely shift in authority which such a top-down managerial system might bring about through increasing the role of central health and safety decision makers in the Council, and which could in effect diminish the authority of adventure leaders themselves in the front-line. So the question, not answered, was: where is the evidence that this new emphasis would reduce risk? Nobody from the outdoor world believed it would work. Some thought it was a dangerous gamble not to be countenanced.

As for management systems, NYCC's approach was examined by the prosecution in minute detail in court and compared with that set out in HSG65 (HSE, 1997). However, just as with risk assessment, there is more than one approach to management, as first discussed in chapter 5. In rudimentary terms it can be said that some systems are autocratic, some paternalistic and some democratically inclined. One size does not fit all organizational contexts. The style set out in HSG65 appears most closely to resemble the autocratic mode: a system best-suited for low-trust organizations employing low-skilled workers; for example, a factory making knick-knacks and relying on casual labour.

It has to be questioned whether such a system is appropriate for the education sector, the health service or local government, where highly educated, motivated, professional people are employed. Apart from the cost implications, the impact upon working relationships and the ability of a chosen system to get the best out of staff deserves careful consideration. It would appear unlikely that this kind of approach could be beneficially applied to adventure activity leaders of all people, who have by the very nature of their work to be able to make minute-by-minute decisions as they ply their trade, and this is in accord with AALA's proposition, described in chapter 8, that within the outdoor sector the availability of competent individuals as leaders might permit these to take 'a more autonomous approach to how they operate' (AALA, 2001: 7).

It is also consistent with the analysis by Hood and colleagues of regulatory regimes as first set out in chapter 5:

> *Indiscriminate or inappropriate application of corporate risk management approaches could detract from, rather than augment, the quality of government of risk by putting more emphasis on existing bureaucratic tendencies to blame-avoidance. What seems to be needed is an approach to business risk management in government that is neither an unreflective adoption of private business practice nor based on an unrealistic view of organizational behaviour in the public sector ... (Hood et al, 2004)*

It was interesting to observe that, during cross-examination, the HSE witnesses did not dispute that the management approach described in HSG65, which had been presented by the prosecution as some kind of gold standard, was in fact only some undisclosed person's opinion of what constituted a good system, nor was compliance with it mandatory. The latter, of course, is as it should be. All of these systems are to some extent experimental and there is no system which fits all circumstances.

Summary

Adventure sports, in common with other public activities, including children and young people's play and outdoor activities in general, involve exposure to obvious hazards. What is notable about adventure sports, although not unique to them, is the severity of the potential consequences. Undoubtedly, with a risk-minimization frame of mind and no consideration of benefits, there is no way that such activities should be permissible. However, there is growing reaffirmation of the copious benefits these activities yield for all age groups in comparison with an infrequency of serious harms, and it is to be hoped that this will eventually help the UK to reclaim its former position as a world leader in this area.

There exists a number of other debates within the sector, but with wider implications. One is about whether risk is a key motivation for engaging in these activities, or whether it is better understood as a by-product. What is clear is that at least part of the allure for individuals is the chance to test themselves against real hazards in powerful natural environments. Participants see this as something altogether significant, and worthy of the sacrifices and countless hours spent honing skills and physical ability. If one were to consider this commitment as evidence of the level of 'willingness-to-pay', then one could only conclude that the benefits of these activities are very highly valued.

So far as AALA is concerned, it is a relatively new organization in a world of shifting politics and priorities, and one which is perhaps now reaching the end of its lifetime as a consequence of the Young review which seeks its abolition. Evidence described here, however, leads to the conclusion that its early strategy supported the adventure sector in a way valued by the majority of its members, and which was beneficial to the sector. A likely explanation of this favourable reaction, bearing in mind that it is unusual to like regulators, is that AALA itself has been staffed by recognized adventure experts with appropriate 'interactional and contributory expertise' of the kind described by Collins and Evans (2007), and thus it did not usher in an alien and inappropriate culture as has happened in public life more widely. It could perhaps be described as 'specialist sector regulation'; that is, inspection *by* the sector but *answerable to government*, as opposed to self-regulation, meaning inspection *by* the sector but answerable *to the sector*, and also as opposed to inspection *by a generalist regime lacking interactional and contributory expertise*. There is perhaps here a message for future designers of regulatory regimes.

However, whilst the AALA approach seemed to be functioning effectively and is even now typically well received, there remains a concern that continuing pressure to find simplistic solutions to what were complex issues would ultimately have threatened that position. For example, one key debate is over the relative importance of the competence of adventure leaders versus the amount of control exercised over them by health and safety professionals with no particular knowledge of adventure activities. Another relates to the degree of freedom which adventure leaders should have in order to make decisions in the field, and the degree to which their freedom should be constrained by prior risk-assessment documentation and systems, including imposed 'go/no-go criteria' and the like.

AALA has itself written:

> However perhaps the best way of thinking of a written risk assessment is as a checklist of things you would mention to new activity leaders during their induction period. (AALA, 2001: 18)

This position contrasts with the official, mainstream view of risk assessment, which is that it is the bedrock upon which all safety systems are founded. Within the world of adventure activities, however, it may be that risk assessment has met its nemesis. The true bedrock, as many would see it, is in fact the experience, competence and real-time decision-making ability of the leaders. Britain has an enviable record in producing high-calibre persons with these characteristics. What goes on inside their heads is not something that can be recorded on paper, however voluminous. It might appear that the current tendency to make risk assessments ever more elaborate is a partial recognition of the true complexity of the process of decision making in the face of exposure to risk and uncertainty; that is, it is not such a simple process to explain after all. If so, it is unlikely to succeed.

A further vulnerability for the sector is the occurrence of events as at the 2008 OMM, which inevitably will sometimes happen and which tend to unleash hugely adverse publicity on the whole sector, leaving it exposed to the threat of outside intervention. This is particularly true for adventure sports, given that they are not considered mainstream and that the majority of the population are not directly involved with them, and tend to have little or no direct understanding. As with other public sector groups, the adventure sports sector would do well to continue to promote clearly why these activities are worthwhile and should be supported. This has been achieved with good effect in other sectors, such as children's play and countryside management.

While the HSE has broadly supported risk-taking activities, it has at times veered away from accepting the fact that in unpredictable environments, serious consequences have sometimes to be expected, and that these can even occur in the seemingly most benign of environments. Indeed, HSE literature, even in the adventure sector, is largely rooted in ideas of risk reduction without much reference to benefits, although HSE leaders have recently voiced their recognition of the benefits of leisure activities. Often, though, the literature transmits the mixed and dubious message that risk exposure is good, as long as it is managed and will not lead to serious harm. Can one learn about real risk by unreal exposure? Would adventure sports have the same meaning if they took place in sanitized, totally controlled environments? We think not.

10
Risk-Benefit Assessment

As has been seen, risk-benefit assessment (RBA) has been around for a long time, and while the Play Safety Forum cannot be credited with its genesis, it certainly gave a mighty boost to its prominence in the UK's public sector when it produced its 2002 position statement (PSF, 2002), with the follow-up by DCSF, DCMS and Play England in 2008, of the implementation guide (Play England, 2008b). Since then other public sector bodies, such as the Forestry Commission (2006), have shown considerable interest because the issues addressed were by no means peculiar to play but common across public life. Thus, the education sector, land-owners, initially in relation to the management of trees, and those providing outdoor activities, have all responded positively and with enthusiasm. So what is risk-benefit assessment and what does it entail?

Over 40 years ago the American scientist Chauncey Starr authored a seminal paper on societal benefit versus technological risk (Starr, 1969). By analysing the activities in which Americans engaged, such as hunting, skiing, smoking, using electrical power, driving a car or riding in a plane, even fighting a war in Vietnam, Starr concluded that so far as the American public were concerned, they were prepared to accept risky activities in exchange for the associated benefits, real or imagined.[1] What holds for Americans in this respect probably holds for others. Risk-benefit was firmly on the agenda, if with patchy acknowledgement.

MRPP's approach to RBA

Managing Risk in Play Provision: Implementation guide (MRPP) and its sister publication, *Design for Play – A guide to creating successful play spaces*, were created by two groups of authors, but it might be noted that essential input was received during drafting from numerous agencies across the nation with interests in play provision *and* child safety and well-being, such that as close to a consensus as possible could be achieved amongst all key stakeholders. This was not always an easy journey. People care passionately about children and anything posing a challenge to conventional wisdom on the topic had sometimes to advance under heavy fire. One might ask: 'How were the final products received?' The following observations suggest that the messages in the documents fell on fertile ground, though it is of course early days yet:

- The endorsement of *Managing Risk in Play Provision*, by the HSE and other key national agencies (including the Department for Health and RoSPA), was said to be 'ground-breaking'.
- A national stakeholder described the change in attitude amongst local authorities, government and the HSE as 'striking'.
- The publication generated debate around risk and play, with one local authority area saying that legal teams had begun to create policies around incorporating risk in play.
- Around nine out of ten local authorities that responded to a survey by Play England reported that its guidance had 'some influence' or 'considerable influence' (this question was not asked in relation to any specific publication, so this is a result that cannot directly be linked to *MRPP* in particular).

Overarching issues

During the work on these publications, a number of key issues emerged relating to RBA as follows:

- that risk-benefit assessment must be conducted against a policy background;
- that it is nothing new for most policymakers, who will already be doing it implicitly if not explicitly (though some things might change);
- that children's play (as with public life generally) is an unpredictable and complex process which has its own implications;
- the novelty of risk benefit assessment is that it restores risk-management decision making to its former equilibrium by highlighting that decisions are about an appropriate balance between the benefits and risks of public space and activities.

The first point, about the need for a policy background, is important in a number of respects. As David Seedhouse (2004) has said in the context of healthcare provision (chapter 7), you need to have a philosophy, a rationale or an agreed purpose, and to state what it is. It is simply not possible to make a decision purely on the basis of some evidence, whatever its quality. Furthermore, without a clearly expressed policy there is an ever-present risk of confusion over objectives, making it impossible to set priorities, and with a serious potential for mission drift.[2] For example, the underlying primary goal of the play sector has always been to enable children to fulfil their right to play,[3] but for several decades this mission was relegated to second place by a quest for safety, apparently at any cost or consequence.[4] In effect, other people's interests and philosophies had taken up the slack. Because the aims of the quest for safety were overstated, this also led to false expectations about injury prevention and no doubt contributed to the litigation which followed. But the most serious consequence was borne by children and young people – the true purpose of play having been demoted on the agenda. It is encouraging to note that the recently published international standard on risk management is totally unequivocal on the need to relate risk management to organizational policies when, for example, it says: 'Management should align risk management objectives with the objectives and strategies of the organisation' (ISO, 2009: 9).

Now it should go without saying that you need to be careful about the wording of your policy, but it is not unusual in the age of spin for slips to be made in the desire to have something simple, or which sounds snappy, media-friendly or politically correct. The substance, though, is important. As has already been discussed in chapter 7, HSG65 provides examples of health and safety philosophies which might be alright in a factory, but may be considered less so in public life where safety is but one of many objectives. Two of these are as follows:

> *We believe that an excellent company is by definition a safe company. Since we are committed to excellence, it follows that minimising risk to people, plant and products is inseparable from all other company objectives.*
>
> *Total safety is the ongoing integration of safety into all activities with the objective of attaining industry leadership in safety performance. We believe nothing is more important than safety ... not production, not sales, not profits. (HSE, 1997)*

On the face of it these statements seem admirable. Maybe, in a factory, they are. They certainly appeal to moral sensibilities. But scrutiny soon shows them to be opinions from a narrow perspective and, in some instances, of unclear logic. The first statement offers what is an opinion when it says, 'an excellent company is by definition a safe company'. Subject to a definition of what is meant by 'safe', the opinion might well be judged to be a reasonable one. But the follow-up sentence, about minimizing risk, stirs up a host of now familiar issues.

What, for instance, if minimizing one risk creates another and possibly even bigger risk elsewhere, or for someone else? It has been estimated that the initial blanket closure of UK airspace in Spring 2010 during the eruption of Eyjafjallajökull resulted in 500,000 Britons being stranded abroad, and thereby placed at some risk. Also, in the transportation sector, the present 'Vision zero' policy of the Highways Agency (DfT, 2010) to aim for the elimination of fatalities and serious injuries to road workers, in part by not permitting workers onto live carriageways, could, if not carefully managed, mean more road closures and consequent diversion of traffic onto less suitable and less familiar roads, and, were this so, more risk to drivers and the public. Many authors have warned how there are numerous ways in which one intervention can generate undesirable unintended consequences in some other arena (e.g. Graham and Wiener, 1995; Elvik, 1999; Haythornthwaite, 2006).

The House of Commons Regulatory Reform Committee (RRC, 2009) concluded, in its investigation of the financial crisis, that regulators needed to observe the following lessons:

1. Seek to understand risk more fully and develop the resources to do that, where appropriate looking at whole systems rather than individual problem areas.
2. Focus more on assessing possible future risks.
3. Identify areas of hidden risk.
4. Identify possibilities of conflict of interest in taking decisions.
5. Seek to anticipate unintended consequences of regulation.
6. Develop mechanisms for challenging prevailing wisdom and political pressure.
7. Involve representatives of consumers in such challenges.
8. Be willing to use their powers more effectively.
9. Seek to match the experience and weight of those they regulate.

The emphasis in this list upon 'whole systems', 'hidden risk', 'conflicts of interest', and especially 'unintended consequences', mirrors the issues raised here, and recently by Lord Young (HM Government, 2010). The RRC went on to encourage other House of Commons Select Committees to use these criteria in assessing the performance of regulators in their own inquiries.

As for the second of the philosophies from HSG65 listed above, it is clearly a political choice whether safety from injury should trump, say, the economic well-being of an organization providing employment, supplying needed goods or providing public services.

As David Stuckler and colleagues (2010) have demonstrated in a recent paper in the *British Medical Journal*: 'Adults in secure and safe employment, receiving wages above the level merely to survive, are less likely to adopt hazardous lifestyles, and can expect to live longer.' This broad position, that economic well-being contributes positively to human health, is not new. For example, an important conclusion of the work of Aaron Wildavsky, who researched this topic for many years, is simply that 'A little richer is a lot safer' (Wildavsky, 1980). The inference is that economic well-being itself is beneficial to health, so the act of prioritizing minimization of injury risk over production, sales and profits could conceivably be tantamount to increasing health risk in the wider population. What is obviously needed is a more holistic view, which could be achieved by observing and implementing the above lessons identified by the RRC.

It is self-evident that public bodies have far more needs to serve than injury prevention, as Lord Hoffmann and others have made clear. It would be better, perhaps, depending on an agency's role, to have a philosophy, so far as the safety element is concerned, along the lines of:

> *Our aim is to manage public space in order to enable public enjoyment and activities to the full. In doing this we will do everything that is reasonable to ensure safety from harm while seeking to maximise positive social outcomes.*

This position is, possibly, subject to some interpretation, not that far removed from that expressed in the introductory words of HSE's guidance on the Adventure Activities Licensing Regulations, namely:

The aim of the adventure activities licensing scheme is to provide assurance that good safety management practice is being followed so that young people can continue to have opportunities to experience exciting and stimulating activities outdoors while not being exposed to avoidable risks of death and disabling injury. (HSE, 2007b)

The clear advantage of positions such as these is that they are consistent with the law in recognizing that all that is reasonable must be done to ensure safety, while keeping the benefits of public life, including health, but also enjoyment of art and nature and other things, firmly on the agenda.[5] And for confirmation that these are legitimate considerations, if it were needed, such statements can be linked to the Green Book by HM Treasury (HMT, 2003), which gives a long list of environmental, landscape, biodiversity and recreational amenity considerations which warrant attention in public sector decision making.

It may also be that an overt public policy position along these lines would serve also to deter undeserving compensation seekers: this because it would be crystal clear that policy is unavoidably about accepting some risks in order to procure some benefits. This should be a much more straightforward position to defend than one which purports to be about creating total safety or minimizing risk, which is anyway an impossibility. Furthermore, once it is widely known that the policy is to tolerate some risks in exchange for the benefits of public space, there is encouragement for the public to take back a degree of responsibility for their actions, and perhaps even for the compensation society to begin to retreat. This in itself could combat moral hazard and thereby create a safer society.

Moving to the second of the overarching issues – that is, the need to try to avoid yet more administrative burden – it was felt important that any new initiative such as a shift to RBA should not generate a whole new raft of paperwork, of which the society we have created is already heavily endowed. The *Principles of sensible risk management* (HSC, 2006b) stand out against this, and no doubt they are right to do so. Lord Young also has identified the need to simplify risk assessment and reduce the huge amount of form-filling which currently goes on (HM Government, 2010: 36). Administration cuts into front-line activities, and arguably it is the front-line presence which works and gives the public confidence, whether it is connected with policing, social work or public services. It is also costly. Unfortunately, as Tim Gill (2010) has commented: '... in recent years the trend has been to conduct ever more detailed risk assessments, because of the fear of litigation'.

It seems unlikely that RBA itself can do much to reverse this trend because the pressure for paper and audit trails of everything has become a way, and even a means, of existence for an ever-growing number of followers. For some agencies, notably some insurance companies, it has become a way of life, apparently *sine qua non*. That particular battle will have to be taken up on a wider front, which examines the cost to society of this administrative burden and decides whether it is producing adequate returns to justify itself. As noted already, the RRAC has said that the UK spends around £100 billion a year on

the administrative cost of regulation.[6] Per family, this amounts to a charge of several thousand pounds per year.[7] Some of such money could instead be spent on social welfare programmes, education, better lifestyles, the arts or a better environment.

The third and fourth points, about unpredictability and complexity, and the restoration of decision making to a previous equilibrium, will be discussed in chapter 11. Firstly, it is appropriate to take a closer look at RBA.

Carrying out RBA

It is important at the outset to be clear that RBA is about a form of decision making which compares (trades-off) risks of harm associated with space and activities against their benefits, and then decides, on balance, whether to go ahead, or to make changes to the balance or not to proceed. It is *not*, as some appear to think, about making a prior judgement on the desirability of something on the basis of its benefits and then switching back to the currently practised mode of risk assessment which pays no obvious heed to benefits, even when they include health benefits.

Thus, supposing your village football team had just had an unlikely victory in the UEFA Champions League and you were faced with the decision whether or not to permit a victory parade, you would weigh up the benefits of the activity against the associated risks.

Alternatively, you might be trying to regenerate an area of land, and develop a sustainable community by integrating housing with green space and natural water features, as has happened at The Hamptons, near Peterborough. Obviously, nature can be cruel and harbours hazards, but it is also beneficial in numerous ways and people value naturalness, so the desire of some to fence or block things off from public access from a safety perspective should be considered alongside the benefits derived from easy access and open vistas.

The crucial point is that some justification is needed for having made a decision to permit, modify or not permit something to go ahead. As we have remarked earlier, Professor Christopher Hood and colleagues have said:

> *What are needed are public statements of how assessors reasoned about the issues, to avoid the impression of ad hoc political judgements masquerading as technocratic expertise. (Hood, Rothstein and Baldwin, 2001)*

It should not be overlooked that the primary purpose of doing this of course is to 'manage risk properly', by which is meant looking after the safety, *and* health *and* welfare, of the public, these being *the primary concerns*. This is not to be confused nor supplanted by ulterior motives such as avoidance of liability (i.e. *the secondary risks*). The fact is that if you do the former, the latter should fall into place by itself. Unfortunately, society has committed itself to providing audit trails, ever more extensive ones, which serve the latter purpose, and sometimes this takes over from the real job. Recall what was said by Simon Jenkins (The *Guardian*, 2010) about the social workers in the Baby P case, who, one suspects, and perhaps through no fault of their own, were stuck at their desks for far too long rather than visiting clients.

On occasion, prosecutors appear, in legal cases, to be asking for comprehensive documentation when elsewhere the message is to keep it simple. One admittedly needs to be wary in current circumstances, where trust in professionals is at a low level and the reaction to anything less than immaculate paperwork is to assert that the job was not done. One can easily understand why insurance companies have joined the throng demanding 'independent' audits and flawless paper trails (accepting for the moment that there is such a thing as a 'flawless paper trail'), though one may also worry about the unintended consequences for others, including the public, as ultimate customers of the services being provided.

The advice given in *Managing Risk in Play Provision* (MRPP) is to list the benefits of the place or activity and link this where possible to reputable sources or publications. And then to assess the risks. Risks could be assessed using historical injury records for the site or activity in question, if available. This approach is recommended in an HSE research publication on risk assessment, which includes the following statement:

> *It is possible to derive incident frequencies directly from the historical record if there are sufficient and accurate data available, and the data are relevant and applicable to the particular process/hazard under review. The 'historical approach' to derivation of incident frequencies based on appropriate data has the advantage that it is not limited by the imagination of the analyst in deriving failure mechanisms and therefore the assessment will not omit any significant routes to failure. The data should already encompass all common relevant contributory aspects including: reliability of equipment, human factors, operational methods, quality of construction, inspection, maintenance and operation, etc ... (HSE, 2003b)*

Box 14 *Benefit assessment of Plas Dol-y-Moch
Outdoor Education Centre*

Plas Dol-y-Moch has a long and successful history of providing outdoor and adventure education activities to young people. The benefits of these activities for participants are numerous and include:

- Increased levels of trust and opportunities to examine the concept of trust (us in them, them in us, them in themselves, them in each other).
- Involvement in activities leading to greater academic and vocational learning with improved achievement and attainment across a range of curricular subjects. Students are active participants not passive consumers and a wide range of learning styles can flourish.
- Enhanced opportunities for 'real world' 'learning in context' and the development of the social aspects of intelligence.
- Increased risk-management skills through opportunities for involvement in practical risk-benefit assessments ('what do we want to do and what do we need to do to make it safe enough?'). Giving learners the tools and experience necessary to assess their own risks in a range of contexts.
- Opportunities to practically examine the components of challenge (i.e. chance of gain or benefit / risk of loss or harm / accurate goal setting and judgement / willingness and commitment / activity outside the comfort zone (physical and/or emotional)).
- Greater sense of personal responsibility.
- Enhanced emotional intelligence (including a greater awareness of their own needs and the needs of others).
- Possibilities for genuine teamworking including enhanced communication skills.
- Improved environmental appreciation, knowledge, awareness and understanding. Including opportunities to interact with a wild environment.
- Improved awareness and knowledge of the importance and practices of sustainability in the modern world.
- Physical skill acquisition and the development of a fit and healthy lifestyle.

These benefits inform the centre's risk-management policy. The centre's aim is to achieve an appropriate level of challenge to maximize the learning for each participant. The aim is not to make the learning environment as safe as possible, but as safe as it needs to be.

Clearly, adventure activities involve an element of challenge and, therefore, risk of loss or harm. This could involve participants, visiting staff, centre staff or members of the public in proximity to the activity.

Using the following strategies the centre will balance the benefits and risks in such a way as to bring the residual level of risk to an appropriate and tolerable level for each group and individual:

- Employment / deployment of competent staff.
- Induction and initial / ongoing training.
- Agreed and regularly reviewed operating procedures and practices.
- Peer and management monitoring of delivery.
- Awareness of, and involvement in, regional and national developments in activity delivery and management.

All teaching staff at the centre are competent to lead their programmed activities. Competent means they:

- Either hold an appropriate NGB award or have been judged competent by a technical adviser / head of centre.
- Have been inducted into the centre's procedures.
- Have received additional training appropriate to their role, including first aid, minibus training, manual handling and management of the water environment, as appropriate.

Source: with permission of David Crossland, Head of Outdoor Education Service, Plas Dol-y-Moch

The approach has some potential deficiencies, but one very significant bonus is that it measures actual experienced risk and not someone's perception of risk, which, as described in chapter 2, is vulnerable to all kinds of biases. Furthermore, it factors in human behaviour, which addresses the problem of the complex interaction between people and hazardous objects or situations which assessors can only dream about.

If no data are available, statistics for comparable circumstances elsewhere might give a clue. For some people, this kind of information-driven, evidence-based or actuarial approach is much preferred to the completion of the kind of risk-consequence matrices described in chapter 2, which are, by their nature, highly subjective. This is because of all the difficulties associated with the matrices, plus the unpredictability of situations involving the public who may or may not have good coping skills, or who may engage in things like risk compensatory behaviour. However, collecting and using numerical data has its own drawbacks, and one needs to be aware of the limitations.

For this reason, local experience is often going to be the least worst and in many cases the best way of assessing what might be the reality in these complex situations. If special expertise is deemed necessary, either to assess benefits or risks, it is worth bearing in mind that the HSE has said that local expertise is again preferable. This is for the obvious reason that local people know the local situation. A second advantage is that they are more likely to be familiar with local policy objectives too.

One valuable way of approaching the issue, and the decision about whether the benefits warrant the risks, is by examining precedents and comparisons with other similar circumstances from around the country, or sometimes abroad if you are anywhere near leading the way. Having done these things, you will be in a better position to make and justify your decision.

Weighing risks against benefits

When faced with a decision which involves comparing the risks of some public place or activity with its benefits, you may feel this is a difficult thing to do, rather like comparing the proverbial apple with the pear. This in a sense is absolutely correct.[8] It is undeniably a complex decision because you are comparing two things with widely differing characteristics. One is likely about the risk of someone being hurt. The other is about benefits which might include any number of items from the following list, which itself does not pretend to exhaust the possibilities: potential for public enjoyment, naturalness, sustainability, supports community values, beauty (natural or manufactured), potential to inspire, encourages healthy exercise, allows people freedom, wilderness value, and so on.

Risk assessors often avoid the matter by the subterfuge of using some published advisory document or standard, and comparing the situation with that. This can be problematic for any number of reasons: there may be no advice which is well-tailored to your situation; the thinking behind the advice may not be made clear, so you don't know if it is any good in the circumstances; the advice may have been written at a distance by someone with no idea of your particular needs or policy objectives.

How on earth can risks and benefits be compared? Perhaps a surprising port of call in search of an answer to this practical question is research into neuroscience, and the inner-workings of the human brain. This subject has already been raised in chapter 8 under the heading 'Psychology and decision making', from which it emerged that broadly speaking the brain has two ways of making decisions. One relies upon so-called 'rational thought' and calculation, such that in making choices we consciously analyse all the options and weigh the pros and cons, akin to the deployment of some kind of mental mathematics. This is undoubtedly an important ability and one which is essential for human survival. Its primary advantage is that it uses evidence and is thereby more objective, if not totally so.

Within the western world there has been a lasting emphasis upon the desirability of this kind of objectivity in decision making, going back to the times of The Enlightenment and far beyond, through thinkers such as René Descartes to Plato. This way of thinking, that careful analysis leads to wisdom, has been so entrenched that essentially it has become a given of western society (Jaeger et al, 2001). Now, through neurological research, this type of thinking is known to be associated with a part of the brain called the prefrontal cortex (Lehrer, 2009). This part of the brain, however, is not without its shortcomings. Research suggests that its calculating capacity is limited, and that it can easily be overwhelmed by choices which have many dimensions and exhibit complexity, and which may lead it astray through a tendency to adopt default positions. It is also comparatively slow in reaching conclusions. You could not rely upon it, for example, to play badminton. There your reactions have literally to be ahead of the game, not mired in some involved thought process on how to angle your racket and how hard to hit the shuttlecock.

As an example of how complexity challenges the prefrontal cortex, Lehrer cites several pieces of research. One is about the seemingly mundane task of selecting a jar of strawberry jam from an assortment of such products in the supermarket.[9] Back in the 1980s a US magazine (Consumer Reports) had invited a panel of experts to sample 45 different jams, scoring them on 16 characteristics such as sweetness, fruitiness and so on, and then to total the scores to give an overall ranking. A few years later a university psychologist replicated the test using his students. The students, using the same methodology as the experts, came up with more or less the same ranking. The results seemed reasonable too, because what were widely believed to be the best and worst jams got the relevant ratings. However, a second group of students was asked to repeat the test with the additional requirement to explain why they preferred one brand over another, through being forced to write down their reasoning as they went. In this way they were being asked to consciously explain their impulsive judgements. The result was entirely different, even to the point of placing what most people thought to be the worst-tasting jam first!

The explanation, which has been supported in other experiments, is that too much thinking about the strawberry jam causes you to put undue emphasis on variables which may in reality not matter that much, in comparison with those which do.[10] So how should the brain best make these decisions? The answer was alluded to in chapter 8, with reference to the second way in which the brain makes choices – termed its emotional mode of operation, and which gave rise to terms like 'affect' and 'gut feelings'. This way of thinking is now believed to be as essential to survival as that provided by the analytical power of the prefrontal cortex. What this seemingly constitutes is some alternative way of mental functioning which is also highly sophisticated. However,

because its output is not expressed as a detailed 'rational' discourse revealing its internal logic, but as a feeling, one which moreover is reliant upon the so-called 'emotional part of the brain', it has suffered some bad press from pro-analytic thinkers. Aristotle though, and David Hume, might have had something to say about the casual dismissal of this way of thinking.

So what has the so-called emotional part of the brain got going for it? It seems it is a rapid processor of information, even able to forecast events, including, say, the trajectories of shuttlecocks flying through the air, so if you play badminton this is certainly for you. And what skills are good for badminton are by and large also essential for everyday living, so we are all very reliant upon it all of the time. Thus, the emotional brain is constantly making rapid decisions, usually based on fleeting and surprisingly limited information of which you may not even be consciously aware. Evidence suggests that in some situations, though not all, it out-computes the rational brain, partly because the rational brain is poor at disregarding non-key information which distracts it from core issues, which leads to its propensity to overload.

In chapter 8 the example of buying a car was given. There were lots of characteristics to consider, as with the strawberry jam story. The argument is that too much information can prevent you from seeing the wood for the trees, and that complex decisions with lots of variables and unknowns are best resolved using your instinctive feelings. Of course, we live in the 'information society', and in an age where information and logic, or what masquerades as such, is still held to be paramount. But the evidence that this is not so is all around us.

A major asset of the emotional brain is that it learns from errors. In the event that it forecasts something which does not turn out to be, it will readjust to accommodate that new information. This process goes on from the day of birth and throughout one's life; some may even be stored in our genes. So what it holds is what in more familiar language is known as experience or a different kind of logic, but still logic. It is akin to what Harry Collins and Robert Evans (2007) called ubiquitous tacit knowledge (as referred in chapter 8), or 'contributory expertise' if it is something with which you have been closely engaged. As they said, we have boundless amounts of this knowledge and without it we could not survive.

What has this to contribute to risk-benefit assessment? In public life decisions are complex because people are involved, giving rise to unknown behaviours including risk-compensatory behaviour, and because the environment is ever-changing. If you are intent, say, upon creating a new space, possibly a shared-space or a public garden, in an inner-city area, you cannot forecast with reliability the outcome – how safe it will be or whether it will function as desired. You may review the working of other similar places and this might give a partial insight, but to think that the outcome could be forecast scientifically, except for the most obvious hazards, would be illusory. The only way to make the decision then is to rely upon accumulated experience or 'contributory expertise' – from your locality – and perhaps drawing upon comparable experiences from elsewhere.

Lehrer (2009) provides a couple of important tricks to help decision makers avoid over-confidence and test themselves, this being important because of the known fallibilities of the human brain in whatever mode of operation. One is to always consider alternative perspectives, and the other is to remind yourself constantly of what you do not know. These are things to do from the ex ante position. In chapter 11 some important, ex post, actions which can be taken will be described.

Record keeping – *a thorny topic*

In 2010, Lord Young said of children's outings:

> *The process for taking children on educational visits involves a huge amount of form-filling – ranging from consent forms to risk assessments – and the valuable time of education officials including school governors, the head teacher, group leaders and the educational visits coordinator. This process can involve excessive bureaucracy that is not proportionate to the role it plays in reducing the risk of accidents. It merely serves as a deterrent and an excuse to do nothing. (HM Government, 2010: 36–37)*

The HSC (2006b) also railed against the accumulation of mountains of paper-work, as with considerable persuasiveness has Michael Power (1994, 2004). As argued in this book, excessive paperwork is not only expensive but may also be undermining of purpose. This is because it is arguably more about managing the secondary risk of liability, as opposed to the primary concern of public health and well-being, so it takes people's eyes off the primary target, and this has in some cases led to a premature sense of 'a job being done'. Secondly, even if it were argued that it does make some contribution to managing primary risks, its utility may be exaggerated. This is because the things that actually make life work, as argued by Collins and Evans (2007), are too complex and numerous ever to write down on a piece of paper.

The difficulty currently faced is that the pressure to keep copious records is all around. Insurers often demand it. In legal cases prosecutors are prone to insist it is produced as evidence of all that was reasonably practicable having been done. HSE's *Five steps to risk assessment* (HSE, 2006a) notes that if you have five or more employees you must write down your assessment, a require-ment which can be traced back through the Management of Health and Safety at Work Regulations to European Council Directive 89/391/EEC (although the latter is not, in fact, about risks to the public).

While Lord Young has urged that this matter be challenged, the current situation remains problematic for service providers. With this in mind, *MRPP* (Play England, 2008b) recommends that risk-benefit assessment records be kept, but in a *narrative form* which identifies the factors considered and the judgements made. This emphasis on a narrative form, while it will not be universally welcomed, is sensible considering the difficulty and meaningfulness of applying numerical, or quasi-numerical, methods to something as elusive as public safety and health, and the potential for numbers to take on a life of their own, even if of dubious validity. *MRPP* provides a series of hypothetical, narrative-style RBA's indicating how this might be done.

The organization PLAYLINK has also provided on its website[11] a draft narrative-style Risk Benefit Assessment Form as an opening suggestion, and which it expects will be modified by service providers based on their individual needs and gathering experience. PLAYLINK itself has considerable unease that the use of pro formas for risk-benefit assessment (like those for risk assessment), whether in quasi-mathematical or narrative form, may not ultimately be beneficial. For one thing they tend to promote a kind of 'tick box' mentality, which likely detracts from the application of true thoughtfulness of the kind sought by Lord Robens all those years ago. Nor, it recognizes, are the proposed forms necessarily less time-consuming than the previous forms, although they should be more realistic and thereby serve a more useful purpose. Why generate them at all then? The answer is that in the absence of authoritative and consistent advice on what is required, it provides something for service providers to cling to, a secondary motive of course, but understandable in the circumstances.

Interestingly, Luke Bennett, of Sheffield Hallam, has ushered in a welcome breath of fresh air in reporting a 2008 junior court legal case (Atkins v. Scott) involving an injury to a party arising from a falling tree (Bennett, 2010). The land-owner, who was acquitted, was in what might have been thought to be a weak position because his tree inspection regime (risk assessment) was undocumented and carried out by 'non-specialists' (persons lacking arboricultural training). However, as Bennett records, the judge in his summing up stated that:

> ... it is important not to become lost in procedures and ease of proof. What is important is whether or not the [landowner] discharged his duty to take such steps to protect passers-by on the highway from danger as a reasonable man in [his] position would have taken.

The judge went on to say that the land-owner's system had been found to be:

> an unrecorded but well-understood and adequate system for obtaining specialist assistance in respect of any trees thought to present problems.

Opposition to unconstrained record-keeping has also been forthcoming from the HSE's Chief Executive, Geoffrey Podger, who agreed with the RRAC that a 'lighter touch' should be possible in the case of the public risk posed by trees:

> In 2007 HSE became concerned that uncertainty was causing some organisations to over-react to the low risk from falling trees. HSE therefore produced guidance for its inspectors on

what is required by the law we enforce – the Health and Safety at Work Act 1974. It makes the point that the risk is generally extremely low. For most trees around the countryside HSE does not believe any action at all is reasonably practicable under the 1974 Act. Where trees are in very public places we suggest that non-specialist staff with a working knowledge of trees should look out for obvious problems as part of their everyday work. Inspection by tree experts is likely to be appropriate only in very limited circumstances, for example where a tree in a very public area is known to be unstable but is kept for heritage or other reasons. There are several other relevant pieces of non-HSE law; we have encouraged stakeholders to agree a simple and proportionate approach to cover all the legal duties. We hope that by sharing our own guidance we have provided a useful starting point. (RRAC, 2009)

In passing, it may be noted that this statement itself makes reference to the potential benefits of trees when it mentions 'heritage or other reasons'.

The business of sensible and proper risk-benefit assessment and risk management does not end here. It might, if you were dealing with a predictable system such as launching a space probe to the outer reaches of the solar system such that its course, once it has left the earth's atmosphere, is predictable with near-total accuracy. With public activities the truth is entirely different because of their complexity and hence their unpredictability. This has some very important implications which are discussed in chapter 11.

Summary

Risk-benefit assessment is absolutely not something that can be meaningfully carried out without a policy background. It must be linked closely to your purposes. It is suggested that a suitably worded policy document, linked to actions, could make useful contributions to restoring any lost balance in public sector decisions about public space, and possibly in dealing with the worst extremes of the so-called compensation culture. That aspect of the compensation culture which generates voluminous paper trails and auditing requirements, sometimes at the expense of front-line services, needs to be addressed from a wider perspective.

Risk-benefit assessment is a simple process to describe, but less so when thought about in detail. The fact is, however, that conventional risk-assessment procedures are not in reality simple either, although they may at times have been presented as such. This still leaves the key challenge of how to compare risks of public space, which largely result in bodily harm, with benefits which come in a variety of forms from health to beauty.

Common sense and neurological research suggest that this cannot sensibly be done using analytic procedures alone, partly because the situations being examined are complex, but also because they are so numerous. That is, many aspects of public life are not readily amenable to scientific analysis and prediction except in some obvious circumstances, at least without considerable uncertainty. Shockingly, perhaps, human beings also rely heavily upon intuitive decision making for most of their choices, these being built upon lifelong learning through experience. This type of knowledge is akin to that described as tacit knowledge, or maybe contributory expertise. It appears that in public life this is likely the first port of call for risk-benefit decision making. However, evidence, and hence analysis, should still be used to the extent that it is available, providing always that it is genuinely relevant.

11
In Search of a New Agenda

What can be done to restore a sense of proportion to decision making on safety, health and risk in public life?

The key issue to be addressed appears to be the failure to recognize that important though safety is, it is not the only commodity which people value, particularly in public life. As Rick Haythornthwaite said of the speed of movement of road traffic in towns (Box 9), there is a trade-off to be made between the level of risk to pedestrians, which reduces if speeds are lowered, and the time taken by motorists to get from one place to another. The choice over which speed to set as the limit is thereby a balancing act. If you exclude from the consideration the benefits of travel by car, then it is entirely logical to set the speed limit very low indeed, or ban cars altogether. The problem is that this is essentially a political judgement. It is not a decision to be taken purely on health and safety grounds. Indeed, it is not a decision that *can* logically be taken on health and safety grounds alone because such a decision would leave out half of the equation – the part contemplating the benefits.

The Risk and Regulation Advisory Council considered a similar issue which was topical in 2008 and continues to be so; namely, the safety of trees in areas visited by the public. At Middlesex University the Centre for Decision Analysis and Risk Management (DARM) has been conducting research for the National Tree Safety Group (NTSG), itself set up to address this issue, on the inspection and management of trees from a public safety perspective. The problem is that trees, as a part of their normal life cycle, shed branches and eventually fall down, and very occasionally this harms somebody or something. Following a number of legal claims by injured parties, actions by the police, and the threat of criminal prosecution by the HSE against some estate wardens and land-owners, a fear of liability developed which had the unintended, undesirable consequence of trees being felled precipitously in various places around the country under the pretext of 'managing public safety' (Bennett, 2010).

In this example, some factual information is available. Research finds that the risk of any tree causing a fatality in Britain is exceedingly small. The historical record shows, during the decade ending on 31 December 2008, that there had been 64 fatalities associated with falling trees. Meteorological data indicate that at least 18 of these fatalities occurred during very windy weather and it is likely that this is an underestimate of the number of wind-related cases. For example, although over the ten-year period there was roughly one fatality per two-month period, on one day in October 2002 five people were killed during windy weather, and this happened again in January 2007 when three people were killed on a single, windy day.

As it stands, it would seem that the mean annual fatality rate in the UK is about six, but falling to about four if high-wind events are excluded. Taking the UK population as 60 million over this period leads to an estimate of 1 in 10 million per year individual risk of death from this cause, or less if high-wind occasions are discounted. This places the risk at a very low level indeed compared with other risks to life (e.g. see Table 2.1), and well down in the 'broadly acceptable' region of the Tolerability of Risk framework shown in Figure 4.1. Nonetheless, individual incidents, such as one which occurred on National Trust land at Dunham Massey on 1 January 2005, in which a child was killed by a falling tree during a storm, have led to calls for systems of tree monitoring which would 'ensure the safety of the public', and for more inspections and record keeping.

There is, of course, no possibility that given the billion plus trees in Britain that the six which will on average kill someone each year can be identified before the event. Tree risk assessment is more of an art than a science for one thing. The sheer number of trees, coupled with the scarcity of incidents, is the other. The odds of finding those trees, even armed with all available expert knowledge, are far less than the chance of winning the jackpot in the lottery with a single ticket. On the other hand, the cost and administrative effort involved in stepping up the level of inspections, and the amount of record keeping, over and above that already done could be enormous. Furthermore, to even attempt to fulfil the impossible dream to 'ensure the safety of the public' would also mean dealing with trees which might fall or shed a substantial limb, even in high winds. Thus, many otherwise beneficial trees would have to be removed if it were not possible to put in place plans to cordon them off during windy weather. In this way the nightmare of unrealistic aspirations spirals out of all proportion. Not only that, but trees are of course immensely valuable to the ecosystem, to human beings for environmental and health reasons, and to the climate. We suspect that a stronger case can be mounted for the planting of more shade-giving trees in cities and towns than for removing them.

It was therefore of great relief to many land-owners, whether having a large estate or just a small garden with a single tree, when the RRAC orchestrated its measured public awareness campaign to deter the British Standards Institution from creating a new standard on tree risk management, which, effectively, would have imposed a new tree inspection regime upon every householder and land-owner in the nation. This was achieved by the RRAC providing facts to the media on the threat to trees from the over-prescription of control measures. As a consequence, the BSI received a flood of letters, so encouraging it to more carefully consider the issue (RRAC, 2009).

Best practice and the highest standard of care

In response to the incident at Dunham Massey, the National Trust's regional director, Tiffany Hunt, made the following statement:

We are very sorry that this tragic event occurred. I do wish, though, to assure everyone that the NT always strives to work to the highest standards of care and safety for our visitors and takes its responsibilities very seriously.

No one who knows the National Trust would harbour the least doubt over its sincerity in this respect. But the statement does highlight a very interesting general question about the definition of 'highest standard of care', which in turn brings up the meaning of another term which is often encountered in the safety world; namely, 'best practice'.

Often, in workplace health and safety, the impression is given that best practice is perceived as that practice which minimizes risk. In other words, the most stringent safety regime that is feasible. However, even in the workplace this position is open to challenge as readers will now know. This is because the legal requirement, in most circumstances and in the broader interests of society, is to fulfil a balancing act such that, in considering whether some safety measure should be implemented, the beneficial effect of the measure in terms of reducing risk to health and safety is weighed against its cost in terms of money, time and trouble. Were the measure in this way to provide poor return such that it was excessively costly and troublesome to implement, and did little to enhance safety or health, then it may not be deemed reasonably practicable, and if that were so would not be required by law.[1]

Nonetheless, the response of some agencies to this situation is that doing what the law requires should therefore be regarded as a minimum standard. This, indeed, appears at times to be HSE's position:

However, in practice, legislative compliance should be regarded as the minimum acceptable standard. (HSE, 2009: 10)

While the presence of the word 'acceptable' in this sentence opens the door for debate as to what exactly is being said, a plausible implication of this statement in the minds of readers would be to legitimize the implementation of measures which go beyond reasonableness, *as defined by the courts*, and also beyond what the man on the Clapham omnibus, the archetypal reasonable man, would himself recommend. It should be recognized that, were this inference taken, the reasonable man would find himself reclassified as lacking in reason! This, it has to be said, would amount to a departure from the centuries-old practices of rational decision making in Britain. The counter-argument to the demand to do more than is reasonable is simply that all of these measures have, ultimately, to be paid for by society, whether they are implemented in the private or the public sector. Therefore, the aim should be to allocate resources with due wisdom, and not in the quest for some private goal.

Returning to the expression, 'the highest standards of care ...', and thinking specifically once more about public space and public activities, how should this be interpreted? It would seem, bearing in mind that public space provision is about providing public benefits, that the highest standard of care could be described as that which:

sets the appropriate balance between benefit and risk, and is neither that strategy which promotes benefit and ignores risk, nor that which minimizes risk at the expense of benefits.

The truth of this should be clear the moment it is acknowledged that just one of the benefits of public space and activities is to promote health and well-being, though these are far from the only benefits and are not always the most important.

Alternative paradigms

The American physicist, Thomas Kuhn, contributed significantly to the understanding of how science progressed. This was not, as might at one time have been supposed, by gradual eking out of progress, but rather by momentous leaps in which previous ways of thinking were overturned and replaced with new ones which had earlier been either unthought of, or thought to have been wrong – hence the term 'paradigm shift'. Kuhn also observed that scientists, even, were prone to infiltrating their own subjective views into their work, and for that reason science could not be labelled as fully objective. The recent furore over 'Climategate' is one case in point, whereby scientific objectivity has come under the spotlight.

The corollary to this is that even if scientists with all their supposed objectivity are biased, then risk assessors may also be associated with paradigms which are rooted in their own subjective views. This is by no means to imply that scientists and risk assessors are blind or bigoted. Everyone is prone to blindness to arguments that others see as self-evident and important. The way to fight this, as Seedhouse would say, is to be aware of one's own prejudices and make sure that they are ones which can be supported by reason, and if at some point that reason fails, to abandon them in favour of a more realistic perspective. Holding some prejudice is not in itself bad – in fact, you need it to decide about anything – but always subject to the proviso that it is *reasoned* prejudice and not *blinkered* prejudice (Seedhouse, 2004).

In cases where the removal of blinkers proves difficult, Howard Margolis has described an interesting approach for understanding environmental conflicts; for example, over the need to control cigarette smoking in public places or the siting of wind farms (Margolis, 1996). The approach can be adapted to analyse the rift within the world of public safety over the risk-minimization versus risk-benefit approaches. Rifts arise, in his terminology, because different persons occupy 'polarized' states. It could be said, for instance, that those who seek to minimize risk would subscribe to the adage 'better safe than sorry', and no doubt this expression is sometimes deployed. On the other hand, unless a safety measure averts some meaningful risk, most people would not logically want to incur the cost or the inconvenience, and it could be said that their position is consistent with a different adage 'waste not, want not'.

Figure 11.1 sets these propositions into a new kind of 2×2 matrix, which is quite different from those described for risk assessment purposes in chapter 2.

	Opportunity cost of safety measure	
	Recognized	Not recognized
Recognized **Danger**	Fungibility 1	'Better safe than sorry' 2
Not recognized	'Waste not, want not' 3	Indifference 4

Figure 11.1 *Recognition, or not, of risks and benefits.*
Adapted from Margolis (1996)

The vertical axis here is about the danger associated with some hazard and not whether it is large or small, but whether it is *getting attention* from the person considering it. On the horizontal axis is the opportunity cost of the safety measure, and whether this is *getting attention or not*. Opportunity cost here includes two kinds of consideration. These are the actual monetary costs of the safety measure, plus any time spent or inconvenience associated with it, *and* any negative impact of the safety measure on the benefits of the public place or activity.

Now for different people there are four possible combinations into which they can slot, depending on whether these two dimensions of the issue are a focus of attention or not. In the bottom right cell (number 4), neither the costs of some new safety precaution nor the danger of not taking the precaution is prominent in that person's mind. The person is basically indifferent to the issue. This is not an unusual situation for anyone to be in. If you are happy with the status quo regarding some issue, or if it has no implications for you because it is, say, far away, then this is the cell in which you would find yourself. In contrast, any person in cell 1 is fully aware of both issues – the opportunity costs of control (including the effect of the control on the benefits of the place) and the dangers posed by the risk if not controlled. Because this person is aware of both dimensions of the situation, it is a situation characterized by *fungibility*, as encountered in chapter 8. That is, the person can see both sides of the equation and hence is aware of the need for some kind of trade-off which weighs up the advantages of caution against its disadvantages.

For the other two cells (2 and 3), one but not both of these factors is recognized. Cell 2 is occupied by those bent on minimizing risk, irrespective of any other consideration – 'better safe than sorry', regardless of cost or disruption to public life. Cell 3 is for those who are indifferent to the hazard, and their intuition says that to spend time or money on it is a wasted resource, and anyway to meddle with it might damage the enjoyment of it in some way. For example, for some people the attempt to block off public access to water-side locations or wild country comes into this cell. They recognize the value of beautiful and natural places, but are relatively indifferent to the normally small but finite risk to which these places give rise.

As Margolis puts it, persons with one kind of experience may find them-selves in cell 2, while others of equal intelligence and motivation may find themselves in cell 3. The view, from either side of the divide, is of someone whose judgement is perverse, narrow and untrustworthy! This is a fine recipe for conflict, and perhaps goes some way to offering an explanation for some origins of 'elf and safety over the top'.

The reality is that we are almost always in a state of fungibility where some trade-off has to be made between the costs of averting and the costs of accepting a risk; that is, there are no free lunches. But within public life, situ-ations are arising frequently where the cost of a safety precaution (here the cost referred to is primarily the impact of the intervention on the benefit of the place or activity) lies outside the professional repertoire and training of the risk assessor. As noted in chapter 7, under the heading 'safety versus health', health and safety professionals are, so far as health is concerned, primarily interested in risks to health from hazards and not benefits to health from public life, nor the other countless benefits public life brings, which can make them insensitive to these factors. This has a number of implications, one of which is how to legitimize the overlooked dimensions of decisions and thereby restore fungibility.

Restoring fungibility

Margolis has had some very interesting ideas on the restoration of fungibility. Although it is an obvious thing to want to do, it is not easy because the 'better safe than sorry' mantra makes a powerful appeal to our sense of morality, especially in the aftermath of some dreadful accident. As Margolis said:

> Consequently, a critical element for reform proposals will be whether they encourage noticing fungibility, but in a way that does not defeat itself by provoking a moral response that makes talk of efficiency seem irrelevant or perverse. To restate that important point: it will be especially hard to promote fungibil-ity if that effort is vulnerable to attack as just an attempt to rationalize why victims be allowed to suffer so that those who are not victims can prosper even more than they already do. And of course that turns on what is cognitively realistic, which is not the same as what is logical. (Margolis, 1996)

He also points out that politically sensitive agencies will be understandably hesi-tant to sign up to any agenda that could be described, by their critics, as being indifferent to suffering. In the UK context, this may be why it has taken RoSPA some time, and heart-searching, to adjust its own position, which it is now bravely doing, and why the HSE has at times apparently edged in the opposite direction as it has made its own interpretation of the political tea leaves.

Margolis' interesting proposition is that regulators of risk should be encouraged to adopt the Hippocratic oath; that is, 'do no harm'. The context in which Margolis was thinking, as noted, was that of environmental protection and public health. In terms of public activities, this could be adapted to a rule which says that if a measure is to be introduced to protect public safety, then there should be reasonable confidence that the measure would, in fact, produce a safety benefit which was not *outweighed* by unintended, detrimental consequences of the measure on, say, public health or quality of life. The point of the 'do no harm' proposition is that in a temperate way it encourages decision makers to be sensitive to both sides of an issue; in other words, to make them aware of its fungibility.

To do this is important because, aside from the possibility that measures adopted in the name of public safety from injury may introduce new risks which are greater than those being managed, they may in some way damage people's enjoyment which amounts to a form of psychological harm. It might be said, of course, that psychological harm is off the radar or otherwise not the responsibility of safety advisers, but in general this would not be true. HSE, for example, has included workplace stress within its concerns. The counter to stress is relaxation and enjoyment, which is what public places largely provide, unless, as described by Patmore (2006), you get enjoyment out of stressing yourself; so the 'do no harm' rule should require this to be considered in the balance.

Some statements by Margolis have immediate resonance in the context of public space and risk assessment. For example:

> *'Do no harm' ... seeks to build a measure, albeit only a partial measure, of fungibility deeply into the process of risk assessment and risk management in a way that appeals to everyday intuitions about fairness. (Margolis, 1996: 167)*

There are two detailed points signalled by this statement. One is that the recommended measure is only 'partial'. What this means is that it is not being proposed that a fully fledged cost-benefit analysis of the type recommended by HM Treasury for major policy decisions in its Green Book (HM Treasury, 2003)[2] should be undertaken for all issues. This would be totally impractical. In addition, some consequences might, intellectually, be too remote from the decision to seem sufficiently plausible to win the argument or might not be sufficiently proven scientifically, and hence open to uncertainty and dispute.

Secondly, the statement flags up the notion of 'do no harm', which is less easily assigned to the dustbin by proponents of 'better safe than sorry' because it has a certain appeal to common sense and fairness. This thereby gives it some stake in the high moral ground normally held by those seeking to minimize risk. In fact, it could be said that all this alternative thinking is doing is to broaden the focus of 'better safe than sorry' to consider other contributions to well-being besides injury prevention.[3]

Managing complex systems

Whether you are a company director trying to improve sales performance, or a politician trying to win an election, there are various strategies that you can adopt. From a management perspective it would be careless if not negligent to fail to measure the progress of the various initiatives which are tried. This could be done by recording sales statistics or by carrying out periodic opinion polls. The reason you have to make these observations is obvious. It is because it is not possible to predict with certainty how your initiatives will pan out. They might be successful, or they might fail. Almost certainly they will not quite hit the hoped-for target and some adjustments to strategy will be required. You have essentially to 'trim the sails'. The reason that accurate predictions cannot be made in advance, even in the age of computers, is that the systems being dealt with are unpredictable and volatile because of their complexity.

It has been argued throughout this book that the provision of public space and activities is also a complex system. This is because it involves people, with all their vagaries, and their interaction with objects and activities, and the environment, built or natural. In these settings a few things can be confidently predicted to work in a certain way, but many cannot. The way to deal with this, as with the director and his sales records, or the politician and his opinion polls, is to monitor the situation.

HM Treasury (2003), in its Green Book, gives guidance on appraisal and evaluation of policies, programmes and projects, and has proposed use of the ROAMEF cycle (see Figure 11.2 for an explanation of the acronym) for this purpose. Although most individual public safety issues are fairly small beer and do not warrant the full treatment of the kind set out in the Green Book, nonetheless the ideas involved are notionally valid even for small-scale activities. There is nothing radical about these ideas, which are common sense and can be found in similar form in countless management texts.

Basically, your starting point is to have a rationale, or policy position, a point already emphasized in this book. This is essential, for without it you have nothing to which to anchor your objectives or subsequent actions. The

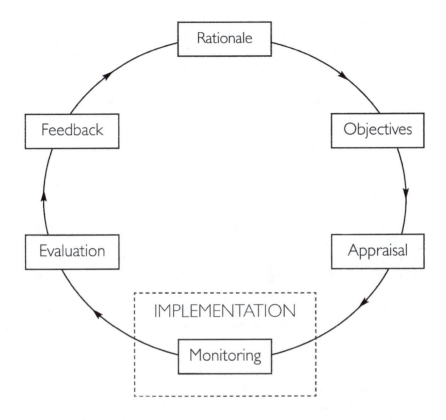

Source: Crown Copyright, HM Treasury (2003)

Figure 11.2 *The ROAMEF management cycle*

HSE, in HSG65 and subsequent publications, is rightly dynamic about the need for unambiguous policy statements which set a clear direction for an organization to follow, as is the new International Standard on risk management (ISO, 2009). Even so, it is not uncommon for some health and safety proponents to operate in an alleged policy vacuum, and even to deny that health and safety is in any way impacted by policy. This is entirely wrong, unless you are deluding yourself that the goal is risk minimization irrespective of all else, which is in fact a policy position in its own right.

The HM Treasury approach has been adapted for public life, in the context of children's and young people's play, in the publication by the DCSF, DCMS and Play England (2008a) on the design of play space. What adults do in public space is analogous to play and the same model can be applied there too. The adoption and adaptation of the Treasury model was deemed essential, firstly, to dispel the falsehood that successful play spaces are simply ordered from a catalogue, put in the ground, and left for no more than occasional maintenance and inspection.

As the guide says, designing for play is an ongoing process, requiring careful thought and planning against a policy background, followed by continued care and maintenance, and periodic review, to ensure that you are providing the best possible play opportunities for children and young people.

A second important message to glean from the ROAMEF cycle is the essential need for monitoring as an aid to evaluation. In practice, that would mean finding out how well the space or activity is doing in providing whatever benefits you were seeking, and additionally to see how it is performing with regard to safety. Given you are dealing with a complex system, monitoring will be the most reliable guide to its actual performance. Something that appears dangerous from a factory-style risk-assessment perspective may in fact not be dangerous at all, whereas something that appears innocuous might lead to accidents.

As Professor John Adams has said, people compensate for things that look dangerous by adjusting their behaviour, whereas things that appear benign may lull them into a false sense of security (Adams, 1995). These behaviours, which differentiate human beings from robots, make it very difficult to forecast how a measure aimed at injury prevention will work out. And as Professor Kip Viscusi (Viscusi, 1992) has said in relation to product safety regulations, which are not that dissimilar from engineering solutions to the safety of public space, their effect:

> ... depends not only on the engineering standards mandated ... but also on the interaction of product characteristics with consumers' precautionary behaviour ... The net effect of these influences may be counterproductive. (Viscusi, 1992: 224)

Source: Crown Copyright, Play England (2008a)

Figure 11.3 *The 'Design for play' play space design cycle (Stage 1, prepare; Stage 2, design; Stage 3, construct; Stage 4, use; Stage 5, maintain; Stage 6, review)*

Now it might be argued that to apply anything approaching the ROAMEF cycle to public space will require more and not less resources because we are no longer talking of, to put it crudely, an 'install and forget' philosophy, but one which involves provision of ongoing checks and balances. There are several responses to this position:

- If you want to get the best out of public space and activities then you must do this.
- If you are genuinely concerned about public safety, however you define that, you must do it.
- There are other positive benefits of various kinds to be accrued.

The other benefits are, firstly, that you are both in practice and visibly more in control of what you are doing. Secondly, a positive and proactive management regime allows you to experiment with new ideas. Thirdly, you are likely to have a better defence when, from time to time, things go wrong, as they always will when you get involved with complex systems. This is because, in following the new protocol, you have shed the mythical quest for total safety and replaced it with a more realistic proposition which acknowledges that accidents are inevitable from time to time, and that you are doing your best to control them while recognizing that public life must go on.

Expertise and competence – local and external

The introduction of risk-benefit assessment, and the acknowledgement of the complexity of decision making in relation to public space, has implications for the kind of expertise needed for judgements over what is provided and sanctioned, and who is competent.

As noted, inter alia, by Lord Young (HM Government, 2010: 15), it has been the pattern in recent years for agencies providing public services to contract out some of their risk assessments to external organizations. In reality, this has always been problematic because external agents often have their own ideas and biases.[4] Their interest may be more to do with warding off liability, what Michael Power would term 'secondary risk management', rather than managing safety. Or, for instance, they may belong to single interest groups whose aims are, by definition, narrow. Potentially, any external group that enters into your decision process is likely to bring its own culture and philosophy. This may be acceptable if its position is either consistent with your own policy position and objectives, or if it is able to recognize that policy position, when presented with it, and conduct its review against those policy objectives. Failure to do this will simply lead to confusion, even subversion of the host organization's policy position, if these differences are not clearly identified and addressed.

However, the advent of risk-benefit assessment throws up other issues. In order to make judgements about the balance of risks and benefits in some setting, it is obvious that you need to know about both risks *and* benefits. It is probably the case, though, that many risk assessors have no particular knowledge of benefits, including those to health. It is not normally part of their training. Collins and Evans (2007), in their study of types of expertise, describe the lowest rung of the ladder as 'beer-mat knowledge'. Beer-mat knowledge is just what it says; namely, the amount of knowledge you pick up about, say, global warming by reading the information supplied on the back of beer mats in public houses. This level of knowledge might make some people feel informed, but it cannot enable people to make a sensible contribution to debates about the nature and consequences of such a complex problem. Regrettably, experience has shown that beer-mat knowledge aptly describes the state of knowledge of some risk assessors when it comes to the benefits of public activities, although others aspire to higher levels such as 'popular understanding', 'primary source knowledge', and in some cases to the highest level of 'contributory expertise' when they are actually immersed in that kind of work. The HSE, for example, has been entirely open and straightforward about its position regarding the benefits of large-scale industrial, major hazard sites, which also need to be subject to risk-benefit assessment prior to approval. Its position is that the final decision on the benefit-risk balance, and hence whether the activity should be sanctioned, has to be made by the local or regional planning authority. This is because, while HSE has immense expertise at assessing risk, the benefits dimension is outside its normal area of expertise.

The second issue is complexity. The only way of dealing with systems which are unfathomable at the outset is to try them and see what happens – to experiment. Not, to paraphrase Nassim Taleb, 'to fool ourselves with simple stories that cater to our thirst for easy explanations'. Rather, the solution to this fallacy is 'experimentation over storytelling' (Taleb, 2007). Thus, Hans Monderman, the Dutch road traffic engineer who introduced the concept of shared space, had to experiment in order to find out what would happen to road traffic accident rates in real communities if the engineering paraphernalia were replaced with more ambiguous settings. Healthcare agencies also have to conduct drug trials, even after they have exhausted all other means of testing. And in the context of children's play, the quest for more exciting play will also require experimentation.

Given this, the only responsible position to adopt is to monitor carefully the effect of these interventions, as in the ROAMEF cycle, and be ready to intervene. As the HSE has said in its advice to external providers of health and safety assistance:

> **Finally** ... Follow up, if possible! It is helpful to see whether your advice has been understood, that any problems with implementation are overcome and the impact you and the employer intended has been achieved.[5] (HSE, 2007c)

The problem this throws up for external assessors is that they may typically only be on location for a few days at most. How, therefore, can they assess the effect of an intervention? It is clearly not possible to do it on this timescale in most circumstances.[6] This suggests that either they need to make return visits, or that local people should take on this responsibility. The use of local expertise is in fact preferred by the HSW Act, which established 'the simple yet enduring principle that those who create risk are best placed to manage it' (HSE, 2009: 4), and the logic of this is clear to see. From the legal perspective, too, it is the duty holder (the provider) who is liable should something be judged to have been inadequately done, and not a third-party external assessor.

It would seem, in most cases at the public sector level, that the people who have the real expertise to weigh the risks and benefits of service provision are the local, front-line professionals. In recent years, during an era which some see as one in which such front-line expertise has been less trusted and more emphasis has been placed upon checks, auditing, use of external inspections and the like, this position has been eroded. But there are signs of a growing unhappiness with this position from some sectors of society, including the judiciary, politicians, social commentators in the media and academics (Power, 1994). The failure to bring down injury rates is another factor.

The HSE's own definition of competence is as follows:

- relevant knowledge, skills and experience;
- the ability to apply these appropriately, while recognising the limits of your competence; and
- the necessary training (HSE, 2007b).

As the HSE has also observed, the Management of Health and Safety at Work Regulations do not spell out how to achieve competence, nor do they require particular qualifications. Its view appears to have been that competence is a goal, not something to be benchmarked by, say, the requirement of particular qualifications.

The HSE goes on to say that employers are more likely to turn to external providers in the case of more complex situations, where a higher level of competence, involving a greater depth of understanding of the issues and an ability to judge and solve problems from first principles, is required (HSE, 2007b). How this should be interpreted in the context of providers of public space and activities is to some extent open to question. It is probably not the case that the kind of 'complexity' referred to by the HSE here is the same kind as that discussed in this book as characterizing public space. The former is more to do with the type of hazards found on an industrial plant (flammable chemicals, heavy machinery involving sophisticated control systems etc.), whereas the latter is about complexity attributable to human interactions with more familiar hazards and the changing environment.

Summary

To restore a sense of balance to decision making on safety from injury, it is suggested that careful attention is warranted to the meaning of widely used expressions such as 'best practice' and 'highest standard of care'. In an environment where there is just one priority, the meaning of these terms is fairly obvious, but it is less so in most real-life situations, including the provision of public space, where multiple objectives are sought.

Thought also needs to be given to the position, sometimes encountered, that the standard set by the courts should be seen as a minimum standard, with the implication that, preferably, something more stringent should necessarily be sought. This may be wrong in situations where a balance has to be made between competing objectives, say, safety from injury versus public health and liberty. In that case, it can be argued, the optimum position is that which would be chosen as reasonable by the courts, or the proverbial reasonable man, and not something which deviates one way or the other from that.[7]

On reflection, it is obvious that different people have different perspectives on issues, and some of this is down to prejudice. Prejudice, per se, is not necessarily bad – you need some prejudice to make any decision. What should be avoided, however, is blinkered prejudice. All prejudice should be reasoned and capable of change in the light of fresh evidence.

Howard Margolis' work on environmental conflicts has highlighted how the failure to recognize all the key elements in a decision can give rise to disagreement and sub-optimal decision making. His proposition is that most decisions involve trade-offs and that these are characterized by what he calls 'fungibility'. However, those seeking a pristine environment, or, by extrapolation, total safety, can wield rhetorical statements such as 'better safe than sorry' to considerable advantage. Because of their ethical appeal, such statements are hard to contest. Margolis suggests that a plausible counter is to seek to 'do no harm'. This too has ethical appeal, and simultaneously opens the door to the consideration of more than one dimension. It restores an element of fungibility.

To manage public space is to manage a complex system. Complex systems are not fully predictable. This requires managers to: a) have clear policy objectives; b) monitor the effects of changes made; and c) trim the sails accordingly.

The issue of expertise and competence is impacted by the use of risk-benefit assessment. Obviously, to do RBA, you need to know about both risks and benefits. It may be that current-day risk assessors are not sufficiently knowledgeable about benefits, or may not even have thought about them. There is a case for greater use of local, in-house professionals in the assessment of public risks, as opposed to externals. Local people have local knowledge, will be 'immersed' in local life, are more likely to be aware of policy objectives and will be around to observe the impact of decisions they make, all of which are essential when dealing with complex systems.

12
Final Thoughts and Résumé

Why did public safety become a contested issue?

Various explanations have been advanced to account for the situation in the UK where the public safety issue is most apparent. Some have proposed that the UK's problem with public health and safety originated in continental Europe and in particular European law, and that without that intrusion the situation would not have developed as it has.[1] There are some arguments in favour of this: the timing is about right. European Council Directive 89/391/EEC on workplace safety was passed in 1989. As described in chapter 8, this directive is not couched in terms of reasonable practicability, but more in terms of avoiding risks if at all possible, or otherwise combating them without reservation. This angle was soon taken up in UK regulations such as the 1992 version of the Management of Health and Safety at Work Regulations, and important advisory documents such as the HSE's *Successful Health and Safety Management* (HSE, 1997), which was first published in 1991.

However, as noted earlier, EC Directive 89/391/EEC is *not* aimed at risks to the public. It talks exclusively about risks to workers at work. Furthermore, it obviously applies to all Member States of the European Union, yet the problems being experienced in the UK over public safety are not, by and large, observed in other Member States to the same degree, though they are present. So what might be the explanation? One possibility is that the EC Directive's workplace risk philosophy is leaking through into public life in the UK via Section 3 of the HSW Act, which, as described in chapter 5, says as follows:

> It shall be the duty of every employer to conduct his undertaking in such a way as to ensure, so far as is reasonably practicable, that persons not in his employment who may be affected thereby are not thereby exposed to risks to their health or safety.

Although, unlike the EC Directive, this paragraph does invoke the qualification of 'reasonable practicability', the more important issue here is that public safety gets drawn into the same net as workplace safety, just as noted by the HSE in *Thirty years on and looking forward* (HSE, 2004a).

Thus, Section 3 provides a channel for workplace ideologies and approaches to safety to invade public life. This leakage would be conveyed by risk assessors and health and safety personnel, who carry the workplace approach with them into public life. This is a plausible route – most health and safety training starts in the workplace and propagates from there. Thus, the seemingly shifting emphasis in the workplace from doing what is reasonably practicable, as in the HSW Act, to the Directive's comparatively unqualified risk minimization formula has a route, in the UK, for impacting upon public life. To this effect, we note, and are in agreement with, the TUC's evidence to Lord Young's 2010 inquiry into the management of public safety:

> The TUC does believe that there is a case for looking at the issue of public safety. The wide-ranging coverage of Section 3 of the HSWA, which applies to the duties of employers to persons other than their employees, is problematic. While it is quite right that employers should owe a duty to the public from their activities, this section has led to some confusion as to the role of the HSE/C in issues of public safety. This is particularly the case in respect of areas where the risk is secondary to the work-relatedness of the activity, such as hospital-acquired infections, deaths in residential homes etc. We believe that public safety issues and public health issues are important, but, unless they relate primarily to the process of work, should be dealt with separately from work-related health and safety matters. (TUC, 2010)

In accord with this, and as we said in chapter 6:

> The way (Section 3 of the HSW Act) is interpreted is that this applies not just when workers are present, for example, cutting the grass or doing maintenance, but even when people are visiting the space and no work is being carried out. Little Suzie, playing in the sandpit in the local authority-owned public playground, is thereby covered by the HSW Act.

Notwithstanding this, we have grave doubts that the authors of the Act ever intended it to be used for such purposes.

The psychology of risk assessment

In chapter 1 we referred to many other potential causes or partial causes of the public safety dilemma in the UK. These included things like some health and safety professionals lacking qualifications or experience; the so-called 'ignorant' public; exaggerated media stories; the 'litigation society'; the behaviours of insurers; self-protectionism by some agencies; 'soft-hearted' courts that favour the claimant's perspective; and 'unaccountable' advisory and regulatory agencies. We said that it is probably true that all of these things have at times contributed in varying extent to the situation which now exists. In passing, however, one factor to which we would also draw attention is the issue of the psychology or 'world view', which we suspect tends to go along with the business of safety management and risk assessment.

Research by American psychologist Paul Slovic and his colleagues has found that different sub-groups of the population have different attitudes to risk and how it should be managed. In particular, their research found that there is a sub-population of white males (as opposed to black males and females in general) who have views about risk, and how it is managed, which are different from that of the rest of the population (Flynn et al, 1994; Slovic, 2000; Rivers et al, 2010). This phenomenon has come to be known as the 'white male effect' (WME). The interesting feature of the WME in relation to public safety is that members of this category 'can be characterised by trust in institutions and authorities and by anti-egalitarian attitudes, including a disinclination toward giving decision-making power to citizens in areas of risk management' (Slovic, 2000: 401). Rivers and colleagues go on to describe this group as 'males who place a high degree of trust in experts and authority figures, who possess an above average level of education, and identify with a conservative political orientation ...'. They also point to the consequences of this as follows: '... its implications are quite clear in that many of those males responsible for making risk management decisions on behalf of society were also members of that group' (Rivers et al, 2010: 76).

The hint is that by some mechanism or other, there is a tendency for the profession of risk management, and presumably thereby those who engage in public safety, to be of a particular world view, one which by its nature has a predilection for external control over personal control and personal responsibility. This possibility is consistent with the work of philosopher David Seedhouse as described in chapter 5; namely that people – that is, all of us – tend to approach a problem from a pre-selected personal perspective such that:

> a preconceived notion + a bit of evidence = a decision about what
> to do

The business of world views or attitudes might also come to bear in the general approach taken by Britain to European Directives, such as 89/391/EEC. There is a view that in Britain when a European Directive is passed, Britain will implement it to the letter, whereas other European Member States will be more flexible in their interpretation.[2] Lord Young implied as much during his recent investigation of health and safety rules, as reported in The *Telegraph* (2010):

> *He also wants to stop Whitehall officials from 'gold plating' or over-interpreting European Union rules, adding to the burden of red tape on small firms and charities.*

Not everyone accepts that this tendency exists in Britain. The Trades Union Congress, in its submission to Lord Young's inquiry, has said that it is a misperception that the UK behaves in this way (TUC, 2010). The truth, we suspect, is intricate and may vary from situation to situation.

Too much of anything, not excluding 'health and safety', is harmful

In public life, 'health and safety' is mainly about safety from injury and less, if at all, about the health of people. Strategies that focus on injury reduction (or any other single commodity) may initially be beneficial, but if pursued too far will have unintended consequences ranging from disproportionate cost to reduced health or loss of amenity. They may also damage the environment. That this is so is a direct result of one of the most famous laws of economics – the law of diminishing returns (e.g. Ferguson, 2002).

All of these effects are consequential for public health. This can happen at the local or regional level, as well as at the macro level through wider misallocation of society's resources. Numerous examples of local level penalties of safety interventions have been listed in chapter 1, with consequences ranging from comic to tragic. The regional scale manifestation was summed up in chapter 5 by reference to Suffolk County Council's chief executive, who observed that:

> *Our structures have responded to new central government requirements, an ever-growing regulatory culture and ring-fenced funding opportunities. We have an overly complex organisation. Inspection, performance management and audit have begun to dominate the local government culture to such an extent that our council is more focused on the regulator than the consumer. (The Times, 2010: 16)*

And at the societal level there has long been recognition that resources spent on one thing cannot be spent on another, and that to spend beyond the point where marginal gains exceed marginal costs is counterproductive[3] (e.g. Aaron Wildavsky on environmentalism (1997) and Rune Elvik's case study of Vision Zero for road traffic accidents (1999)). This indeed lies behind the concept of reasonable practicability (or just reasonableness as in common law), and the interest in placing a monetary value on a human life or in the use of QALYs for health service decision making, as described in chapter 3. The aim is to provide some means of judging what expenditures are reasonable in each sector, so that no sector loses out, and other sectors are not impoverished or disadvantaged by the demands of one.

The recent paper by David Stuckler and colleagues (2010) in the *British Medical Journal* provides further important evidence of the societal level impact of resource allocation, in terms of the relationship between public health and social welfare spending. The clear inverse relationship they found between social spending per capita and mortality rates – the greater the spending on social welfare the lower the mortality rate – is very suggestive. The implication is that if these budgets are cut, then there will be measurable health consequences – people will die younger. The same is true if expenditure on regulation, of which dealing with safety from injury is a part, becomes inefficient and thereby excessive, and at the expense of public health more widely.

Treating the whole patient

In their book on protecting health and the environment, John Graham and Jonathan Wiener (1995) observe that risk trade-offs – that is, the inadvertent substitution of one risk for another[4] – are pervasive and fundamental problems of decision making in almost every circumstance, from the care of individual hospital patients to the preservation of the entire planet. This they ascribe to systematic shortcomings in the ways decisions are made, due to an overly narrow focus by decision makers.

The way out of this dilemma is, they say, to adopt a more holistic paradigm, which seeks to 'treat the whole patient' rather than some fragment of it. Indeed, they point out how, as with risk-benefit assessment, this is nothing new at all, already being practised in fields as diverse as Gestalt psychology, ecology and international relations.

Achieving this, however, is not easy. Stuckler and colleagues (2010), like Graham and Wiener, warn of 'pervasive silo mentalities' which impede holistic practices. This, they note, can lead to such dire consequences as 'the high profile deaths of young children at the hands of their carers where problems were missed because of poor communication between several agencies'. In the present era of spending cuts, they warn that these could accentuate the problem by encouraging individual organizations to behave opportunistically and focus on 'the narrow targets they can use most easily to justify their existence'.

Graham and Wiener identify several reasons for these failures to act in the best interests of society, a number of which have resonance in the current discussion on public safety. These include what they call 'omitted voices'. This refers to the absence of affected parties from key decision processes, such that organized interests have disproportionate sway, as is thought to have happened in the case of children and young persons' play provision during the final decades of the last century, during which play value lost out to a quest for risk minimization. Only in the last decade has this trend showed signs of reversing, having required great efforts from the Play Safety Forum and Britain's national play agencies, and other concerned parties. That this has proved so difficult should be of no surprise, as it is costly and time-consuming for private parties to make themselves heard in arenas dominated by powerful commercial interests, as exemplified by Jerome Mayhew's account of his own experience of dealing with standards setters (chapter 7).

A second source of systematic shortcomings in decision making, according to Graham and Wiener, is what they call 'heuristics'. These manifest themselves in several ways. One is via our common tendency, when confronted with a complex problem (as public safety arguably is), to attempt to disaggregate and simplify it, addressing each category as if it were unconnected with others, when the truth more likely is that all things are in some way interconnected. In a similar vein, Nicholas Taleb (2008), author of *The Black Swan*, referred to the 'narrative fallacy'.[5] By this he meant our love of summarizing and simplifying complex phenomena in order to present them as supposedly logical sequences, but which in reality give only an impression of understanding. Another heuristic mechanism operates through fixation upon a dramatic event, such as a terror attack, or a particular symptom, such as accidental injury to the exclusion of public health.

A third cause is termed 'bounded oversight', which Graham and Wiener described as rampant and pathological in the executive branch of their (US) government. The issue here is that the proliferation of regulatory bodies, each with its own mission, tends to foster competition to tackle one's own target risk to the neglect of side effects which this might have. This is obviously relevant in the context of public space and activities if one agency's mission is to reduce risk, and another's is to provide services.

How can these problems be tackled? Suggested remedies include requiring agencies to reduce *overall* risk of harm rather than to allow themselves to become preoccupied with a single problem in isolation. Stuckler and colleagues (2010) provide examples of schemes in England trying to do just this – the Total Place programme – whereby agencies, including local government, primary care trusts, police and fire authorities and others, join forces to work across institutional boundaries. Another measure is to screen proposed safety interventions for unintended consequences, as also recommended by the House of Commons RRC. In this regard, risk-benefit assessment, as advocated in chapter 10, could be used to further this purpose.

Reclaiming the high moral ground

There are obvious difficulties involved in adopting policies counter to those of agencies whose avowed aim is to eliminate some evil. Elimination of evils is generally seen to be a good thing and morally desirable, and accounts for the occasional, usually temporary, flirtation of public and some private bodies with 'zero tolerance' or risk minimization policies. Therefore, to suggest otherwise, might place you on seemingly weak ground in the eyes of some commentators. With regard to injuries to the public, to go against the advice of agencies seeking to prevent accidents can easily be portrayed as callous if not negligent. In this respect, the thinking of Howard Margolis is helpful.

As recounted in chapter 11, Margolis proposed that some measure of 'fungibility' (a restoration of balanced decision making which recognizes both the dangers *and* opportunities of, for example, public space) might be restored without prompting a moral backlash by incorporating a sense of 'do no harm' into risk-assessment and risk-management decision making. 'Do no harm' approaches, as opposed to those anchored in 'injury prevention', would necessarily require the weighing of the costs and benefits of public space provision, including their social, psychological and physical health benefits, which have so often of late been given inadequate attention or even disregarded altogether.

The advantage here of 'do no harm' is that it has its own ethical roots which can be traced back, if one wished, as far as ancient Greece and likely further, and that it is a widely quoted and respected position, being one of the most esteemed ethical principles in the field of medicine. 'Do no harm' requires the physician to think about both the benefits and the harms associated with a medical intervention. It also accords with Graham and Wiener's concern for 'treating the whole patient', and Stuckler and colleagues' support for reducing the overall risk of harm rather than one aspect of harm in isolation, all of which positions are eminently sensible and rational in a holistic sense. The application of this thinking to public space and activities would clearly require benefits as well as risks to be considered, providing for potentially better decisions.

Questions about risk assessment

In chapter 2 an examination of the types of risk assessment commonly used in the public sphere did not find these to be either simple or unproblematic. Frequent failure to adequately define terms was just one precursor to problems and is symptomatic of the fundamental subjectivity of most assessments, which are, as research in psychology and decision making has shown, subject to numerous biases. As Cox said (of risk matrices): 'these do not necessarily support good (e.g. better-than-random) risk management decisions' (Cox, 2008). The problems do not stop there. The conflation of technical risk assessments with value judgements, which should properly be a part of risk management and policy, further renders many of these procedures suspect. As we pointed out earlier, Deirdre Hutton, Chair of the UK Food Standards Agency, has rightly said of the latter problem:

> *Essentially: risk assessment belongs to science but does not give the answer as to the 'right' level of risk – that judgement belongs to society and involves trade-offs between risk and benefit ...* (Hutton, 2009)

Overall, these matters should generate a cascade of questions about the conduct, validity and utility of these assessments. We are by no means the first to point this out. Apart from the recent, and some would say, long overdue technical inquiries by Cox (2007, 2008) into some risk assessment practices, reported in chapter 2, social scientists have been stressing the subjectivity of the assessment of these kinds of risks for decades (Douglas and Wildavsky, 1983; Schwartz and Thompson, 1990; Adams, 1995; Adams and Thompson, 2002), so prompting deep inquiry by national and international agencies (Royal Society, 1992; NRC, 2003; IRGC, 2005), though it would appear that the resulting messages are failing to get through or are being ignored.

Recently, in a review of the status of risk assessment for environmental protection purposes, Eileen Abt and colleagues (2010) expressed their position succinctly as follows:

> *... that risk assessment be viewed as a method for evaluating the relative merits of various options for managing risk, that is, as a means to an end, rather than an end in itself.*

They also warned, as might we in the context of public space though subject to other reservations, that:

> *... much work is needed to improve the scientific status, utility, and public credibility of risk assessment.*

In addition, and at the heart of public sector safety decision making, we also observe that despite all the issues around risk assessment, this does not deter many of its followers from proposing 'solutions' or 'fixes'. Yet, as we reported in chapter 5, the historical position is that we lack knowledge of solutions to public safety that actually work. In a recent update of this, in November 2010, NICE decided not to publish guidance on preventing unintentional injuries among under-15s during outdoor play and leisure, as it had earlier set out to do. The reason given was:

> ... a lack of effectiveness evidence, the low numbers of serious injuries and deaths during outdoor play and leisure, and concerns that standalone guidance might encourage unwarranted risk aversion (with negative consequences for physical activity and play). (NICE, 2010)

On what basis, therefore, do the many recommendations for improving public safety actually rest? If, as NICE and others have said, evidence is lacking, one can only surmise that decisions are being made on the basis of the preconceived notions of the assessors themselves, which is Seedhouse's version of how decisions are made (chapter 5). One is left to contemplate, therefore, what might be the actual role being played by risk assessment? Is it really to identify priorities as is normally supposed, or is it to give legitimacy and a quasi-justification for choices separately made?

Taken together, these issues imply that the subjective style of risk assessment, as used in public sector decision making, is overrated and over-sold. The kinds of decisions which public officials have continuously to make about the care and safety of the public are predicated upon too many considerations ever to fit into the simplistic risk assessment schemas in widespread circulation. As Collins and Evans might aver, the thought processes are too complex to put on paper – a position which chimes with AALA's propositions about the need for autonomy of outdoor adventure leaders and the relegation of risk assessment from its current pinnacle to a more mundane checklist status (chapter 8).

Risk assessment is, in any event, a tool to *help* decision makers decide – it does not generate answers of itself. Decision makers obviously need to be aware of its limitations which might be procedural (e.g. commonly used risk matrices are incapable of capturing the complexity of public safety decision making), technical, or which might equally be related to the process of deciding what to do in the light of a given assessment. This process, of weighing risks and deciding what to do, or of comparing risks with benefits of some place, requires social and ethical as well as technical contributions. This, presumably, is what led Professor Hood and colleagues to sum up in this way:

> What are needed are public statements of how assessors reasoned about the issues, to avoid the impression of ad hoc political judgements masquerading as technocratic expertise. (Hood, Rothstein and Baldwin, 2001)

This statement, seemingly, supports the view expressed in this book (and *Managing Risk in Play Provision*) that what are needed are justifications, in narrative form, of public sector decisions, for the simple reason that such decisions could not be recorded in another way.

Of fundamental importance, if the benefits of public space and activities are to be put back on the agenda, is a supplementary need for clear, fit-for-purpose, policy statements, against which risk-benefit assessments can be conducted. There has been a tendency for such statements in recent years to be polished and given the PR-treatment, but this can generate a missed opportunity if the meaningfulness and precision of the message is lost. As it says in HSG65 (HSE, 1997), having a guiding policy is an essential, maybe even the first, component of a management system. Yet many assessments appear to be conducted against only vaguely discerned policy objectives, many of which policies are weak on the benefits of service provision if these are mentioned at all.

It is also self-evident, as HSE has recognized in the context of the major hazard industries but which is true elsewhere, that risk-benefit assessment also requires knowledge not just of risks but also of benefits. Most risk assessors, as currently trained, have no particular knowledge of benefits, which may in part explain why benefits tend to be sidelined. The problem is of the same nature as one identified by Graham and Wiener (1995), regarding the proliferation of specialists in the American medical service and the dearth of generalists. What is needed in healthcare, and, by extrapolation, in the provision of public space and activities, is the empowerment of more holistic thinking incorporating knowledge and awareness. This should bridge the divide between risk of harm and benefit of provision, and permit the making of reasoned, articulated judgements about the appropriate trade-off in the context of the relevant institutional policy position.

The requirement for broad, generalist knowledge also has implications for the selection of risk assessors. The HSE has always been of the view that wherever possible local or in-house expertise is preferable, and that position continues to be sound, even more so with this requirement in mind. Firstly, this is because local professional people know the local situation through 'immersion', and to some degree all local situations will be unique. Secondly, local people will be more familiar with local policy objectives. Thirdly, they will be able to monitor the effects of any steps that are taken, which, as discussed in chapter 11, is essential for proper management of systems which incorporate complexity.

Management and auditing

In chapter 9 one of the issues to come to the fore, prompted by a particular legal case, was management styles and auditing requirements. However, this issue had been around for a long time prior to that, having been picked up by research (e.g. Power, 1994, 2004 and 2009; Hood et al, 2001) and many commentators on social affairs.

At the sharp end, the effects of the administrative burden, posed by autocratic management systems on staff time, on freedom to use initiative and sheer cost, are being noted, and questions are rightly being asked about effectiveness and value for money (e.g. Suffolk County Council, as in chapter 5 and this chapter).

Power noted as long ago as 1994 that we need to start looking beyond audit since it is not a passive practice, but one which displaces trust from the front line to second-order verificatory activities. To rehabilitate trust (and arguably to improve risk management) we need, he says, the following:

> ... a broad shift in control philosophy: from long distance, low trust, quantitative, disciplinary and ex-post forms of verification by private experts to local, high trust, qualitative, enabling, real time forms of dialogue with peers. In this way we may eventually be in a position to devote more resources to creating quality rather than just policing it. (Power, 1994: 40)

There are indeed signs, if isolated, that these thoughts are beginning to be put into practice – for example, in the approach of Central Surrey Health to the empowerment of front-line professionals (chapter 8) – and the way in which the adventure activities sector continues to stand up for the importance of adventure leaders' skills and experience over managerial tendencies, which would increase paperwork and undermine authority.

Taking care with advice and standards

Statutes and regulations must obviously be obeyed, but as discussed in this book, they still need to be interpreted thoughtfully and with regard to all the relevant circumstances. Various agencies and experts have sought to put their own interpretation on these directions, but it should not be overlooked that the final arbiter in the interpretation of the written law is neither a regulator nor some expert, but the courts.

As discussed at length, a key issue in relation to public safety revolves around the issue of the recognition, in law, of the benefits of public space and activities. Under civil law it appears well established that the courts, in deciding whether reasonable measures have been taken by a responsible person to protect the public, are likely to consider, inter alia, the effect of control measures upon the benefits or social utility of the place or activity. So far as the HSW Act is concerned, the situation is less clear. The role of social utility in determining what measures are reasonably practicable still retains an air of uncharted territory. Different views exist and these may well be evolving gradually with time. The courts will determine the outcome, and no doubt their decision will reflect to some extent public opinion:

> Judges interpret the legislative and common law principles and hence determine the level of risk which should or should not have been taken in given cases, thereby setting common law precedents. They are not however detached from the reactions

> *of the wider public, nor would they wish to be, since accept-*
> *ability of risk is intrinsically a socioeconomic-political issue.*
> *(Ball, Maggs and Barrett, 2009)*

In addition to the primary legislation, there is also a plethora of published guidance of an advisory nature on just about everything under the sun. Some of this advice is of high quality, having been developed over a substantial period of time by recognized thinkers and notably involving key stakeholders. Examples with which we are familiar and to which we have referred in this text include *Managing Visitor Safety in the Countryside* by the VSCG (2005) and the Play Safety Forum's position statement on *Managing Risk in Play Provision* (PSF, 2002).

Not all published guidance should be accepted as necessarily helpful, however, and some of it may simply be no more than an opinion, possibly wrong, and might have been generated to support the interests of some group, or be outdated. Nor is there a guarantee that guidance is necessarily consistent with legal requirements (e.g. to do what is reasonable or reasonably practicable). Although it is often presumed that this is so, even in the case of normally respected documents such as British and European Standards, these may not be based on risk assessment. This creates a paradox because if one's duty of care is supposed to be founded upon a suitable and sufficient risk assessment, and a piece of advice has been used as a surrogate which has no such basis, where does this leave you?

As Tim Gill has said (2010):

> *Such materials should be helpful and supportive. However,*
> *guidance can only go so far, and can never deal fully with all the*
> *possible circumstances and situations that may arise on a visit*
> *or during an activity.*

Although this was written in the context of adventure activities, the parallels with public space are clear enough. Guidance generated by some remote agency may contain useful messages of a general nature, but these may not be totally applicable to local circumstances. Nor need it necessarily be consistent with your own policy agenda. Given, for example, the shifting political opinion in Britain about the need for children and young people to enjoy a more exciting and challenging outdoor life, this implies that the existing industry standards on things like play equipment might need to be revised. This, however, is likely to take some time, as the writing of such standards is now a pan-European activity.

The clear message would appear to be: be thoughtful and selective in the advice you accept. Rely preferably upon your own agency's assessment of risks and benefits if you can. If you wish to deviate from what is seen elsewhere as established practice, as Hans Monderman bravely did with his concept of shared space, document why you are doing this based substantially upon your own analysis.

What to do in the event that health and safety demands seem excessive

The problem of public safety is not going to be solved overnight, and in the event that one is the recipient of a health and safety demand which seems to go beyond the bounds of plausibility, what can one do? The answer will obviously depend on the circumstances, but one action might be to ask appropriate questions, a perfectly legitimate activity and entirely justifiable (if you are the duty holder it is your responsibility anyway to decide what to do). A sample of general issues, some of which might be relevant depending upon circumstances, is as follows:

• Does the assessment consider benefits *and* risks to the public?
• What qualifications does the originator have in respect of both benefits assessment and risk assessment?
• Are the recommendations based on a legal requirement, if so which?
• If they are based on advice or opinion, whose advice and opinion, and is it pertinent in the circumstances?
• If advice used is generated remotely, how does it contribute to local affairs?
• Has the technical justification for the risk assessment been clearly explained?
• Have uncertainties been identified and discussed?
• Are there any omissions from the assessment?
• Has thought been given to the possibility of unintended consequences?
• Does the technical assessment stray into decision making?
• If so, is the assessor qualified and authorized to make those decisions?
• Is the assessor aware of and giving recognition to the policy position of the provider?

Managing complex systems

In chapter 11 it was described how those managing public safety are, in fact, dealing with a complex system such that the success or otherwise of interventions made is unpredictable, being subject to uncertainty. The conclusion which can be drawn is that 'install and forget' strategies, as they might loosely be called, should be supplanted with strategies which monitor the performance of interventions, both in terms of their effectiveness in combating risk and in providing benefit. Although such monitoring figures as an essential ingredient in all management cycles (e.g. HMT's ROAMEF cycle as in HMT, 2003), this approach is seldom used to its full capacity, and sometimes is not used at all. For those who are genuinely interested in the proper management of risks to the public, and the provision of the public benefits of community space and activities, this situation needs to be addressed. The results of these monitoring activities should, of course, be interpreted against the backdrop of overarching policy objectives, as described here, and as stipulated in the new international standard on risk management (ISO, 2009).

Not throwing the baby out with the bathwater

As observed in chapter 1, occupational health and safety in Britain made huge advances during the 20th century and has saved many thousands of lives through reductions in accidents. Even though the true figure is hard to discern because of the parallel decline of many forms of heavy industry and the growth of mechanization, which would also have served to reduce the toll of accidents, the fundamental truth of this is not questioned. Towards the end of that century and during the early years of the new one, the pace of improvement as measured by the number of accidental workplace deaths slowed considerably, although in 2010 provisional figures show a further decline which, however, might be attributable to the recession. The number of workplace deaths as a result of occupational disease, on the other hand, has not declined as much, and some believe it is higher than ever before, prompting the TUC to say: 'Sadly we have a society that seems to see preventing injury as being more important than preventing illness' (TUC, 2010).

While the TUC is referring to workplace illness, the same could be said of public life, where, as we have argued, injury prevention has in some cases been pursued to such a degree that it is likely undermining health and welfare. There is a second threat, however, which we identified in chapter 1. That is that the entire social movement to protect people against risk of any kind could lose its momentum through being discredited. As Graham and Weiner have put it, in the US context:

> *Unless risk tradeoffs are acknowledged and addressed forth-rightly, the national campaign to reduce risk may ultimately come to be viewed as oversold, or even viewed with cynicism that forfeits its legitimacy and public support. (Graham and Wiener, 1995)*

Should this come to pass in the UK it would be a costly and unnecessary tragedy. We have eminently sensible statutes in the form of the HSW Act and the Occupiers' Liability Acts, which basically ask for that which is reasonable to be done. Nothing could be more reasonable than that. We also have a primary regulator in the Health and Safety Executive which is of undeniable world class and professionalism. The courts, too, are well aware of the importance of public life and the benefits, including health, which they bring, and have put immense effort into deliberating how unavoidable trade-offs should be made.

Sorting out what has happened and is happening seems primarily to require a more thinking approach against the backdrop of an otherwise enviable framework. It is perhaps salutary to reflect that back in the days of the Robens Committee, one of the objectives of their recommendations, and of the subsequent principled-approach of the Health and Safety at Work etc. Act, was to encourage a more thoughtful approach to health and safety. That wheel appears to be turning full circle.

Notes

Chapter 1 Clear and Foreseeable Danger

1. Such as ISO 31000:2009 on risk management and ISO/IEC 31010:2009 on risk assessment.
2. As remarked by Lord Young, the government's investigator: 'It took me five long years to qualify as a solicitor before I could practice and it takes doctors even longer. Yet, I can set up as a health and safety consultant tomorrow with no qualifications in the field' (IoSH, 2010).
3. Also referred to as the 'compensation culture', a rather vague term which somehow impugns blame, not necessarily correctly, for a supposed rash of litigation on the workings of the legal system.
4. Suggesting that health and safety education may be missing some essentials.
5. Early 'risk assessments' were etched onto clay tablets.
6. In 2001 the *British Medical Journal* proclaimed in an editorial: 'For many years safety officials and public health authorities have discouraged use of the word "accident" when it refers to injuries or the events that produce them. An accident is often understood to be unpredictable – a chance occurrence or an "act of God" – and therefore unavoidable. However, most injuries and their precipitating events are predictable and preventable. That is why the *BMJ* has decided to ban the word accident' (*BMJ*, 2001).
7. Under Section 18 of the HSW Act, the Secretary of State can make local authorities responsible for the enforcement of the Act to whatever extent is prescribed.

Chapter 2 Risk Assessment – *A Simple Tool?*

1. The Factories Act (1961) and the Offices, Shops and Railway Premises Act (1963).
2. Lord Robens' report (Robens, 1972) had implications far beyond the UK, particularly through its advocacy of *self-regulation* by duty holders (those responsible for hazards).
3. Matthew Leitch points out, for example, that the new international standard on risk management (ISO 31000:2009) defines risk as: 'Effect of uncertainty on objectives' (Leitch, 2010). This is itself a complex construct, perhaps because the ISO is trying to cover as many kinds of hazard as possible.
4. But not always. Some people use risk = (probability × consequence). For example, if the annual likelihood of a flood in your town were one in 1000 and the consequence, when it happened, was property damage of £1 million, then by this formula the risk could be described as amounting to £1000 per year. This approximates to

the approach which insurers use to set insurance premiums, and is known as the 'expected value of loss' approach.

5. A useful reference for engineering-style risk assessment is ISO/IEC (2009).

6. http://www.hse.gov.uk/research/misc/vectra300-2017-r03.pdf

7. Elsewhere, HSE has acknowledged the importance of the benefits to society of activities and the need to make trade-offs (HSE, 2001: para. 13, p8).

8. A full explanation of the meaning of this term will be given in chapter 6.

9. Strictly this only applies to risk matrices where something more tangible than 'low', 'medium' and 'high' has been used, but even where it is not it is likely the case that users are thinking along these same lines because matrices have to cover everything from the very small to the very large in a few steps.

10. Ordinal numbers are of the form first, second, third etc. Cardinal numbers are ones denoting quantity; for example, a kilogram of rice, a wind speed of 50 knots, a risk of injury of one in a thousand per year.

11. It has been surmised that the 2000 Hatfield rail crash also resulted in thousands of commuters being scared away or prevented from travelling by rail, forcing them to endure the higher risks of road travel.

12. There are also more straightforward but nonetheless serious misunderstandings. Lord Hobhouse, in the House of Lords case 'Tomlinson v. Congleton B.C. and others', noted that there was fundamental confusion over the concept of risk: 'It is a fallacy to say that because drowning is a serious matter that there is a serious risk of drowning' (House of Lords, 2003, para. 79).

13. Conventional risk assessment is here taken to be that process described in HSE's *Five steps to risk assessment* or similar.

14. In fact, what Fischhoff et al described was the more sophisticated form of risk analysis used in some industries, which deal with more serious hazards, or with major policy decisions such as whether or not to restrict flights after a volcanic eruption. This involves specialist forms of risk assessment which have names like 'event tree analysis', 'fault tree analysis', 'hazard and operability' studies (HAZOP), and so on. These risk assessments then feed into yet more highly structured forms of decision making, often involving some form of systematic cost-benefit analysis or decision analysis.

Chapter 3 Is Safety Paramount?

1. Things that are traded, or bought and sold on the market, have a 'market price', but people also value other non-traded things like peace and quiet, an ancient woodland, good health, and all the Treasury is saying here is that these should be included in the consideration of whether to go ahead or not.

2. The arguments over the cost to individuals and the economy over measures to eliminate the risk posed to aircraft by volcanic ash provides a recent example of the seriousness of this debate.

3. ATP would not have prevented the Clapham Junction disaster itself, which was attributed to defective wiring of signals and poor maintenance.

4. A less expensive system, known as the Train Protection and Warning System (TPWS) with most of the capability of ATP, was fitted to the rail system by the end of 2003.

5. Though this does come up in the often-debated case of helicopter emergency services which should be subject to the same debate as ATP.

6. For a fuller account of NICE's decision process, see Appleby, Devlin and Parkin (2007).

7. There are occasional exceptions to this requirement – see chapter 6.
8. In the nuclear industry the term ALARA (as low as reasonably achievable) is used, though with very similar meaning to ALARP.
9. It is like saying if one-quarter of a cake is worth £1 then the whole cake should be worth £4.
10. To calculate your own values of your own life (in £s), just multiply your answer to Question 1 (expressed in £s) by 100,000 and your answer to Question 2 (expressed in pence) by 120,000 (i.e. 400 × 30,000/100).
11. This figure should not be regarded as the value of someone's life (although it is often referred to as 'the value of a life' for convenience), but a figure which represents the value of small changes in risk of death. For example, the figure of £1 million corresponds to a reduction in risk of one in a hundred thousand being worth £10 to an average individual.

Chapter 4 Risk and Safety – *A National Philosophy*

1. HSE published a simplified version in 2001 with the same essential features (HSE, 2001), but the original is preferred here, having greater clarity.
2. But see later in this chapter the complication of 'gross disproportion'.
3. In 1952 the Department of Transport had set the value of preventing a fatality at about £40,000 (this value is the adjusted value to 2008 prices), based on lost earnings only which may be compared with the current value of roughly £1.5 million, which includes both lost earnings and the much larger contribution derived from WTP. The pre-WTP valuations were indeed niggardly.

Chapter 5 What Works in Public Life?

1. A similar hierarchy appears in the 'Management of health and safety at work regulations 1999', under the heading 'Principles of prevention to be applied' (HSE, 2000: para. 30). It is offered there as *guidance* on how to comply with Regulation 4 of the MHSWR.
2. A position by no means restricted to the UK. Herrington and Nicholls (2007) identify existence of a similar perspective in Canada, though it is much more widespread than that.
3. The descriptor 'engineers' is used very loosely here to encapsulate what might otherwise be described as those with a technical and/or reductionist approach to thinking. Such approaches can also be discerned, occasionally, in economics, medicine and other disciplines.
4. This is similar to 'moral hazard' in insurance dealings. When people buy insurance, they may be prone to be less careful, or so insurers suspect.
5. In the world of safety, these approaches are often referred to as 'environmental' and 'behavioural'.
6. http://www.urbannous.org.uk/udlhm1.htm
7. Lord Young reports that the UK market for health and safety support is worth over £700 million, and possibly as much as £1 billion in annual sales (HM Government, 2010: 31). This excludes the duty holders' costs of compliance and administration.
8. Regrettably the government stopped funding the leisure accident database in 2003. This saved around £1.5 million per annum, but meant that the main source of information on the overall effectiveness of public space injury prevention schemes was terminated.

9. Lord Young himself has criticized the similar tendency of insurance companies to require full health and safety risk assessments by external consultants before offering insurance cover to SMEs (HM Government, 2010: 32). These pressures come from other places too; for example, some British and European Standards.

10. http://www.whycycle.co.uk/safety_and_security/cycling_helmets/

Chapter 6 Legal Matters

1. The Occupiers' Liability Act (Scotland) 1960 in the case of Scotland.

2. In some situations the requirement may be absolute, or to do whatever is practicable, as opposed to reasonably practicable. These requirements are more demanding. Absolute requirements apply where the risk of injury is inevitable unless a precaution is taken. Practicable requirements, if required, must be carried out if they are feasible, and considerations of difficulty, inconvenience and cost are not relevant. But in most circumstances, the requirement is the lesser one – to do what is reasonably practicable.

3. 'At the time' – there is now!

4. In November 2010, at the United in Play conference in Fremantle, Australian lawyer Robert Samut identified the same four factors as being relevant under Australian civil law claims.

5. A reference to the Occupiers' Liability Act 1957.

6. The Visitor Safety in the Countryside Group provides a valuable account of legal responsibilities for countryside managers, including a list of recent court rulings (VSCG, 2005).

Chapter 7 Advice – *Whose Advice?*

1. A term used by John Graham and Jonathan Wiener (1995).

2. An issue peripheral to the main argument here, though not necessarily inconsequential, is that the burden of this extra work falls upon one party, the insured, whereas what is being required is demanded by the other for whom it is a free good. In this way the insured becomes vulnerable to excessive demands, as also noted by Lord Young (HM Government, 2010: 32).

3. The writing of Standards documents can also be a scene of conflict, particularly where committee members bring different philosophies to the table. In the case of the new ISO 31000:2009 Standard on Risk Management, it has been said that the International Electrotechnical Commission's Advisory Committee on Safety (ACOS) withdrew its support because 'it believed that (so-called) safety risks are a special case and should be generally excluded from the generally applied risk management process in ISO 31000. The central argument of ACOS was that any risk to people is unacceptable' (Purdy, 2010).

4. Much to its credit, from our perspective, RoSPA has of late started to talk more of 'as much safety as necessary' as opposed to accident prevention. This is a difficult transition for any agency to make.

5. Ken Ogilvie, outdoor adventure leader, also records how practitioners and official guidance tend to see risk in a very narrow light of physical things, when in reality it is far more complex (Ogilvie, 2005: 165–167).

6. It is interesting to note that while RoSPA has been adjusting its position to become more accommodating of the benefits of public space, the HSE seems at times to be heading on an opposite tack. According to HSE's website in 2010: 'Our mission

is to prevent death, injury and ill health in Britain's workplaces.' Previously, HSE's position was better described as 'managing risk properly'.

7. Often referred to, with affection, as R2P2.

8. An earlier version neglected to mention it at all.

9. On 13 January 2010, Judith Hackitt, Chair of the HSE, was interviewed on BBC Radio 4's Woman's Hour, where she expressed the view that there was a 'grain of truth' in the stories about health and safety, but that they 'were exaggerated'.

10. HM Treasury provides a straightforward description of the process in chapter 4 of its guide on managing risks to the public (HMT, 2005).

11. The term 'risk based society' is a descriptor used by the HSE in its publication *Thirty years on and looking forward*. *Risk Society* is also the title of an influential book by German sociologist Ulrich Beck (1992), from which the term may have originated.

12. In fact, HSE statistics also show the number of fatal injuries to have been virtually level from the mid-90s until 2004 (HSE, 2004a), suggesting a longer period of stagnation.

13. The man on the Clapham omnibus is a hypothetical, reasonably educated and intelligent but non-specialist person, against whom a defendant's conduct might be judged in an English civil law trial for negligence. The standard of care required is that which might be exercised by 'the man on the Clapham omnibus'. Thus, a person has acted negligently if she has departed from the conduct expected of a reasonably prudent person acting under similar circumstances. The reasonable man concept exists in other countries too, including Australia and the USA. The Australian equivalent is 'the man on the Bondi tram'.

Chapter 8 A Closer Look at Decision Making

1. Some people prefer the term benefit-risk assessment. RBA or BRA, it's the same thing.

2. Here it is important to be clear that exposure to risk means exposure to *real* risk, not fantasy risk.

3. Conventional workplace risk assessment should in reality also be about trade-offs because 'reasonable practicability' is itself a trade-off between the benefits of a control measure (benefits here refers to the amount of risk reduction it provides) and the cost, time, difficulty etc. of implementing it. In the risk-minimization culture this trade-off is not, however, consciously acknowledged.

4. http://www.ispor.org/sigs/rm.asp

5. In 2005 the Better Regulation Task Force reported that complying with just the information requirements of UK regulations was estimated to cost some £20–40 billion per annum (BRTF, 2005).

6. See, for example, Michael Power's *The risk management of everything* (2004) for a critique of this approach.

7. Marcus Bailie expands upon the use of risk assessments as checklists in *Horizons* (Bailie, 2006).

8. Interestingly, Lord Young has now endorsed the use of checklists for some activities and the need to get away from the plethora of regulations which has been generated (HM Government, 2010: 15, 39).

Chapter 9 Adventure Activities – *A Hard Case*

1. Listed amongst these persons are supporters of the 'Campaign for Adventure', whose numbers include HRH Prince Philip, Rt Hon Tony Blair, Sir Bobby Robson CBE, Douglas Keith Scott, Ken Livingstone, Libby Purves, Sir Christian Bonington, Dr K. B. Everard, Professor Frank Furedi, Dr Bob Sharp, Roger Orgill MBE, Roger Putnam OBE, Jonathan Dimbleby and Sir Paul Judge (http://www.campaignforadventure.org/).
2. Adventure sports are not to be confused with the modern phenomenon of certain spectacular pursuits, conducted in purpose-built venues designed to provide exhilaration, but at reduced levels of risk.
3. From time to time, especially in the aftermath of a serious incident, there are always some who proclaim that even these activities should be free of risk.
4. The FAR for mountaineering is based on data for Scotland from the Scottish Sports Council.
5. These estimates do not apply to elite groups, say of Everest climbers or cave divers, who can be exposed to much higher risks.
6. The adverse reaction to licensing when it was first introduced is quite different from the current-day reaction to the proposition by Lord Young to abolish AALA (HM Government, 2010). This is partly because those subject to licensing have now got used to the system, but more likely because AALA's regime has been fair and reasonable, and, somewhat unusually, gave recognition to the benefits of adventure activities. This is not to say that licensing was not a step too far nor that AALA's balanced regime would have persisted indefinitely.
7. A not unreasonable viewpoint in the circumstances. Hood and colleagues (2004) have coined the term 'tombstone' process to describe how unexpected tragedies and disasters engender public reaction, which in turn allows a policy 'window' of opportunity to open, thus creating opportunities for new initiatives or policy development. This, they contend, is the way in which risk regulation regimes commonly develop and evolve, a process bearing some similarity to Kuhn's 'paradigm shifts'. It is not the best way to make policy which should entail calm and careful consideration, although in the case of the Activity Centres (Young Persons' Safety) Act 1995 a period for this quiet reflection appears to have been afforded.
8. There have been six fatalities to under-18s at licensed centres since 1996, three being from natural causes, two from drowning, and one a fall from a height onto rocks.
9. It is the function of the HSE and not AALA to bring these prosecutions.
10. And as it says in the Approved Code of Practice accompanying the Management of Health and Safety at Work Regulations (1999) (para. 15): 'There are no fixed rules about how a risk assessment should be carried out; indeed it will depend on the nature of the work or business and the types of hazards and risks.'

Chapter 10 Risk-Benefit Assessment

1. More precisely, Starr found that the acceptability of risk appeared to be proportional to the third power of the benefits (real or imagined). That is, if the perceived benefit doubles, then eight times the level of risk is tolerated.
2. The RRAC uses a similar term when it talks of 'regulatory creep'. As they put it: 'Under the influence of risk actors and risk-mongers, rules, guidelines, procedures and conditions are created that make people believe that they are obliged to do more than is strictly required by law – for example a health and safety consultant

might promote guidelines that they saw as best practice in a way that made businesses think that they were required to follow these guidelines. In an environment in which zero failure is allowed, rules, guidelines and procedures tend to be tightened rather than relaxed. When there are a number of varying sources of advice and rules on how to handle a risk, there is a pressure to follow the most cautious and risk-averse. All of this reduces the ability to innovate, and means that constraints that are put on people go beyond what law-makers originally intended. This can make people feel that their lives are being over-managed and that their liberties are being curtailed' (RRAC, 2009: 21).

3. This is set out in Article 31 of the UN Convention on the Rights of the Child. An interesting aspect of the UN's perspective is that play includes activities which are not controlled by adults (UN, 2007), a notion which sits uneasily with other perspectives that seek even to manage play as if it were a goal-driven work activity.

4. Classically, the then European Standard on play equipment (BSEN 1176-1:1998) went so far as to proclaim that it did not even consider play value in arriving at its recommendations (BSI, 1998).

5. Unless the provider of public services flags up the benefits of an activity, there is a fair chance that, should an accident happen and a court case ensue, no one else will. Thus, a jury would tend not to consider the risk-benefit balance. In the R (HSE) v. North Yorkshire County Council case, described in chapter 9, the defence team were very good in identifying the benefits of school trips into the natural environment and the jury were then minded to decide if they agreed with the assessment. This does not always happen.

6. BBC News has reported in 2010 that regulations cost UK firms £88.3 billion in 2009: http://www.bbc.co.uk/news/business-10878262

7. HSE (2009) has reported that the cost of work-related accidents is £20 billion per year. This figure may not be strictly comparable with the RRAC figure. What is more important than the estimated £20 billion price tag, though, is the marginal-cost to marginal-benefit ratio for workplace safety. That is, how much safety gain would there be for every additional £1 spent? Even if the cost of accidents is as high as suggested, spending more money may not produce a net gain if strategies do not produce sufficient benefit. Plus, of course, would there be any other unintended impacts of proposed interventions, good or bad?

8. The sentence is qualified with 'in a sense' because traditionally practised risk assessment of public activities itself suffers from its own problems including this one of the comparison of incommensurables; namely, the cost of control versus their safety benefit. As described in chapter 3, attempts have been made by economists to value things like human safety in order to put the costs and benefits of control into the same units (£s). But while these things may be useful for decisions where massive computational power is warranted due to the scale of the problem, like the safety of a town from flooding, or the provision of some new treatment on the NHS, public services involve endless small-scale decisions of similar nature, but which have almost to be made on the hoof because it is unrealistic to try to apply mathematical techniques to all of these circumstances, even if it were possible. In its alternative mode of use in which risk assessment ducks comparison with cost of control, the other problem emerges of how far a risk should be reduced, itself imponderable for those who are alert to this difficulty.

9. This task is, in fact, quite complex because of the number of varieties of jam, and the number of factors which can be considered. It's enough, it seems, to overwhelm the prefrontal cortex.

10. Rather like some systems for rating hotels, which include on their checklist items like 'Is a trouser press provided?'
11. PLAYLINK can be found at http://www.playlink.org.uk

Chapter 11 In Search of a New Agenda

1. The issue of gross disproportion is omitted here because it has been discussed in chapter 4. Also note that it is arguably a distortion so far as public sector decision making is concerned, where risks are generally low and accepted in exchange for benefits.
2. One could resort to a full-cost benefit analysis in which an attempt is made to monetize and compare all the pros and cons of a decision, or one could resort to some form of multicriteria decision analysis in which monetization is not required, but weighting factors are used instead (as discussed in chapter 8).
3. Something akin to this happened in the field of environmental pollution control when, in 1988, the government adopted the principle of 'best practicable environmental option' (BPEO). The aim of BPEO is that when there is waste to be disposed of the BPEO solution should be sought, this being the one which achieves the minimum impact on the environment as a whole through considering all the disposal options – land, air or water. BPEO is therefore strong on fungibility.
4. There is also a fierce debate over the standard of qualifications and experience which should be required of health and safety consultants. It remains possible for persons to set up as health and safety consultants without any qualifications at all, and some have done this, as noted by Lord Young. Some see the solution as further professionalization of health and safety. Others are less sure that this is a good route to take, as it shifts the boundary of everyday, common-sense decision making further into the professional ambit and away from ordinary front-line people, with their potentially copious tacit knowledge and vast resources of inter-actional expertise.
5. We ourselves would modify this recommendation by deleting the words 'if possible'. Follow-up is in our view essential for responsible risk management of complex systems.
6. Nassim Taleb says the same of financial auditors: '... the accounting period upon which companies' performances are evaluated is too short to reveal whether or not they are doing a great job' (Taleb, 2007: 97).
7. The phrase deployed by the HSE itself is actually 'minimum acceptable standard', which may have a different connotation.

Chapter 12 Final Thoughts and Résumé

1. This is not a particularly fair challenge. All Member States have a say in the drafting of directives, and the authors suspect that British delegates had a significant influence upon this particular directive and other crucial developments, such as the introduction of risk assessment and everything that that came to imply. See also the TUC's statement that European safety directives are based largely upon the same Anglo-Scandinavian principles as the HSW Act (TUC, 2010).
2. A less charitable but oft-heard comment is that other Member States just ignore the Directives.
3. That is, beyond the point where for every £1 invested the gain is less than £1. Generally, when investing in some activity, one chooses firstly the measures which bring the biggest benefit for the least cost, followed by those which produce some

benefit at higher cost and so on, until one reaches the break-even point where marginal cost equals marginal gain.

4. For clarity, the term 'trade-offs', as used by Graham and Weiner, refers to the commonplace phenomenon whereby efforts to reduce one risk create another, as in, for example, the unexpected closure of UK airspace in 2010 which stranded thousands of travellers, thereby placing many at some personal risk. Elsewhere in this book, however, the term refers to the trade-offs between the benefits of public life and its risks.

5. Taleb named it a 'fallacy' out of politeness, his personal preference being to call it a 'fraud'.

References

AALA (Adventure Activities Licensing Authority) (2001) *Self Assessment and Guidance for Providers of Adventure Activities*, Cardiff, AALA

Abt, E., Rodricks, J. V., Levy, J. L., Zeise, L. and Burke, T. A. (2010) 'Science and decisions', *Risk Analysis*, vol 30, no 7, pp1028–1036

Acona Ltd (2006) *Defining best practice in corporate occupational health and safety governance*, HSE research report No. 506, Sudbury, HSE Books

Adams, J. (1985) *Risk and freedom – the record of road safety regulation*. Available online at http://john-adams.co.uk/books/ accessed in July 2010

Adams, J. (1995) *Risk*, London, UCL Press

Adams, J. and Thompson, M. (2002) Taking account of societal concerns about risk: Framing the problem, HSE Report 035, Sudbury, HSE Books. Available online at http://www.hse.gov.uk/research/rrpdf/rr035.pdf accessed in August 2010

Appleby, J., Devlin, N. and Parkin, D. (2007) 'NICE's cost-effectiveness threshold', *British Medical Journal*, vol 335, pp358–359

Arrow, K. J., Cropper, M. L., Eads, G. C., Hahn, R. W., Lave, L. B., Noll, R. G., Portney, P. R., Russell, M., Schmalensee, R., Smith, V. K. and Stavins, R. N. (1996) *Benefit-Cost Analysis in Environmental, Health, and Safety Regulation: A Statement of Principles*, Annapolis, The Annapolis Centre

Asquith, L. J. (1946) in Charlesworth, J. and Percy, R. A. (eds) *Charlesworth and Percy on Negligence* (1997), London, Sweet & Maxwell

Asquith, L. J. (1949) '*Edwards v National Coal Board*', 1 KB704, 1 AER743, 65TLR430C.

Bailie, M. (2003) *Lessons from Stainforth Beck?* Available online at http://lessonslearned.org.uk/docs/Stainforth%20Beck.pdf accessed in August 2010

Bailie, M. (2006) 'Risk assessments, safety statements and all that ...', *Horizons*, vol 36, pp13–15

Bailie, M. (2007) 'Beyond the Nanny State', *Horizons*, vol 39, pp4–7

Ball, D. J. (1998) 'Assessing the risks', *J. Sports, Exercise and Injury*, vol 4, pp3–9

Ball, D. J. (2000) 'Ships in the night and the quest for safety', *J. Injury Control and Safety Promotion,* vol 7, no 2, pp83–96

Ball, D. J. (2002) *Playgrounds – risks, benefits and choices*, Sudbury, HSE Books. Available online at http://www.hse.gov.uk/research/crr_pdf/2002/crr02426.pdf accessed in July 2010

Ball, D. J. (2006) *Environmental Health Policy*, Maidenhead, Open University Press

Ball, D. J., Maggs, D. and Barrett, M. (2009) *Judges, courts, the legal profession and public risk*, London, Risk & Regulation Advisory Council. Available online at www.bis.gov.uk/files/file53398.doc accessed in August 2010

Ball-King, L. N. (2009a) *The UK Risk Register Revisited*, London, DARM, Middlesex University

Ball-King, L. N. (2009b) *Finding the Equilibrium: Adventure Sports and Regulation*, London, DARM, Middlesex University

Barrett, M. and Ball, D. J. (2009a) *Insurers and public risk*, London, Risk & Regulation Advisory Council. Available online at www.bis.gov.uk/files/file53392.doc accessed in August 2010

Barrett, M. and Ball, D. J. (2009b) *Experts and public risk*, London, Risk & Regulation Advisory Council. Available online at www.bis.gov.uk/files/file53394.doc accessed in August 2010

Bast, J. L. (2002) 'Why do public health advocates lie about the risks of smoking?', *Health Care News*, September, Chicago, The Heartland Institute. Available online at http://www.heartland.org/policybot/results/10150/Why_Do_Public_Health_Advocat es_Lie_About_the_Risks_of_Smoking.html accessed in September 2010

Beck, U. (1992) *Risk society – Towards a New Modernity*, London, Sage

Bennett, L. (2010) 'Trees and public liability – who really decides what is safe?', *Arboricultural Journal*, vol 33, pp141–164

Bennett, L. and Crowe, L. (2008) *Landowners' Liability? Is perception of the risk of liability for visitor accidents a barrier to countryside access?*, Sheffield, Countryside Recreation Network. Available online at http://shura.shu.ac.uk/678/ accessed in July 2010

Berger, P., Kristol, I., Mills, M., Wildavsky, A., Anderson, D., Le Fanu, J., Skrabanek, P., Browning, R., Finch, P. and Johnstone, R. (1991) *Health, Lifestyle and Environment: Countering the Panic*, London, The Social Affairs Unit

Blalock, G., Kadiyali, V. and Simon, D. H. (2005) 'The impact of 9/11 on driving fatalities: the other lives lost to terrorism', *Applied Economics*, vol 41, pp1717–1729

Bottex, B., Dorne, J. L., Carlander, D., Benford, D., Przyrembel, H., Heppner, C., Kleiner, J. and Cockburn, A. (2008) 'Risk-benefit health assessment of food – food fortification and nitrate in vegetables', *Trends in Food Science & Technology*, vol 19, no 1, ppS113–119

BMA (British Medical Association) (1987) *Living with Risk*, Chichester, Wiley

BMJ (*British Medical Journal*) (2001) 'BMJ bans accidents', *British Medical Journal*, vol 322, pp1320–1321

BRC (Better Regulation Commission) (2006) *Risk, Responsibility and Regulation – Whose risk is it anyway?* Available online at http://archive.cabinetoffice.gov.uk/brc/ upload/assets/www.brc.gov.uk/risk_res_reg.pdf accessed in August 2010

British Railways Board (1994) *Automatic train protection: report to Secretary of State for Transport,* London, BRB

BRTF (Better Regulation Task Force) (2004) *Better Routes to Redress*, London, BRTF. Available online at http://archive.cabinetoffice.gov.uk/brc/upload/assets/ www.brc.gov.uk/betterroutes.pdf accessed in July 2010

BRTF (Better Regulation Task Force) (2005) *Regulation – Less is More: Reducing Burdens, Improving Outcomes*, London, BRTF

BSI (British Standards Institution) (1998) *Playground equipment – Part 1: General safety requirements and test methods*, BSEN 1176–1:1998, London, British Standards Institution

Cabinet Office (2002) *Risk: Improving government's capability to handle risk and uncertainty*, London, Cabinet Office Strategy Unit

Callaghan, B. (2006) 'HSC tells health and safety pedants to "get a life"'. Available online at http://www.hse.gov.uk/risk/statement.htm accessed in August 2010

Charlesworth, J. and Percy, R. A. (1997) *Charlesworth and Percy on Negligence*, London, Sweet & Maxwell

Collins, H. and Evans, R. (2007) *Rethinking Expertise*, London, University of Chicago Press

Copnall, R. (2008) quoted in the *Solicitors Journal*, 31 March 2008. Available online at http://www.solicitorsjournal.com/story.asp?sectioncode=3&storycode=7479&featurecode=14&c=1 accessed in August 2010

Court of Appeal (2008) R v. J. G. J. Porter, case No. 2007/04618/B3, London, Royal Courts of Justice

Covello, V. T. and Mumpower, R. (1985) 'Risk Analysis and Risk Management: An Historical Perspective', *Risk Analysis*, vol 5, no 2, pp103–120

Cox, L. A. (2007) 'Does Concern Driven Risk Management Provide a Viable Alternative to QRA', *Risk Analysis*, vol 27, no 1, pp27–42

Cox, L. A. (2008) 'What's Wrong with Risk Matrices?', *Risk Analysis*, vol 28, no 2, pp497–513

CPAG (Child Poverty Action Group) (2009) *Child wellbeing and child poverty – where the UK stands in the European table*, London, CPAG. Available online at http://www.cpag.org.uk/info/ChildWellbeingandChildPoverty.pdf accessed in July 2010

Dawkins, R. (1976) *The Selfish Gene*, Oxford, Oxford University Press

DfT (Department for Transport) (2004) *Highways Economics Note No. 1*, London, Department for Transport

DfT (Department for Transport) (2008) *Road Casualties Great Britain: 2007 – Annual report*, Norwich, TSO

DfT (Department for Transport) (2010) *Road Worker Safety: Aiming for Zero*, report PR012/10, Bedford: Highways Agency Publishing Group. Available online at http://www.highways.gov.uk/knowledge/documents/Road_worker_Safety_Strategy.pdf accessed in July 2010

Diamond, C., Higashira, T., Olawuye, A., Zhang, J. N. and Soekoe, D. (2009) *Public safety, Risk Assessment and Decision Making*, London, DARM, Middlesex University

DoT (Department of Transport) (1989) *The Hidden Report – Investigation into the Clapham Junction Railway Accident*, London, HMSO

Douglas, M. and Wildavsky, A. (1983) *Risk and Culture*, Los Angeles, University of California Press

Dreyfus, H. L., Dreyfus, S. E. and Athanasiou, T. (1986) *Mind Over Machine: The Power of Human Intuition and Expertise in the Era of the Computer*, New York, Free Press

Elmonstri, M., Ball-King, L. N., Menelaou, C. and Popescu, P. (2009) *Health, safety and public activities*, London, DARM, Middlesex University

Elvik, R. (1997) 'Evaluation of road accident blackspot treatment: a case of the Iron Law of evaluation studies?', *Accident Analysis and Prevention*, vol 29, no 2, pp191–199

Elvik, R. (1999) Can injury prevention efforts go too far? Reflections on some possible implications of Vision Zero for road accident fatalities, *Accident Analysis and Prevention*, vol 31, pp265–286

Environment Agency (circa 1998) *Sustainable Development: Taking Account of Costs and Benefits*, Bristol, Environment Agency

EOC (English Outdoor Council) (2005) *High Quality Outdoor Education*. Available online at http://www.englishoutdoorcouncil.org/HQOE.pdf accessed in August 2010

EU (European Union) (1989) *The EU Workplace Health and Safety Directive 89/391/EEC*. Available online at http://europa.eu/legislation_summaries/employment_and_social_policy/health_hygiene_safety_at_work/c11113_en.htm accessed in August 2010

Evans, A. W. (2005) *Safety Appraisal Criteria*, The 2005 Lloyd's Register lecture, London, The Royal Academy of Engineering

Evans, A. W. and Verlander, N. Q. (1996) 'Estimating the consequences of accidents: the case of automatic train protection in Britain', *Accident Analysis and Prevention*, vol 28, no 2, pp181–191

Ewart, A. (1989) *Outdoor Adventure Pursuits: Foundations, Models, Theories*, Arizona, Publishing Horizons Inc.

FC (Forestry Commission) (2006) *Growing Adventure*, Bristol, Forest Enterprises

Ferguson, K. (2002) *Essential Economics for Business Students*, Basingstoke, Palgrave

Fischhoff, B., Lichtenstein, S., Slovic, P., Derby, S. L. and Keeney, R. L. (1981) *Acceptable Risk*, Cambridge, Cambridge University Press

Flynn, J., Slovic, P. and Mertz, C. K. (1994) 'Gender, Race, and Perception of Environmental Health Risks', *Risk Analysis*, vol 14, no 6, pp1101–1108

Garlick, A. (2007) *Estimating Risk: A Management Approach*, Burlington (USA), Gower Publishing

Gigerenzer, G. (2007) *Gut feelings: Short Cuts to Better Decision Making*, London, Penguin Books

Gill, T. (2007) *No Fear – Growing up in a risk averse society*, London, Calouste Gulbenkian Foundation

Gill, T. (2010) *Nothing Ventured – balancing risks and benefits in the outdoors*, Devon, English Outdoor Council

Graham, J. and Wiener, J. (1995) *Risk vs. Risk: Tradeoffs in Protecting Health and the Environment*, Cambridge, Mass., Harvard University Press

Green, J. (1997) *Risk and Misfortune*, London, UCL Press

Guldberg, H. (2009) *Reclaiming Childhood: Freedom and Play in an Age of Fear*, Abingdon, Routledge

Hackitt, J. (2008) Speech to IoSH. Available online at http://www.hse.gov.uk/aboutus/speeches/transcripts/iosh080508.htm accessed in July 2010

Hackitt, J. (2010) Speech to schools health and safety conference. Available online at http://www.hse.gov.uk/aboutus/speeches/transcripts/hackitt110310.htm accessed in August 2010

Harrington QC, P. and Forlin, G. (2008) 'Child's play', *New Law Journal*, 1 August, pp1102–1103. Available online at http://www.newlawjournal.co.uk/nlj/content/childs-play accessed in April 2011

Hawkes, N. (2 May 2008) *Alzheimer's victory lifts lid on secretive approval of new drugs*, London, *The Times*

Haythornthwaite, R. (2006) *The Regulation of Risk – Setting the Boundaries*, Bath, University of Bath Centre for the Study of Regulated Industries, http://www.bath.ac.uk/management/cri/pubpdf/Occasional_Lectures/16_Haythornthwaite.pdf accessed in July 2010

Hayward, G. (1996) 'Risk of injury per hour of exposure to consumer products', *Accident Analysis and Prevention*, vol 28, no 1, pp115–121

Herrington, S. and Nicholls, J. (2007) 'Outdoor play spaces in Canada: the safety dance of standards and policy', *Critical Social Policy*, vol 27, no 1, pp128–138

Heseltine, P. (1995) 'Safety versus play value', in Christiansen, M. L. (ed) Playground Safety, pp 91–95, Proc. International Conference, Pennsylvania, Penn State University

HM Government (2010) *Common Sense Common Safety*. Available online at http://www.number10.gov.uk/wp-content/uploads/402906_CommonSense_acc.pdf accessed in December 2010

HMT (Her Majesty's Treasury) (1991) *Economic Appraisal in Central Government*, London, TSO

HMT (Her Majesty's Treasury) (2003) *The Green Book – Appraisal and Evaluation in Central Government*, London, TSO

HMT (Her Majesty's Treasury) (2005) *Managing Risks to the Public: Appraisal Guidance*, London, HM Treasury

Hoffmann, L. H. (2005) *The Social Cost of Tort Liability*, speech to National Constitution Center, Philadelphia. Available online at http://commongood.org/learn-reading-cgpubs-speeches.html accessed in July 2010

Hood, C., Rothstein, H. and Baldwin, R. (2001) *The Government of Risk: Understanding Risk Regulation Regimes*, Oxford, Oxford University Press

House of Lords (2003) *Judgments – Tomlinson v. Congleton Borough Council and others*, London, House of Lords. Available online at http://www.publications.parliament.uk/pa/ld200203/ldjudgmt/jd030731/tomlin-1.htm accessed in July 2010

HSC (Health and Safety Commission) (2006a) *Safety pedants told to get a life*. Available online at http://www.hse.gov.uk/risk/statement.htm accessed in July 2010

HSC (Health and Safety Commission) (2006b) *Principles of sensible risk management*, available online at http://www.hse.gov.uk/risk/principlespoints.htm accessed in July 2010

HSE (Health and Safety Executive) (1988) *The tolerability of risk from nuclear power stations*, Norwich, TSO

HSE (Health and Safety Executive) (1992) *The tolerability of risk from nuclear power stations*, revised, Norwich, TSO

HSE (Health and Safety Executive) (1997) *Successful Health and Safety Management*, (HSG65), Sudbury, HSE Books

HSE (Health and Safety Executive) (2000) *Management of Health and Safety at Work Regulations 1999*, Sudbury, HSE Books

HSE (Health and Safety Executive) (2001) *Reducing risk: protecting people – HSE's decision making-process*, Sudbury, HSE Books

HSE (Health and Safety Executive) (2003a) *Adventure Activities Centres: Five Steps to Risk Assessment*, Sudbury, HSE Books

HSE (Health and Safety Executive) (2003b) *Good Practice and Pitfalls in Risk Assessment*, Sudbury, HSE Books

HSE (Health and Safety Executive) (2004a) *Thirty years on and looking forward*, London, HSE. Available online at http://www.hse.gov.uk/aboutus/reports/30years.pdf accessed in July 2010

HSE (Health and Safety Executive) (2004b) *Revitalising health and safety*. Available online at http://www.hse.gov.uk/revitalising/ accessed in August 2010

HSE (Health and Safety Executive) (2006a) *Five steps to risk assessment*. Available online at http://www.hse.gov.uk/pubns/indg163.pdf accessed in July 2010. Note: earlier versions have been published

HSE (Health and Safety Executive) (2006b) *Principles of sensible risk management*. Available online at http://www.hse.gov.uk/risk/principles.htm accessed in July 2010

HSE (Health and Safety Executive) (2007a) *European court supports UK safety laws*, (Case C127-05 European Commission v. United Kingdom). Available online at http://www.hse.gov.uk/press/2007/c07007.htm accessed in July 2010

HSE (Health and Safety Executive) (2007b) *Guidance from the Licensing Authority on the Adventure Activities Licensing Regulations 2004*, Sudbury, HSE Books

HSE (Health and Safety Executive) (2007c) *Statement to the external providers of health and safety assistance*, London, HSE. Available online at http://www.hse.gov.uk/pubns/externalproviders.pdf accessed in July 2010

HSE (Health and Safety Executive) (2008) *Speech by Judith Hackitt to IoSH Annual Honorary Presidents' luncheon.* Available online at http://www.hse.gov.uk/aboutus/speeches/transcripts/iosh080508.htm accessed in April 2011

HSE (Health and Safety Executive) (2009) *The Health and Safety of Great Britain*, Sudbury, HSE Books. Available online at http://www.hse.gov.uk/strategy/ accessed in July 2010

HSE (Health and Safety Executive) (2010) Schools health and safety conference. Available online at http://www.hse.gov.uk/aboutus/speeches/transcripts/hackitt110310.htm accessed in August 2010

Humberstone, B. (1990) 'Gender, change and adventure education', *Gender and Education*, vol 2, no 2, pp199–215

Hurst, N. W. (1998) *Risk Assessment: The Human Dimension*, Cambridge, The Royal Society of Chemistry

Hutton, D. (2009) The risk and benefit assessment landscape, Food Standards Agency. Available online at http://www.food.gov.uk/news/speeches/formerspeeches/deirdrehutton/riskbenefitassessmentlandscape accessed in July 2010

ICA (Institute of Chartered Accountants) (1999) *Internal Control: Guidance for Directors on the Combined Code*, 'The Turnbull report', London, ICA

IoSH (2010) *Health and safety in "crisis" says Lord Young.* Available online at http://www.shponline.co.uk/news-content/full/iosh-10-health-and-safety-in-crisis-says-lord-young accessed in July 2010

IRGC (International Risk Governance Council) (2005) *Risk governance – an integrative approach*, Geneva, IRGC. Available online at http://www.irgc.org/IMG/pdf/IRGC_WP_No_1_Risk_Governance__reprinted_version_.pdf accessed in August 2010

ISO (International Organization for Standardization) (2009) *Risk management – Principles and guidelines*, ISO 31000, Geneva

ISO/IEC (International Organization for Standardization and International Electrotechnical Commission) (2009) *Risk management – Risk assessment techniques*, ISO/IEC 31010, Geneva, International Electrotechnical Commission

Jaeger, C. C., Renn, O., Rosa, E. A. and Webler, T. (2001) *Risk, Uncertainty and Rational Action,* London, Earthscan

Jarvis, S., Towner, E. and Walsh, S. (1995) Chapter 8, in Botting, B. (ed) *The Health of Our Children*, London, Office of Population, Censuses and Surveys

Jones-Lee, M. W. (1984) 'The valuation of transport safety', in *Proceedings of the Annual Transportation Convention*, Pretoria, Department of Transport

Kasperson, R. E., Renn, O., Slovic, P., Brown, H. S., Emel, J., Goble, R., Kasperson, J. X. and Ratick, S. (1988) 'The social amplification of risk: a conceptual framework', *Risk Analysis*, vol 8, no 2, pp177–187

Kimball, R. and Bacon, S. (1993) 'The Wilderness Challenge', in Gass, M. A. (ed) *Adventure Therapy: Therapeutic Applications of Adventure Programming*, Iowa, Kendal Hunt Publishing Company

Kniesner, T. J., Viscusi, W. K., Woock, C. and Ziliak, J. P. (2007) *Pinning Down the Value of a Statistical Life*, Discussion Paper No. 3107, Bonn, IZA (Institute for the Study of Labour)

Krein, K. (2007) 'Nature, risk and adventure sports', in McNamee, M. (ed) *Philosophy, Risk and Adventure Sports*, London, Routledge

Lehrer, J. (2009) *The Decisive Moment: How the Brain Makes Up its Mind*, Edinburgh, Canongate Books

Leitch, M. (2010) 'ISO 31000:2009 – the new international standard on risk management', *Risk Analysis,* vol 30, no 6, pp887–892

Letwin, O. (2009) *Death of Baby P highlights failure of regulation*. Available online at http://www.guardian.co.uk/politics/2009/jan/27/baby-p-oliver-letwin accessed in July 2010

London Evening Standard (2009) 'We support the Kensington Road revolution'. Available online at http://www.thisislondon.co.uk/standard/article-23722080-details/We+must+support+the+Kensington+road+revolution/article.do accessed in July 2010

Margolis, H. (1996) *Dealing with Risk: Why the Public and Experts Disagree on Environmental Issue*, Chicago, University of Chicago Press

Mayhew, J. (2007) 'Are we suffering from mollycoddlitis?', *Safety & Health Practitioner*, vol 25, no 12, pp39–42

Mill, John Stuart (2001) (originally published in 1863) *Utilitarianism*, Indianapolis and Cambridge, Hackett Publishing Company

Millward, A. Associates, Rawlings Heffernan Consultancy Services and Fettes, L. (2003) *Research into Insurance Cover for the VCS in England*, London, Home Office Active Community Unit

Mohr, P. (2000) 'Gauging the risk', *Descent,* vol 153, pp20–22

Mortlock, C. (1984) *The Adventure Alternative*, Cumbria, Cicerone Press

National Audit Office (2001) *Modern Policy-Making: Ensuring Policies Deliver Value for Money*. Report by the Comptroller and Auditor General, HC 289 Session 2001–2, London, TSO

NCB (National Children's Bureau) (2005) 'Cycling and Children and Young People – A Review', London, NCB

Nebelong, H. (2008) 'What good design can do for us', *Horticultural Week*, April, pp 5–7. Available online at http://www.sansehaver.dk/brochurer/what_good_design_can_do.pdf accessed in September 2010

NICE (National Institute for Health and Clinical Excellence) (2010) *Strategies to prevent unintentional injuries among under-15s: guidance*, London, NICE. Available online at http://guidance.nice.org.uk/PH29/Guidance/pdf/English accessed in January 2011

NRC (National Research Council) (2003) *Understanding Risk: Informing Decisions in a Democratic Society*, Washington DC, National Academies Press

Ogilvie, K. C. (2005) *Leading and Managing Groups in the Outdoors*, second edition, Penrith, Institute for Outdoor Learning

ONS (Office of National Statistics) (2005) *Mortality statistics: injury and poisoning*, DH4, no 30, London, ONS

Patmore, A. (2006) *The Truth about Stress*, London, Atlantic Books

Peat, F. D. (1995) *Blackfoot Physics: A Journey into the Native American Universe*, London, Fourth Estate

Play England (2008a) *Design for Play: A guide to creating successful play spaces*, Nottingham, DCSF Publications. Available online at http://www.playengland.org.uk/resources/design-for-play.pdf accessed in July 2010

Play England (2008b) *Managing Risk in Play Provision: Implementation guide*, Nottingham, DCSF Publications. Available online at http://www.playengland.org.uk/resources/managing-risk-play-provision-guide.pdf accessed in July 2010

Power, M. (1994) *The Audit Explosion*, London, DEMOS

Power, M. (2004) *The Risk Management of Everything*, London, DEMOS

Power, M. (2009) 'The Risk Management of Nothing', *Accounting, Organizations and Society*, vol 34, pp 849–855

PSF (Play Safety Forum) (2002) 'Managing risk in play provision: A position statement', National Children's Bureau, London. Available online at http://www.playengland.org.uk/Page.asp?originx_4178si_56947549249695b31j_2 0079193740c accessed in July 2010

Purdy, G. (2010) 'ISO 31000:2009 – Setting a New Standard for Risk Management', *Risk Analysis*, vol 30, no 6, pp881–886

Reid (1954) *Marshall v Gotham Co Ltd*, AC 300, House of Lords, available online at http://www.safetyphoto.co.uk/subsite/case%20m%20n%20o%20p/marshall_v_gotham_co_ltd.htm accessed in July 2010

Rivers, L., Arvai, J. and Slovic, P. (2010) 'Beyond a Simple Case of Black and White: Searching for the White Male Effect in the African-American Community', *Risk Analysis*, vol 30, no 1, pp65–77

Robens, Lord (1972) *Safety and Health at Work: Report of the Committee 1970–72*, Cmnd. 5034; London, HMSO

Royal Society (1983) *Risk Assessment: A Study Group Report*, London, The Royal Society

Royal Society (1992) *Risk: Analysis, Perception, Management*, London, The Royal Society

RRAC (Risk and Regulation Advisory Council) (2009) *Response with responsibility – Policy-making for public risk in the 21st century*, London, RRAC. Available online at http://www.bis.gov.uk/files/file51459.pdf accessed in July 2010

RRC (Regulatory Reform Committee) (2009) *Themes and Trends in Regulatory Reform*, Ninth report of the Regulatory Reform Committee, Norwich, TSO. Available online at http://www.parliament.the-stationery-office.co.uk/pa/cm200809/cmselect/cmdereg/329/32902.htm accessed in July 2010

RSA (Royal Society for the Encouragement of Arts, Manufactures and Commerce) (2007) Risk Commission Conference, speech by Judith Hackitt. Available online at http://www.hse.gov.uk/aboutus/speeches/pdfs/hackittrsa3110.htm accessed in August 2010

Sapolsky, H. M. (1990) 'The politics of risk', *Daedalus*, vol 119, no 4, pp83–96

SCES (Select Committee on Education and Skills) (2004) Second report. Available online at http://www.publications.parliament.uk/pa/cm200405/cmselect/cmeduski/120/12005.htm accessed in August 2010

Schwartz, M. and Thompson, M. (1990) *Divided We Stand: Redefining Politics, Technology and Social Choice*, London, Harvester Wheatsheaf

Scottish Sports Council (2007) *Scottish Mountaineering Incidents 1996–2005*, Edinburgh, Scottish Sports Council

Seedhouse, D. F. (2004) *Health Promotion: Philosophy, Prejudice and Practice*, Chichester, Wiley

Seigneur, V. (2006) 'The problems of defining risk: the case of mountaineering', *Forum of Qualitative Social Research*, vol 7, no 1

Slovic, P. (2000) *The Perception of Risk*, London, Earthscan

Spectator (2003) 'Health and safety spell danger', Rachel Royce, 6 December. Available online at http://www.spectator.co.uk/essays/all/11517/part_2/health-and-safety-spell-danger.thtml accessed in August 2010

Starr, C. (1969) 'Social benefit versus technological risk – What is our society willing to pay for safety?', *Science*, vol 165, pp1232–1238

Stuckler, D., Basu, S. and McKee, M. (2010) 'Budget crises, health, and social welfare programmes', *British Medical Journal*, vol 341, 10 July, pp77–79

Taleb, N. N. (2007) *The Black Swan: The Impact of the Highly Improbable*, London, Penguin Books

Tejada-Flores, L. (1967) 'The Climbers Game', *Ascent*, vol 1, pp 23–25

Tejada-Flores, L. (1990) 'Beyond Climbing Games: Alpinism as Humanism', *Summit Magazine*, Fall 1990

The *Guardian* (2008) 'Safety fears rule out United parade', 22 May. Available online at http://www.guardian.co.uk/uk/2008/may/22/championsleague accessed in July 2010

The *Guardian* (2010) 'Straw has left justice to the tender mercies of the press', 10 March. Available online at http://www.guardian.co.uk/commentisfree/2010/mar/09/jack-straw-jon-venables-the-sun accessed in July 2010

The Independent (1997) 'Too many 'ologists make you boring', 4 April

The Independent (2008) 'The extreme world of mountain marathons'. Available online at http://www.independent.co.uk/sport/general/others/the-extreme-world-of-mountain-marathons-975372.html accessed in August 2010

The Telegraph (2010) 'Health and safety rules should be removed from offices, says David Cameron Adviser', http://www.telegraph.co.uk/news/newstopics/politics/7826183/Health-and-safety-rules-should-be-removed-from-offices-says-David-Cameron-adviser.html accessed in August 2010

The Times (2006) 'Our cotton-wool kids'. Available online at http://www.timesonline.co.uk/tol/life_and_style/article689316.ece accessed in December 2010

The Times (2007) 'Outcry after Unicef identifies UK's "failed generation of children"'. Available online at http://www.timesonline.co.uk/tol/news/world/europe/article1384238.ece accessed in July 2010

The Times (2008a) 'Plans to check safety of all garden trees will cost homeowners dear'. Available online at http://property.timesonline.co.uk/tol/life_and_style/property/article4176060.ece accessed in July 2010

The Times (2008b) 'Dangerous trees: barking mad'. Available online at http://www.timesonline.co.uk/tol/comment/leading_article/article4175187.ece accessed in July 2010

The Times (2009) 'Stop, get ready, go: let common sense begin'. Available online at http://www.timesonline.co.uk/tol/comment/article6216262.ece accessed in July 2010

TUC (Trades Union Congress) (2010) Submission by the Trades Union Congress. Available online at http://www.tuc.org.uk/h_and_s/tuc-18203-f0.cfm accessed in August 2010

UDC (Urban Design Compendium) (2009) *New Road – Key Principles Designing streets for Different Users*. Available online at http://www.urbandesigncompendium.co.uk/newroad accessed in July 2009

UN (United Nations) (2007) *Implementation Handbook for the Convention on the Rights of the Child*. Available online at http://ipaworld.org/category/un-convention/ accessed in August 2010

UNICEF (2007) *Report on Childhood in Industrialised Countries*, York, UNICEF. Available online at http://www.unicef.org.uk/press/news_detail_full_story.asp?news_id=890 accessed in January 2010

Viscusi, W. K. (1992) *Fatal Tradeoffs: Public and Private Responsibilities for Risk*, Oxford, Oxford University Press

VSCG (Visitor Safety in the Countryside Group) (2003) *Managing Visitor Safety in the Countryside – Principles and Practice*. Available online at http://www.vscg.co.uk/ accessed in July 2010

Walker, B. (2005) 'Heads up', *Cycle*, June, pp42–45

Wheatley, S. (2008) 'Occupiers' Liability: An historical victory', *Personal Injury Law Journal*, Dec–Jan 2008

WHO (World Health Organization) (1987) *Air Quality Guidelines for Europe*, Copenhagen, WHO

Wildavsky, A. (1980) 'Richer is Safer', *Public Interest*, vol 60, pp23–29

Wildavsky, A. (1997) *But is it True? Citizen's Guide to Environmental Health and Safety Issues*, Cambridge, Mass., Harvard University Press

Young, Lord (2010) *'Health and safety in "crisis"'*. Available online at http://www.shponline.co.uk/news-content/full/iosh-10-health-and-safety-in-crisis-says-lord-young accessed in July 2010

Zhang, A., Boardman, A. E., Gillen, D. and Waters II, W. G. (2004) *Towards Estimating the Social and Environmental Costs of Transportation in Canada*, Vancouver, University of British Columbia

Index

AALA (Adventure Activities Licensing Authority) 108, 114–115, 125–129, 131, 132–133, 172
AALR (Adventure Activities Licensing Regulations) 126, 138–139
Aberfan disaster 3
accidents
  black spots 61–62
  causation 53–57
  cost of 95, 97, 184
  perspectives on 10
  trends in 58, 95
  use of data 141, 158–163, 176–177
Activity Centres (Young Persons' Safety) Act 125
Adams, John 54–55, 123, 160, 171
adventure sports
  attitude to risk 118–120, 130
  licensing regulations 138–139
  nature of 118, 120
  risks of 123–125
  version of 'Five steps to risk assessment' 105–106
advice, plethora of 81, 109, 174–175
affective reasoning 110–112
  see also analytic reasoning
AHOEC (Association of Heads of Outdoor Education Centres) 127–129
air pollution control 20, 37–38
ALARA (As Low As Reasonably Achievable) 180
ALARP (As Low As Reasonably Practicable) 16, 38–39, 46, 65–67, 79, 86
  challenge by European Commission 67
Alkali Inspectorate 38
Alzheimer's disease 37
ATP (Automatic Train Protection) 35–36

analytic reasoning 110–111
  see also affective reasoning
ancient monuments *see* safety
aspirin 101
Asquith, Cyril (Baron Asquith of Bishopstone) 50, 66, 67, 69, 71, 72
auditing 59–60, 80–81, 107, 141, 173–174
autonomy of specialist sector leaders 131, 133, 172

Baby P. 11, 57, 107, 141
Bailie, Marcus 3, 127, 129
Ball, David 63, 79, 123
Ball-King, Laurence 26, 127–128
banking crisis 11, 57, 137–138
Beck, Ulrich 182
beer mat knowledge 162
beliefs, role of prior 53–57, 88, 92, 111, 154–156, 167, 169
benefits
  knowledge requirements 173
  Plas Dol-y-Moch assessment 142–143
  of public life 24, 68–69, 73, 84, 142–143
  of risk reduction 50, 66–67
  trade-off against risk 140, 144–147
Bennett, Luke 76, 148
Bentham, Jeremy 46
'best practice' 30, 152–154, 163–164, 183–184
  contribution of monitoring 162, 176
Better Regulation Commission 58, 72, 126
'better safe than sorry' 154–157, 164, 170–171
  see also 'do no harm'
bias 28, 31, 50, 51, 92, 110, 112, 143, 154, 161, 166–167, 171

Blair, Tony 7
bootstrapping 30
bounded rationality 78, 170
BPM (Best Practicable Means) 38
British Railways Board 36
'broadly acceptable risk' 47–48
BSI (British Standards Institution) 11, 81, 152
bureaucracy 1, 5, 94, 107, 147–149

Cabinet Office 21–22, 25–26, 102
Callaghan, Bill (former Chair of HSC) 2, 7, 86
Cameron, David (Prime Minister) 1
carcinogens 20, 100–101
CARR (Centre for Analysis of Risk and Regulation) 80
caving, comparative risks of 124
Central Surrey Health 107, 174
chemicals *see* toxic chemicals
childhood
   play provision in 55–56, 169
   right to play 136
   state of 13–14, 136, 169, 175
Children's Play Council 14
Children's Society 14
Civil Aviation Authority 36
Clapham Junction rail crash 35
Clapham omnibus, man on the 95, 153, 182
climbing, comparative risks of 124
coal industry
   Edwards case 50, 66–67
   safety record 2
Codes of Practice (CoPs) 16, 30–31, 80, 174–175
Collins, Harry 112–115, 126–127, 146–147, 162, 172
communication 169
Compensation Act, The 74–76
compensation culture 1, 10, 149, 178
   deterring 139, 161
competency 108, 161–163, 173
consultation
   'omitted voices' 169
consumer product safety *see* safety of consumer products
Consumer Safety Unit (DTI) 29–30
contributory expertise 113, 146, 162
   see also tacit knowledge; specialist tacit knowledge

cost-benefit analysis 35, 36, 45
   case studies 35–39
   ethical challenges of 39–40, 46
   official values of 'safety' 44
   use by HSE 39
Court of Appeal 11, 13, 73, 74, 75, 76
Covello, Vincent 9, 101
Cox, Louis 28–29, 171
CPAG (Child Poverty Action Group) 14
cycle helmets 61

DARM (Centre for Decision Analysis and Risk Management) 151
Dawkins, Richard 103
DCSF (Department for Children, Schools and Families) 100, 127, 135, 159
DCMS (Department for Culture, Media and Sport) 100, 135, 159
Decision Analysis 101–102, 110
decision making
   approaches to 30–31, 109–112
   modified Pareto rule 34–35
   neuroscience contributions to understanding 144–147
   Pareto efficiency principle 34
Dejevsky, Mary 5
Department for Health 136
Department for Transport 35–36, 44, 124
DES (Department for Education and Skills) 125
Design for Play 57, 135, 160
diminishing returns, law of 168
'do no harm' 157, 164, 170
   see also 'better safe than sorry'
DoT/DfT (Department of/for Transport) 35–36, 44, 124
Dunham Massey 152
duty of care to visitors *see* Occupiers' Liability Acts
dynamic risk assessment 108

economics of safety 33–44
Edwards v. National Coal Board 50, 66–67
Elvik, Rune 62, 168
empowerment 107, 131, 173–174
English Outdoor Council 108, 120–121
Environment Act 38
Environment Agency 38
environmentalism 168

environmental protection 37–38
ethics 39–40, 46, 170–171
 regaining the high moral ground
  156–158, 170–171
 in risk management 21–22
European Commission 67
European Court of Justice 67
European Directive 89/391/EEC 104,
  147, 165, 167
European Food Safety Authority 102
Evans, Andrew 36, 51
Evans, Robert 112–115, 146–147, 162,
  172
excessive demands 176
experts and expertise
 categories of 112–115
 contributory 113, 133, 146, 162
 requirements of 112, 161–163, 173
Eyjafjallajökull 20, 135

false expectations
 as a cause of litigation 136, 161
 as a route to unintended consequences
  152
FARs (Fatal Accident Rates) 123–125
Fischhoff, Baruch 30
Five steps to risk assessment 22–24, 86,
  89, 105, 147
food safety, *see* safety
Food Standards Agency (UK) 102, 171
Forestry Commission 135
fungibility 112, 113, 155–156
 restoration of 156–157, 164, 170–171

Garlick, Andy 27–28
Gigerenzer, Gerd 110–111
Gill, Tim 13, 63, 108–109, 139, 175
Glenridding tragedy 129
'gold-plating' 167
good life promotion *see* positive health
  promotion
governance 57–58
Graham, John 59, 137, 169–170, 173,
  177
greatest happiness principle 46
Green, Judith 10, 62
gross disproportion 49–52
Guldberg, Helene 13–14, 63

Hackitt, Judith (Chair of HSE) 7, 8, 62,
  92–94

Hampstead Heath ponds 68–69
Haythornthwaite, Rick (Chair of RRAC)
  12, 58, 72, 97, 104, 151
Hayward, Gordon 29–30
hazards
 definition, *see* risk terminology
 prioritization 23
health and safety
 challenges to 1–8, 177
 ethical issues 39–40
 impact on public life 1–14, 168
 see also safety versus health
 pricing of 35–40
 success of 2, 177
Health and Safety of Great Britain
  94–97, 104
healthcare *see* National Health Service
Heseltine, Peter 14
heuristics (mental) 110, 169–170
Hicks, John *see* Pareto efficiency
Hippocratic oath 157
HM Treasury
 broad remit of 69
 the Green Book 139, 157, 158
 *Principles of Managing Risks to the
  Public* 95–96
 monitoring and the ROAMEF cycle
  158–161, 176
 valuation of safety and 'non-market'
  goods 35
Hoffmann, Leonard (Lord) 2, 3, 33,
  68–69, 73–74, 84–85, 94, 100, 138
holistic paradigms 169–170, 170–171
Hood, Christopher 59–60, 132, 141,
  172
House of Commons Regulatory Reform
  Committee 137–138, 170
'How safe is safe enough?' 19–20
HSC (Health and Safety Commission) 2,
  85–87, 103, 147
HSE (Health and Safety Executive) 8,
  39, 46–47, 49, 50, 54, 85–86, 97,
  126, 129–130, 141, 148, 153, 159,
  162–163, 177
HSW Act (Health and Safety at Work etc
  Act)
 origins 3, 10, 16
 philosophy 16, 46, 177
 Section 3, impact of 10, 165–166
 spill-over into public life 11, 65–66,
  103–105, 165–166

Hunt, Tiffany 152–153
Hutton, Deirdre 102, 171

injury prevention
  origins 10
  versus 'do no harm' 156–157, 164,
    170–171
  versus health 9, 68, 83–85, 138,
    170–171, 177
insurers 10, 22, 28, 78, 80, 139, 141,
  147, 166
international aspects 1–2, 9, 16, 21, 39,
  52, 67, 169, 171, 176
IoSH (Institution of Occupational Safety
  and Health) 6, 7
IRGC (International Risk Governance
  Council) 171
ISO 31000 21, 137, 159, 176

Jenkins, Simon 5, 6, 107–108
Jones-Lee, Michael 40
judgement
  lay v. professional 31, 110–112

Kaldor, Nicholas *see* Pareto efficiency
Kaletsky, Anatole 4
knowledge
  categorization of 112–115
  specialist 113
  tacit 113
Kuhn, Thomas 154

land owners 135, 148, 151–152
law 65–77, 174–175
  as a minimum standard? 153, 164
  uncertainty of outcome 76
Layfield, Frank (Sir) 46
legal cases
  Atkins v. Scott 148
  Bolton v. Stone 70–71, 74
  Daborn v. Bath Tramways Motor Co.
    Ltd. 71–72
  Edwards v. National Coal Board 50,
    66–67, 71
  Latimer v. AEC Ltd 71
  Morris v. West Hartlepool Steam
    Navigation Co. Ltd. 69, 70
  Paris v. Stepney Borough Council 71
  Poppleton v. Trustees of the
    Portsmouth Youth Activities
    Committee 75

Regina (HSE) v. North Yorkshire
  County Council 92, 129–130
Regina (HSE) v. Porter 11, 13, 15, 28
Tomlinson v. Congleton Borough
  Council, 73–74, 76
Lehrer, Jonah 144–146
Letwin, Oliver (MP) 11, 56
local authorities 10
Löfstedt, Ragnar 65
Lyme Bay tragedy 125–126

managing risk *see* risk management
management systems 57–61, 131–132,
  173–174
Managing Risk in Play Provision 29,
  135, 141, 148, 173, 175
Margolis, Howard 44, 49, 112,
  154–157, 164, 170–171
Marine and Coastguard Agency 36
Mayhew, Jerome 76, 81–82, 169
media influences 1, 4–7, 117, 121–123
memes 103–104
MHSWR (Management of Health and
  Safety at Work Regulations) 10, 16,
  66, 105–106, 147, 163, 165
Mill, John Stuart 46
mission drift 107, 136, 166
Monderman, Hans 56, 162, 175
Moore, Victoria 6
moral hazard 139, 180
Mumpower, Jeryl 9, 101
myth of the month 8, 87

Nanny State, causes of 3
narrative fallacy 162, 169, 179, 186
  see also risk assessment, complexity of
  and risk management of complex
    systems
National Audit Office 69
National Coal Board 3, 50
National Health Service
  use of drug trials 162
  use of evidence 109
  use of QALYs 36–37, 168
National Research Council (US) 171
National Tree Safety Group 151
National Trust 152–153
Nebelong, Helle 55
neuroscience 144–147
NFARs (Non-Fatal Accident Rates)
  123–125

NICE (National Institute for Health and Clinical Excellence) 37, 59, 172
North Yorkshire County Council 92, 129–131

obesity, health effects of 84
  linked to exercise 126
Occupiers' Liability Acts 65, 69–70
OMM (Original Mountain Marathon) 117, 121–123
opportunity costs, recognition of 154–156
outdoor learning 120
overspecialisation 173
ownership of risk 107

Pareto efficiency 34–35, 46, 88
perceived risk *see* risk perception
personal responsibility 88
Peterborough, The Hamptons 140
philosophy of safety *see* safety, philosophy of
Plas Dol-y-Moch, benefits assessment 142–143
Play England 29, 100, 120, 135
  Design for Play 57, 135, 159–160
  Managing Risk in Play Provision 29, 135, 141, 147, 173, 175
playground safety 55, 63
PLAYLINK 148
Play Safety Forum 100, 120, 135, 169, 175
Podger, Geoffrey (Chief Executive of the HSE) 148
policy
  design of 137, 173
  ethical implications 137
  importance of 136, 149, 158–159, 164, 173, 176
  monitoring 158–163
  need for public statements of 141
positive health promotion 86, 89, 92, 104
Power, Michael 59–61, 80–81, 147, 161, 173–174
prejudice 154, 164
Principles of Managing Risks to the Public 96
Principles of Sensible Risk Management 8, 86–87, 89, 90–91, 105, 139
prioritization 23

pro-activity, need for, *see* risk management
psychological harm 157
psychology of decision making 28, 109–112, 144–147, 166–167, 170–171
public concern *see* societal concerns
public safety
  credibility of 2–3, 14
  dangers of 14–15
  impacts on public life 1–8, 11–14
  importance of 1, 177
  issue of paramountcy 33–34
  questioning simplicity of 105, 109, 116, 158, 162
Purves, Libby 5, 7, 88

QALY (Quality Adjusted Life Year) 36–37, 41, 44, 79, 168

radiation 19, 52, 100–101
reasonable practicability *see* ALARP *and* Tolerability of Risk
reasoning 28
  affective 109–112
  analytic 109–112
red tape 1, 4, 94, 123, 167
Reid, James (Lord) 67, 69, 70
Reducing Risk Protecting People 20, 39, 86, 94
regulation
  costs of 58, 97, 104–105, 139–140, 184
  creep of 95, 97, 183–184
  rule-based 11
  regimes 59–60, 132–133
  vested interests 104–105
right to play 136
risk
  definition *see* risk terminology
  how low is low enough? 24–26,
  primary and secondary 141, 161
risk amplification 123
risk assessment, definition *see* risk terminology
  complexity of 16–30, 105–106, 109, 114–115, 131, 169–173
  contrasting views on 108, 131, 133, 169
  difference from risk management 21–22, 102

risk assessment, definition (*contd*)
  different techniques of 22, 105, 133, 141
  Five steps to 22–24, 86, 89
  history of 9–10
  minimisation of risk 24, 53, 65, 117, 130, 132, 153, 166
  as *part* of a process 21–22, 102
  public credibility 171–172
  questions about 8–9, 171–172, 173
  requirement for 16
  requirement to record 105–106, 147–149
  'scores' 27–28,
  subjectivity of 8, 28–30, 133, 141, 154–156
  substitution by standards or advice 82–83, 99, 144
  use of accident data 141
risk assessors
  ideology 166
  questions for 176
  selection of 173
risk aversion 27, 76
risk-benefit assessment
  attitudes to (early) 135–136
  complexity of 109, 136, 158–161
  conduct of 140–147, 173
  expertise in 161–163, 173
  HSE support for 100
  issues 136–143, 173
  logic of 151
  as a meme 105
  ordinariness of 99–101, 136
  origins of (recent) 63
  policy requirement 136, 149
  trade-off of risks and benefits 102, 144–147
  use of accident data 141
  vis-à-vis risk assessment 140
risk communication
  omitted voices 81–82, 169
risk control, hierarchy of 54
risk management, definition *see* risk terminology
  approaches to 30–31, 156–157
  beliefs about 31, 51, 60, 130–131
  communication of decisions 171–173
  of complex systems 62, 158–161, 177
  difference from risk assessment 21–22, 102

House of Commons (RRC)criteria for success 138
HSE's '*Principles of sensible...*' 8, 87, 88–90, 139
international standard on 21, 137, 159, 176
law as a 'minimum' requirement 95–97, 153
policy requirements of 136–137, 158–159, 176
primary and secondary 141, 147
principles of
  HM government 96
  RRC 137–138
pro-activity of 47
'scores' 27–28
values inherent in 21–22
risk matrices
  formats and usage 23–30
  limitations 171–172
risk perception 28
  alternative of objective data 141
  see also psychology of decision making
risk solutions
  conflicting views 53–57
  lack of evidence 172
  management systems 57–61
  'regression to the mean' 62
risk terminology 16–22
  hazard 16
  individual risk 20
  risk 17–19
  risk assessment 21–22
  risk management 21–22
  safe *and* safety 19–20
  societal concerns 20–21
  societal risks 20
ROAMEF cycle 158–161, 162, 176
Robens, Alfred (Lord) 3, 16, 38–39, 107, 109, 131, 148
Robens Commission report 3, 131,177
RoSPA (Royal Society for Prevention of Accidents) 83–85, 136, 156–157
Royal Society 49, 171
R v. Porter 11, 13, 15, 28
RRAC (Risk and Regulation Advisory Council) 8, 12, 58, 95, 139–140, 148–149, 152
RRC (Regulatory Reform Committee of the House of Commons) 138, 170

RSA (Royal Society for the encouragement of Arts, Manufactures and Commerce) 92

safe, definition *see* risk terminology
safety, definition *see* risk terminology
  of adventure sports 117–134
  of ancient monuments 72–73
  approaches to 53–64, 78–79
  of consumer products 29–30, 115, 160
  cost of regulating 58, 97, 104, 139–140, 180, 184
  ethics of 39–40
  of food 102
  meanings of 19–20, 78–79
  paramountcy of 8, 33–44
  philosophy 88, 138
  playgrounds 55, 61
  transport 18–19, 56, 61–62, 72
  valuation of 40–43
  versus health 9, 68, 83–85, 137–138, 168, 177
  see also legal cases *and* risk management
Sapolsky, Harvey 81
SCES (Select Committee on Education and Skills) 120–121
secondary risk management 60, 80, 141, 147, 161
Seedhouse, David 53, 88, 92, 97, 111, 136, 154, 167, 172
SFAIRP (So Far As Is Reasonably Practicable) *see* ALARP
'shared space' concept of 56, 162, 175
Sizewell B Inquiry 46–47
Slovic, Paul 110–111, 167
Smith, Robert QC 130–131
social utility of public activities 71–72
societal concerns 20–21
SPADs (Signals Passed at Danger) 35–36
sports
  adventure 117–134
specialist tacit knowledge 113, 115–116
  see also tacit knowledge; contributory expertise
Stainforth Beck tragedy 129
standard of care 152–154
Standards
  British 2, 12–14, 152, 174–175
  international 21, 55, 184
  interpretation of 174–175

ISO 31000 21, 137, 159
  as surrogates for risk assessment 80–81
Starmer, Keith (QC) 7
Starr, Chauncey 135
Strange, Rob (Chief Executive IOSH) 7
Stuckler, David 138, 168–170
Successful Health and Safety Management (HSG65) 57, 86, 89, 104, 131–132, 137, 159, 165, 173
Suffolk County Council 60, 168

tacit knowledge 113–115
  see also specialist tacit knowledge; contributory expertise
Taleb, Nassim 162, 169
Tejada-Flores, Lito 119
Thirty years on and looking forward 165
Tolerability of Risk, framework 46–52
Tolerability of Risk from Nuclear Power Stations 46
Tomlinson v. Congleton Borough Council 73, 84–85
Total Place programme 170
toxic chemicals 52
trade-offs 94, 98–99, 100, 102, 112, 151, 155–156, 169, 171–173, 177
transport safety, see safety
trees
  climbing 14
  risk from 151–152
  safety of 148–149
  standards 11, 12–13, 81
  unrealistic expectations 152
trust, need to rehabilitate 174
TUC (Trades Union Congress) 166–167, 177
Turnbull report 57

Uncertainty
  of court decisions 76
  of effectiveness of 'solutions' 53–57, 81, 83–85, 98
  of risk assessments of public space 105–106
  role of monitoring 158–161, 176
UNICEF 14
unintended consequences 59, 78, 137–138, 141, 157, 168, 169–170
utilitarianism 46–47, 88

value of life
  methodology 40–43
  official values 44
  relationship to the QALY 44
  value your own life 40–43
Viscusi, Kip 55, 61, 123, 160
vision zero 137, 168
Voce, Adrian 8, 14
volcanic ash 20, 59, 137
Voluntary and Community Sector 80
VSCG (Visitor Safety in the Countryside
  Group) 175, 181

warning notices, proliferation of 115
water bodies 24
welfare economics 41
Wheatley, Simon 72–73
white male effect (WME) 167

Wiener, Jonathan 59, 137, 169–170,
  173, 177
Wildavsky, Aaron 138, 168, 171
willingness-to-pay 41–43, 135
WHO (World Health Organisation) 39
Worcestershire County Council 29
'worst case scenarios,' problems of 27

X-rays 20, 100–101

Young, David (Lord Young of Graffham)
  1, 6, 65, 97, 100, 132, 138–139,
  147, 161, 167
young people *see* childhood

zero tolerance 10, 19, 137, 168, 170
  shedding the myth of 161